Peugeot
Talbot
Diesel
Engine
Owners
Workshop
Manual

A K Legg T Eng MIMI

Models covered
This manual covers the Peugeot/Talbot 1769 cc &
1905 cc (1.7 litre & 1.9 litre) Diesel engines used in the
Peugeot 205 (inc. Van), 305 (inc. Van) & 309, and in
the Talbot Horizon

Covers all components exclusive to Diesel-engined variants
Does not cover the 1548 cc Diesel engine used in early 305 models

(950–9PI)

ABCDE
FGHIJ
KLMNO
PQRS

Haynes Publishing Group
Sparkford Nr Yeovil
Somerset BA22 7JJ England

Haynes Publications, Inc
861 Lawrence Drive
Newbury Park
California 91320 USA

Acknowledgements

Certain illustrations are the copyright of Peugeot Talbot Motor Company Limited and are used with their permission. Duckhams Oils provided lubrication data. Thanks are also due to Sykes-Pickavant who supplied some of the workshop tools, and all the staff at Sparkford who assisted in the production of this Manual.

© **Haynes Publishing Group 1988**

A book in the **Haynes Owners Workshop Manual Series**

Printed by J. H. Haynes & Co. Ltd, Sparkford, Nr Yeovil, Somerset BA22 7JJ, England

ISBN 0 85696 950 8

British Library Cataloguing in Publication Data
Legg, A. K. (Andrew K.). *1942–*
    Peugeot/Talbot diesel engine owners workshop manual
    1. Cars, maintenance & repair. Amateurs' manuals
    I. Title   II. Series
    629.28'722
    ISBN 0-85696-950 8

Contents

Front three-quarter view of Peugeot/Talbot XUD engine. Timing belt cover has been removed

1	Timing belt
2	Oil filler cap and ventilation hose
3	Injectors
4	Diagnostic socket
5	Temperature sensors
6	Fast idle thermo unit
7	Thermostat cover
8	Injection pump (Roto-Diesel)
9	Coolant hose to oil cooler
10	Drivebelt tension adjusting bolt
11	Flywheel
12	Alternator
13	Oil filter
14	Sump
15	Alternator drivebelt
16	Crankshaft pulley
17	Water pump
18	Timing belt intermediate roller
19	Injection pump sprocket
20	Timing belt tensioner
21	Right-hand engine mounting bracket
22	Camshaft sprocket

About this manual

Its aim

The aim of this manual is to help you get the best value from your vehicle. It can do so in several ways. It can help you decide what work must be done (even should you choose to get it done by a garage), provide information on routine maintenance and servicing, and give a logical course of action and diagnosis when random faults occur. However, it is hoped that you will use the manual by tackling the work yourself. On simpler jobs it may even be quicker than booking the car into a garage and going there twice, to leave and collect it. Perhaps most important, a lot of money can be saved by avoiding the costs a garage must charge to cover its labour and overheads.

The manual has drawings and descriptions to show the function of the various components so that their layout can be understood. Then the tasks are described and photographed in a step-by-step sequence so that even a novice can do the work.

Unlike most Haynes manuals, which cover a particular vehicle in different trim levels and engine sizes, this book covers one engine and its associated equipment as fitted to a range of vehicles. Items which are common to Diesel and petrol models – eg bodywork, transmission and running gear – are not covered in this book.

Its arrangement

The manual is divided into seven Chapters, each covering a logical sub-division of the vehicle. The Chapters are each divided into Sections, numbered with single figures, eg 5; and the Sections into paragraphs (or sub-sections), with decimal numbers following on from the Section they are in, eg 5.1, 5.2, 5.3 etc.

It is freely illustrated, especially in those parts where there is a detailed sequence of operations to be carried out. There are two forms of illustration: figures and photographs. The figures are numbered in sequence with decimal numbers, according to their position in the Chapter – eg Fig. 6.4 is the fourth drawing/illustration in Chapter 6. Photographs carry the same number (either individually or in related groups) as the Section or sub-section to which they relate.

There is an alphabetical index at the back of the manual as well as a contents list at the front. Each Chapter is also preceded by its own individual contents list.

References to the 'left' or 'right' of the vehicle are in the sense of a person in the driver's seat facing forwards, but note that, in Chapter 1, references to the 'front' of the engine are in respect of the timing belt end with the engine removed from the vehicle.

Unless otherwise stated, nuts and bolts are removed by turning anti-clockwise, and tightened by turning clockwise.

Vehicle manufacturers continually make changes to specifications and recommendations, and these, when notified, are incorporated into our manuals at the earliest opportunity.

Whilst every care is taken to ensure that the information in this manual is correct, no liability can be accepted by the authors or publishers for loss, damage or injury caused by any errors in, or omissions from, the information given.

Project vehicles

The vehicles used in the preparation of this manual, and appearing in many of the photographic sequences, were a Peugeot 205 GRD and a Talbot Horizon LD.

General dimensions, weights and capacities

Dimensions
Overall length:

205	3.705 m (145.9 in)
305	4.262 m (167.8 in)
309	4.051 m (159.5 in)
Horizon	3.960 m (155.9 in)

Overall width:

205 except GRD	1.562 m (61.5 in)
205 GRD	1.572 m (61.9 in)
305	1.636 m (64.4 in)
309	1.628 m (64.1 in)
Horizon	1.679 m (66.1 in)

Overall height:

205 except Van	1.373 m (54.1 in)
205 Van	1.376 m (54.2 in)
305	1.410 m (55.5 in)
309	1.380 m (54.3 in)
Horizon	1.410 m (55.5 in)

Weights
Kerb weights (approx):

205 except GRD	870 kg (1918 lb)
205 GRD	895 kg (1973 lb)
305 except GRD	985 kg (2172 lb)
305 GRD	1010 kg (2227 lb)
309	950 kg (2094 lb)
Horizon	1021 kg (2251 lb)

Trailer weight limit:

205 except Van	700 kg (1543 lb)
205 Van	900 kg (1984 lb)
305	1051 kg (2317 lb)
309	1000 kg (2205 lb)
Horizon	800 kg (1764 lb)
Maximum roof rack load	75 kg (165 lb)

Capacities

Engine oil (drain and refill)	4.5 litres (7.9 pints)

Cooling system:

205	8.3 litres (14.6 pints)
305	9.5 litres (16.7 pints)
309	8.5 litres (15.0 pints)
Horizon	6.2 litres (10.9 pints)

Fuel tank:

205	50 litres (11.0 gallons)
305	43 litres (9.5 gallons)
309	55 litres (12.1 gallons)
Horizon	45 litres (9.9 gallons)
Manual gearbox	2.0 litres (3.5 pints)

Introduction to the Peugeot/Talbot diesel engine

The 1.9 litre diesel engine was first fitted to the Talbot Horizon in late 1982, then in September 1983 the 1.7 litre version was fitted to the Peugeot 205. In October 1983 both engine sizes were available in the Peugeot 305, and in August 1986 the 1.9 engine was available in the Peugeot 309.

Over the last decade the diesel engine has made a large impact on the saloon car market due mainly to a marked improvement of its performance and economy, and a reduction in noise levels.

Routine maintenance tasks are few and easily carried out, although certain jobs will require the purchase or construction of special tools.

Outside the engine bay the vehicles to which these engines are fitted are much the same as petrol-engined versions. For complete coverage of a particular vehicle, the appropriate manual for petrol engined vehicles will be needed as well.

Buying spare parts

Only Peugeot/Talbot spare parts should be used if the vehicle (or engine) is still under warranty. The use of other makes of parts may invalidate the warranty if a claim has to be made. In any case, only buy parts of reputable make. 'Pirate' parts, often of unknown origin, may not meet the maker's standards either dimensionally or in material quality.

Large items or sub-assemblies – eg cylinder heads, starter motors, injection pumps – may be available on an 'exchange' basis. Consult a

Peugeot/Talbot dealer for availability and conditions. Dismantled or badly damaged units may not be accepted in exchange.

When buying engine parts, be prepared to quote the engine number. This is stamped on the front of the cylinder block.

General repair procedures

Whenever servicing, repair or overhaul work is carried out on the car or its components, it is necessary to observe the following procedures and instructions. This will assist in carrying out the operation efficiently and to a professional standard of workmanship.

Joint mating faces and gaskets

Where a gasket is used between the mating faces of two components, ensure that it is renewed on reassembly, and fit it dry unless otherwise stated in the repair procedure. Make sure that the mating faces are clean and dry with all traces of old gasket removed. When cleaning a joint face, use a tool which is not likely to score or damage the face, and remove any burrs or nicks with an oilstone or fine file.

Make sure that tapped holes are cleaned with a pipe cleaner, and keep them free of jointing compound if this is being used unless specifically instructed otherwise.

Ensure that all orifices, channels or pipes are clear and blow through them, preferably using compressed air.

Oil seals

Whenever an oil seal is removed from its working location, either individually or as part of an assembly, it should be renewed.

The very fine sealing lip of the seal is easily damaged and will not seal if the surface it contacts is not completely clean and free from scratches, nicks or grooves. If the original sealing surface of the component cannot be restored, the component should be renewed.

Protect the lips of the seal from any surface which may damage them in the course of fitting. Use tape or a conical sleeve where possible. Lubricate the seal lips with oil before fitting and, on dual lipped seals, fill the space between the lips with grease.

Unless otherwise stated, oil seals must be fitted with their sealing lips toward the lubricant to be sealed.

Use a tubular drift or block of wood of the appropriate size to install the seal and, if the seal housing is shouldered, drive the seal down to the shoulder. If the seal housing is unshouldered, the seal should be fitted with its face flush with the housing top face.

Screw threads and fastenings

Always ensure that a blind tapped hole is completely free from oil, grease, water or other fluid before installing the bolt or stud. Failure to do this could cause the housing to crack due to the hydraulic action of the bolt or stud as it is screwed in.

When tightening a castellated nut to accept a split pin, tighten the nut to the specified torque, where applicable, and then tighten further to the next split pin hole. Never slacken the nut to align a split pin hole unless stated in the repair procedure.

When checking or retightening a nut or bolt to a specified torque setting, slacken the nut or bolt by a quarter of a turn, and then retighten to the specified setting.

Locknuts, locktabs and washers

Any fastening which will rotate against a component or housing in the course of tightening should always have a washer between it and the relevant component or housing.

Spring or split washers should always be renewed when they are used to lock a critical component such as a big-end bearing retaining nut or bolt.

Locktabs which are folded over to retain a nut or bolt should always be renewed.

Self-locking nuts can be reused in non-critical areas, providing resistance can be felt when the locking portion passes over the bolt or stud thread.

Split pins must always be replaced with new ones of the correct size for the hole.

Special tools

Some repair procedures in this manual entail the use of special tools such as a press, two or three-legged pullers, spring compressors etc. Wherever possible, suitable readily available alternatives to the manufacturer's special tools are described, and are shown in use. In some instances, where no alternative is possible, it has been necessary to resort to the use of a manufacturer's tool and this has been done for reasons of safety as well as the efficient completion of the repair operation. Unless you are highly skilled and have a thorough understanding of the procedure described, never attempt to bypass the use of any special tool when the procedure described specifies its use. Not only is there a very great risk of personal injury, but expensive damage could be caused to the components involved.

Tools and working facilities

Introduction

A selection of good tools is a fundamental requirement for anyone contemplating the maintenance and repair of a motor vehicle. For the owner who does not possess any, their purchase will prove a considerable expense, offsetting some of the savings made by doing-it-yourself. However, provided that the tools purchased are of good quality, they will last for many years and prove an extremely worthwhile investment.

To help the average owner to decide which tools are needed to carry out the various tasks detailed in this manual, we have compiled three lists of tools under the following headings: *Maintenance and minor repair, Repair and overhaul,* and *Special.* The newcomer to practical mechanics should start off with the *Maintenance and minor repair* tool kit and confine himself to the simpler jobs around the vehicle. Then, as his confidence and experience grow, he can undertake more difficult tasks, buying extra tools as, and when, they are needed. In this way, a *Maintenance and minor repair* tool kit can be built-up into a *Repair and overhaul* tool kit over a considerable period of time without any major cash outlays. The experienced do-it-yourselfer will have a tool kit good enough for most repair and overhaul procedures and will add tools from the *Special* category when he feels the expense is justified by the amount of use to which these tools will be put.

It is obviously not possible to cover the subject of tools fully here. For those who wish to learn more about tools and their use there is a book entitled *How to Choose and Use Car Tools* available from the publishers of this manual.

Maintenance and minor repair tool kit

The tools given in this list should be considered as a minimum requirement if routine maintenance, servicing and minor repair operations are to be undertaken. We recommend the purchase of combination spanners (ring one end, open-ended the other); although more expensive than open-ended ones, they do give the advantages of both types of spanner.

> *Combination spanners - 10, 11, 12, 13, 14 & 17 mm*
> *Adjustable spanner - 9 inch*
> *Engine sump drain plug key*
> *Set of feeler gauges*
> *Brake bleed nipple spanner*
> *Screwdriver - 4 in long x $^1/_4$ in dia (flat blade)*
> *Screwdriver - 4 in long x $^1/_4$ in dia (cross blade)*
> *Combination pliers - 6 inch*
> *Hacksaw (junior)*
> *Tyre pump*
> *Tyre pressure gauge*
> *Oil can*
> *Fine emery cloth (1 sheet)*
> *Wire brush (small)*
> *Funnel (medium size)*
> *Chain or strap wrench*

Repair and overhaul tool kit

These tools are virtually essential for anyone undertaking any major repairs to a motor vehicle, and are additional to those given in the *Maintenance and minor repair* list. Included in this list is a comprehensive set of sockets. Although these are expensive they will be found invaluable as they are so versatile - particularly if various drives are included in the set. We recommend the ½ in square-drive type, as this can be used with most proprietary torque wrenches. If you cannot afford a socket set, even bought piecemeal, then inexpensive tubular box spanners are a useful alternative.

The tools in this list will occasionally need to be supplemented by tools from the *Special* list.

> *Sockets (or box spanners) to cover range in previous list, plus 27 mm for injectors*
> *Reversible ratchet drive (for use with sockets)*
> *Extension piece, 10 inch (for use with sockets)*
> *Universal joint (for use with sockets)*
> *Torque wrench (for use with sockets)*
> *'Mole' wrench - 8 inch*
> *Ball pein hammer*
> *Soft-faced hammer, plastic or rubber*
> *Screwdriver - 6 in long x $^5/_{16}$ in dia (flat blade)*
> *Screwdriver - 2 in long x $^5/_{16}$ in square (flat blade)*
> *Screwdriver - 1$^1/_2$ in long x $^1/_4$ in dia (cross blade)*
> *Screwdriver - 3 in long x $^1/_8$ in dia (electricians)*
> *Pliers - electricians side cutters*
> *Pliers - needle nosed*
> *Pliers - circlip (internal and external)*
> *Cold chisel - $^1/_2$ inch*
> *Scriber*
> *Scraper*
> *Centre punch*
> *Pin punch*
> *Hacksaw*
> *Valve grinding tool*
> *Steel rule/straight-edge*
> *Allen keys (inc. splined/Torx type if necessary)*
> *Dial test indicator and stand*
> *Selection of files*
> *Wire brush (large)*
> *Axle-stands*
> *Jack (strong trolley or hydraulic type)*
> *Light with extension lead*

Special tools

The tools in this list are those which are not used regularly, are expensive to buy, or which need to be used in accordance with their manufacturers' instructions. Unless relatively difficult mechanical jobs are undertaken frequently, it will not be economic to buy many of these tools. Where this is the case, you could consider clubbing together with friends (or joining a motorists' club) to make a joint purchase, or borrowing the tools against a deposit from a local garage or tool hire specialist.

The following list contains only those tools and instruments freely available to the public, and not those special tools produced by the vehicle manufacturer specifically for its dealer network. You will find occasional references to these manufacturers' special tools in the text of this manual. Generally, an alternative method of doing the job without the vehicle manufacturers' special tool is given. However, sometimes, there is no alternative to using them. Where this is the case and the relevant tool cannot be bought or borrowed, you will have to entrust the work to a franchised garage.

> *Valve spring compressor (where applicable)*
> *Piston ring compressor*
> *Balljoint separator*
> *Universal hub/bearing puller*
> *Impact screwdriver*
> *Micrometer and/or vernier gauge*
> *Universal electrical multi-meter*
> *Cylinder compression gauge (suitable for diesel)*
> *Lifting tackle*
> *Trolley jack*

Buying tools

For practically all tools, a tool factor is the best source since he will have a very comprehensive range compared with the average garage or accessory shop. Having said that, accessory shops often offer excellent quality tools at discount prices, so it pays to shop around.

Remember, you don't have to buy the most expensive items on the shelf, but it is always advisable to steer clear of the very cheap tools. There are plenty of good tools around at reasonable prices, so ask the proprietor or manager of the shop for advice before making a purchase.

Care and maintenance of tools

Having purchased a reasonable tool kit, it is necessary to keep the tools in a clean serviceable condition. After use, always wipe off any dirt, grease and metal particles using a clean, dry cloth, before putting the tools away. Never leave them lying around after they have been used. A simple tool rack on the garage or workshop wall, for items such as screwdrivers and pliers is a good idea. Store all normal wrenches and sockets in a metal box. Any measuring instruments, gauges, meters, etc, must be carefully stored where they cannot be damaged or become rusty.

Take a little care when tools are used. Hammer heads inevitably become marked and screwdrivers lose the keen edge on their blades from time to time. A little timely attention with emery cloth or a file will soon restore items like this to a good serviceable finish.

Working facilities

Not to be forgotten when discussing tools, is the workshop itself. If anything more than routine maintenance is to be carried out, some form of suitable working area becomes essential.

It is appreciated that many an owner mechanic is forced by circumstances to remove an engine or similar item, without the benefit of a garage or workshop. Having done this, any repairs should always be done under the cover of a roof.

Wherever possible, any dismantling should be done on a clean, flat workbench or table at a suitable working height.

Any workbench needs a vice: one with a jaw opening of 4 in (100 mm) is suitable for most jobs. As mentioned previously, some clean dry storage space is also required for tools, as well as for lubricants, cleaning fluids, touch-up paints and so on, which become necessary.

Another item which may be required, and which has a much more general usage, is an electric drill with a chuck capacity of at least 5/16 in (8 mm). This, together with a good range of twist drills, is virtually essential for fitting accessories such as mirrors and reversing lights.

Last, but not least, always keep a supply of old newspapers and clean, lint-free rags available, and try to keep any working area as clean as possible.

Spanner jaw gap comparison table

Jaw gap (in)	Spanner size
0.250	1/4 in AF
0.276	7 mm
0.313	5/16 in AF
0.315	8 mm

Jaw gap (in)	Spanner size
0.344	11/32 in AF; 1/8 in Whitworth
0.354	9 mm
0.375	3/8 in AF
0.394	10 mm
0.433	11 mm
0.438	7/16 in AF
0.445	3/16 in Whitworth; 1/4 in BSF
0.472	12 mm
0.500	1/2 in AF
0.512	13 mm
0.525	1/4 in Whitworth; 5/16 in BSF
0.551	14 mm
0.563	9/16 in AF
0.591	15 mm
0.600	5/16 in Whitworth; 3/8 in BSF
0.625	5/8 in AF
0.630	16 mm
0.669	17 mm
0.686	11/16 in AF
0.709	18 mm
0.710	3/8 in Whitworth; 7/16 in BSF
0.748	19 mm
0.750	3/4 in AF
0.813	13/16 in AF
0.820	7/16 in Whitworth; 1/2 in BSF
0.866	22 mm
0.875	7/8 in AF
0.920	1/2 in Whitworth; 9/16 in BSF
0.938	15/16 in AF
0.945	24 mm
1.000	1 in AF
1.010	9/16 in Whitworth; 5/8 in BSF
1.024	26 mm
1.063	11/16 in AF; 27 mm
1.100	5/8 in Whitworth; 11/16 in BSF
1.125	11/8 in AF
1.181	30 mm
1.200	11/16 in Whitworth; 3/4 in BSF
1.250	11/4 in AF
1.260	32 mm
1.300	3/4 in Whitworth; 7/8 in BSF
1.313	15/16 in AF
1.390	13/16 in Whitworth; 15/16 in BSF
1.417	36 mm
1.438	17/16 in AF
1.480	7/8 in Whitworth; 1 in BSF
1.500	11/2 in AF
1.575	40 mm; 15/16 in Whitworth
1.614	41 mm
1.625	15/8 in AF
1.670	1 in Whitworth; 11/8 in BSF
1.688	111/16 in AF
1.811	46 mm
1.813	113/16 in AF
1.860	11/8 in Whitworth; 11/4 in BSF
1.875	17/8 in AF
1.969	50 mm
2.000	2 in AF
2.050	11/4 in Whitworth; 13/8 in BSF
2.165	55 mm
2.362	60 mm

Conversion factors

Length (distance)

Inches (in)	X	25.4	= Millimetres (mm)	X	0.0394	= Inches (in)
Feet (ft)	X	0.305	= Metres (m)	X	3.281	= Feet (ft)
Miles	X	1.609	= Kilometres (km)	X	0.621	= Miles

Volume (capacity)

Cubic inches (cu in; in³)	X	16.387	= Cubic centimetres (cc; cm³)	X	0.061	= Cubic inches (cu in; in³)
Imperial pints (Imp pt)	X	0.568	= Litres (l)	X	1.76	= Imperial pints (Imp pt)
Imperial quarts (Imp qt)	X	1.137	= Litres (l)	X	0.88	= Imperial quarts (Imp qt)
Imperial quarts (Imp qt)	X	1.201	= US quarts (US qt)	X	0.833	= Imperial quarts (Imp qt)
US quarts (US qt)	X	0.946	= Litres (l)	X	1.057	= US quarts (US qt)
Imperial gallons (Imp gal)	X	4.546	= Litres (l)	X	0.22	= Imperial gallons (Imp gal)
Imperial gallons (Imp gal)	X	1.201	= US gallons (US gal)	X	0.833	= Imperial gallons (Imp gal)
US gallons (US gal)	X	3.785	= Litres (l)	X	0.264	= US gallons (US gal)

Mass (weight)

Ounces (oz)	X	28.35	= Grams (g)	X	0.035	= Ounces (oz)
Pounds (lb)	X	0.454	= Kilograms (kg)	X	2.205	= Pounds (lb)

Force

Ounces-force (ozf; oz)	X	0.278	= Newtons (N)	X	3.6	= Ounces-force (ozf; oz)
Pounds-force (lbf; lb)	X	4.448	= Newtons (N)	X	0.225	= Pounds-force (lbf; lb)
Newtons (N)	X	0.1	= Kilograms-force (kgf; kg)	X	9.81	= Newtons (N)

Pressure

Pounds-force per square inch (psi; lbf/in²; lb/in²)	X	0.070	= Kilograms-force per square centimetre (kgf/cm²; kg/cm²)	X	14.223	= Pounds-force per square inch (psi; lbf/in²; lb/in²)
Pounds-force per square inch (psi; lbf/in²; lb/in²)	X	0.068	= Atmospheres (atm)	X	14.696	= Pounds-force per square inch (psi; lbf/in²; lb/in²)
Pounds-force per square inch (psi; lbf/in²; lb/in²)	X	0.069	= Bars	X	14.5	= Pounds-force per square inch (psi; lbf/in²; lb/in²)
Pounds-force per square inch (psi; lbf/in²; lb/in²)	X	6.895	= Kilopascals (kPa)	X	0.145	= Pounds-force per square inch (psi; lbf/in²; lb/in²)
Kilopascals (kPa)	X	0.01	= Kilograms-force per square centimetre (kgf/cm²; kg/cm²)	X	98.1	= Kilopascals (kPa)
Millibar (mbar)	X	100	= Pascals (Pa)	X	0.01	= Millibar (mbar)
Millibar (mbar)	X	0.0145	= Pounds-force per square inch (psi; lbf/in²; lb/in²)	X	68.947	= Millibar (mbar)
Millibar (mbar)	X	0.75	= Millimetres of mercury (mmHg)	X	1.333	= Millibar (mbar)
Millibar (mbar)	X	0.401	= Inches of water (inH₂O)	X	2.491	= Millibar (mbar)
Millimetres of mercury (mmHg)	X	0.535	= Inches of water (inH₂O)	X	1.868	= Millimetres of mercury (mmHg)
Inches of water (inH₂O)	X	0.036	= Pounds-force per square inch (psi; lbf/in²; lb/in²)	X	27.68	= Inches of water (inH₂O)

Torque (moment of force)

Pounds-force inches (lbf in; lb in)	X	1.152	= Kilograms-force centimetre (kgf cm; kg cm)	X	0.868	= Pounds-force inches (lbf in; lb in)
Pounds-force inches (lbf in; lb in)	X	0.113	= Newton metres (Nm)	X	8.85	= Pounds-force inches (lbf in; lb in)
Pounds-force inches (lbf in; lb in)	X	0.083	= Pounds-force feet (lbf ft; lb ft)	X	12	= Pounds-force inches (lbf in; lb in)
Pounds-force feet (lbf ft; lb ft)	X	0.138	= Kilograms-force metres (kgf m; kg m)	X	7.233	= Pounds-force feet (lbf ft; lb ft)
Pounds-force feet (lbf ft; lb ft)	X	1.356	= Newton metres (Nm)	X	0.738	= Pounds-force feet (lbf ft; lb ft)
Newton metres (Nm)	X	0.102	= Kilograms-force metres (kgf m; kg m)	X	9.804	= Newton metres (Nm)

Power

Horsepower (hp)	X	745.7	= Watts (W)	X	0.0013	= Horsepower (hp)

Velocity (speed)

Miles per hour (miles/hr; mph)	X	1.609	= Kilometres per hour (km/hr; kph)	X	0.621	= Miles per hour (miles/hr; mph)

Fuel consumption*

Miles per gallon, Imperial (mpg)	X	0.354	= Kilometres per litre (km/l)	X	2.825	= Miles per gallon, Imperial (mpg)
Miles per gallon, US (mpg)	X	0.425	= Kilometres per litre (km/l)	X	2.352	= Miles per gallon, US (mpg)

Temperature

Degrees Fahrenheit = (°C x 1.8) + 32

Degrees Celsius (Degrees Centigrade; °C) = (°F - 32) x 0.56

*It is common practice to convert from miles per gallon (mpg) to litres/100 kilometres (l/100km), where mpg (Imperial) x l/100 km = 282 and mpg (US) x l/100 km = 235

Safety first!

Professional motor mechanics are trained in safe working procedures. However enthusiastic you may be about getting on with the job in hand, do take the time to ensure that your safety is not put at risk. A moment's lack of attention can result in an accident, as can failure to observe certain elementary precautions.

There will always be new ways of having accidents, and the following points do not pretend to be a comprehensive list of all dangers; they are intended rather to make you aware of the risks and to encourage a safety-conscious approach to all work you carry out on your vehicle.

Essential DOs and DON'Ts

DON'T rely on a single jack when working underneath the vehicle. Always use reliable additional means of support, such as axle stands, securely placed under a part of the vehicle that you know will not give way.

DON'T attempt to loosen or tighten high-torque nuts (e.g. wheel hub nuts) while the vehicle is on a jack; it may be pulled off.

DON'T start the engine without first ascertaining that the transmission is in neutral (or 'Park' where applicable) and the parking brake applied.

DON'T suddenly remove the filler cap from a hot cooling system – cover it with a cloth and release the pressure gradually first, or you may get scalded by escaping coolant.

DON'T attempt to drain oil until you are sure it has cooled sufficiently to avoid scalding you.

DON'T grasp any part of the engine, exhaust or catalytic converter without first ascertaining that it is sufficiently cool to avoid burning you.

DON'T allow brake fluid or antifreeze to contact vehicle paintwork.

DON'T syphon toxic liquids such as fuel, brake fluid or antifreeze by mouth, or allow them to remain on your skin.

DON'T inhale dust – it may be injurious to health (see *Asbestos* below).

DON'T allow any spilt oil or grease to remain on the floor – wipe it up straight away, before someone slips on it.

DON'T use ill-fitting spanners or other tools which may slip and cause injury.

DON'T attempt to lift a heavy component which may be beyond your capability – get assistance.

DON'T rush to finish a job, or take unverified short cuts.

DON'T allow children or animals in or around an unattended vehicle.

DO wear eye protection when using power tools such as drill, sander, bench grinder etc, and when working under the vehicle.

DO use a barrier cream on your hands prior to undertaking dirty jobs – it will protect your skin from infection as well as making the dirt easier to remove afterwards; but make sure your hands aren't left slippery. Note that long-term contact with used engine oil can be a health hazard.

DO keep loose clothing (cuffs, tie etc) and long hair well out of the way of moving mechanical parts.

DO remove rings, wristwatch etc, before working on the vehicle – especially the electrical system.

DO ensure that any lifting tackle used has a safe working load rating adequate for the job.

DO keep your work area tidy – it is only too easy to fall over articles left lying around.

DO get someone to check periodically that all is well, when working alone on the vehicle.

DO carry out work in a logical sequence and check that everything is correctly assembled and tightened afterwards.

DO remember that your vehicle's safety affects that of yourself and others. If in doubt on any point, get specialist advice.

IF, in spite of following these precautions, you are unfortunate enough to injure yourself, seek medical attention as soon as possible.

Asbestos

Certain friction, insulating, sealing, and other products – such as brake linings, brake bands, clutch linings, torque converters, gaskets, etc – contain asbestos. *Extreme care must be taken to avoid inhalation of dust from such products since it is hazardous to health.* If in doubt, assume that they *do* contain asbestos.

Fire

Remember at all times that fuel is highly flammable. Never smoke, or have any kind of naked flame around, when working on the vehicle. But the risk does not end there – a spark caused by an electrical short-circuit, by two metal surfaces contacting each other, by careless use of tools, or even by static electricity built up in your body under certain conditions, can ignite fuel vapour, which in a confined space is highly explosive.

Always disconnect the battery earth (ground) terminal before working on any part of the fuel or electrical system, and never risk spilling fuel on to a hot engine or exhaust.

It is recommended that a fire extinguisher of a type suitable for fuel and electrical fires is kept handy in the garage or workplace at all times. Never try to extinguish a fuel or electrical fire with water.

Fumes

Certain fumes are highly toxic and can quickly cause unconsciousness and even death if inhaled to any extent. Fuel vapour comes into this category, as do the vapours from certain solvents such as trichloroethylene. Any draining or pouring of such volatile fluids should be done in a well ventilated area.

When using cleaning fluids and solvents, read the instructions carefully. Never use materials from unmarked containers – they may give off poisonous vapours.

Never run the engine of a motor vehicle in an enclosed space such as a garage. Exhaust fumes contain carbon monoxide which is extremely poisonous; if you need to run the engine, always do so in the open air or at least have the rear of the vehicle outside the workplace.

If you are fortunate enough to have the use of an inspection pit, never drain or pour fuel, and never run the engine, while the vehicle is standing over it; the fumes, being heavier than air, will concentrate in the pit with possibly lethal results.

The battery

Never cause a spark, or allow a naked light, near the vehicle's battery. It will normally be giving off a certain amount of hydrogen gas, which is highly explosive.

Always disconnect the battery earth (ground) terminal before working on the fuel or electrical systems.

If possible, loosen the filler plugs or cover when charging the battery from an external source. Do not charge at an excessive rate or the battery may burst.

Take care when topping up and when carrying the battery. The acid electrolyte, even when diluted, is very corrosive and should not be allowed to contact the eyes or skin.

If you ever need to prepare electrolyte yourself, always add the acid slowly to the water, and never the other way round. Protect against splashes by wearing rubber gloves and goggles.

When jump starting a car using a booster battery, for negative earth (ground) vehicles, connect the jump leads in the following sequence: First connect one jump lead between the positive (+) terminals of the two batteries. Then connect the other jump lead first to the negative (–) terminal of the booster battery, and then to a good earthing (ground) point on the vehicle to be started, at least 18 in (45 cm) from the battery if possible. Ensure that hands and jump leads are clear of any moving parts, and that the two vehicles do not touch. Disconnect the leads in the reverse order.

Mains electricity

When using an electric power tool, inspection light etc, which works from the mains, always ensure that the appliance is correctly connected to its plug and that, where necessary, it is properly earthed (grounded). Do not use such appliances in damp conditions and, again, beware of creating a spark or applying excessive heat in the vicinity of fuel or fuel vapour.

Routine maintenance

The maintenance schedules below are basically those recommended by the manufacturer. Vehicles operating under adverse conditions may need more frequent maintenance. Some of the tasks called up will be described in detail in the appropriate manual for petrol-engined vehicles.

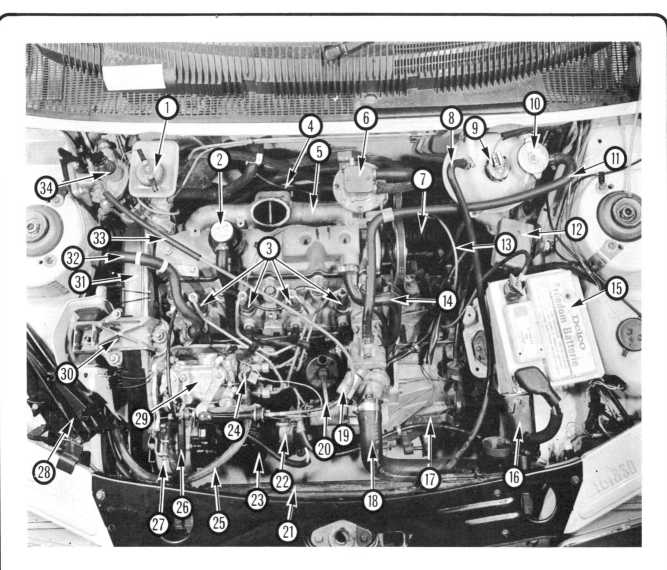

Under-bonnet view of a Peugeot 205 GRD (air cleaner removed)

1 Brake fluid reservoir and filler cap
2 Engine oil filler cap
3 Injectors
4 Speedometer cable
5 Inlet manifold
6 Brake vacuum pump (exhauster)
7 Steering gear
8 Expansion tank vent hose

9 Coolant low level warning switch
10 Coolant filler/pressure cap
11 Expansion tank supply hose
12 Preheater plug relay
13 Reverse gear stop cable
14 Crankcase ventilation hose
15 Battery
16 Electric cooling fan relay box

17 Clutch relay lever
18 Top hose
19 Fast idle thermostatic unit
20 Engine oil dipstick
21 Radiator
22 Starter motor
23 Oil filter
24 Stop solenoid
25 Fuel supply hose
26 Fuel return hose

27 Alternator
28 Vehicle lifting jack
29 Injection pump
30 Right-hand engine mounting bracket
31 Timing cover
32 Coolant bypass hose
33 Accelerator cable
34 Fuel filter

Front end underbody view of a Peugeot 205 GRD

1 Subframe
2 Final drive drain plug
3 Anti-roll bar guide rod
4 Exhaust pipe

5 Exhaust manifold resonator
6 Anti-roll bar
7 Tie-rod
8 Lower suspension arm

9 Lower engine mounting torque link
10 Oil level sensor
11 Right-hand driveshaft

12 Engine oil drain plug
13 Radiator
14 Gearbox
15 Left-hand driveshaft

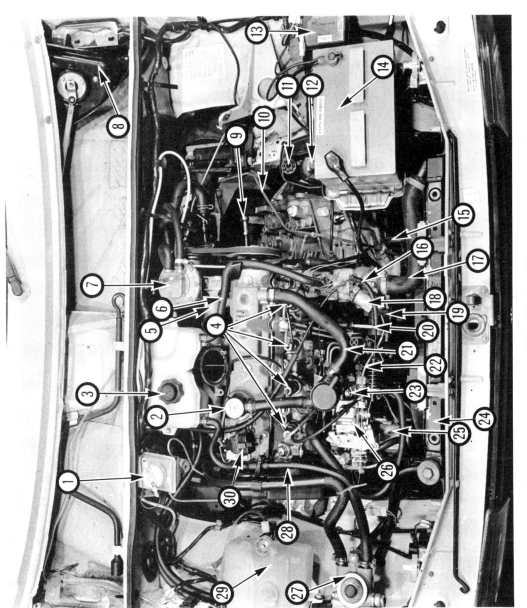

Under-bonnet view of a Talbot Horizon LD (air cleaner removed)

1 Brake fluid reservoir and
   filler cap
2 Engine oil filler cap
3 Coolant expansion tank and
   filler cap
4 Injectors
5 Inlet manifold
6 Expansion tank supply hose

7 Brake vacuum pump
   (exhauster)
8 Windscreen wiper motor
9 Gearchange rod
10 Hydraulic clutch fluid pipe
11 Air cleaner mounting pad
12 Left-hand engine/gearbox
   mounting

13 Preheater plug relay
14 Battery
15 Clutch release lever
16 Accelerator cable
17 Top hose
18 Fast idle thermostatic unit
19 Starter motor
20 Engine oil dipstick
21 Crankcase ventilation hose

22 Fast idle cable
23 Stop solenoid
24 Radiator
25 Alternator
26 Injector pump
27 Fuel filter
28 Expansion tank vent hose
29 Washer fluid reservoir
30 Diagnostic socket

Front end underbody view of a Talbot Horizon LD

1 Torsion bar
2 Anti-roll bar
3 Gearchange control rods
4 Exhaust pipe
5 Crossmember
6 Track rod end

7 Lower suspension arm
8 Lower shock absorber
   mounting
9 Splash shield
10 Bottom hose

11 Lower engine mounting
   torque link
12 Electric cooling fan
13 Engine oil drain plug
14 Right-hand driveshaft

15 Horn
16 Gearbox
17 Final drive drain plug
18 Left-hand driveshaft
19 Steering gear

Weekly, before a long journey, or every 250 miles (400 km)

Engine
Check oil level

Cooling system
Check coolant level

Braking system
Check fluid level

Suspension and steering
Check tyre pressures
Examine tyres for wear and damage

Electrical system
Check operation of lights, horn etc
Check washer fluid level(s)
Check battery electrolyte level (if applicable)

General
Check all systems for condition and security

Every 5000 miles (7500 km) or six months, whichever comes first

Engine
Renew oil and filter (Chapter 1)

Fuel system
Drain water from fuel filter (Chapter 3)

Gearbox
Check oil level (models up to 1988)

Every 15 000 miles (22 500 km) or 18 months, whichever comes first

In addition to the 5000 mile service requirements

Engine
Clean oil filler cap mesh

Fuel system
Renew fuel filter (Chapter 3)
Check condition of accelerator cable

Clutch
Check cable adjustment (not Horizon)

Braking system
Check handbrake adjustment
Check vacuum pump for leaks
Check rear brake shoes for wear

Suspension and steering
Check steering pump fluid level

Electrical system
Check drivebelt tension(s)

Every 2 years

Cooling system
Renew coolant

Braking system
Renew fluid

Every 30 000 miles (45 000 km) or 3 years, whichever comes first

In addition to, or instead of, the previously specified service requirements.

Fuel system
Renew air cleaner element

Gearbox
Renew oil (models up to 1988)

Suspension and steering
Check wheel bearing adjustment
Check steering components for condition and security
Check suspension components for condition and security
Check shock absorbers for leaks and operation

Every 40 000 miles (60 000 km) or 4 years, whichever comes first

In addition to the previously specified service requirements

Gearbox
Check oil level (models from 1988)

Every 50 000 miles (75 000 km)

Engine
Renew timing belt (Chapter 1)

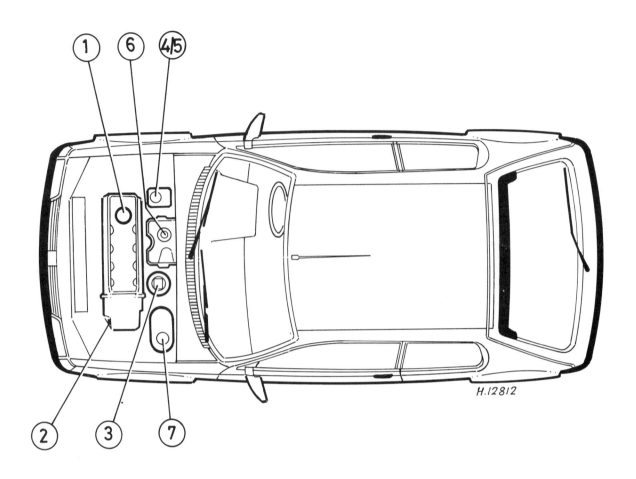

H.12812

Recommended lubricants and fluids

Component or system	Lubricant type/specification	Duckhams recommendation
1 Engine	Multigrade engine oil, viscosity SAE 15W/40 to API SE/CD	Duckhams Hypergrade
2 Manual gearbox:		
Models up to 1988	Multigrade oil, viscosity SAE 15W/40 to API SF/CC	Duckhams Hypergrade
Models from 1988	Gear oil, viscosity SAE 75W/80W to API GL5	Duckhams Hypoid PT 75W/80W
3 Brake vacuum pump	Multigrade oil, viscosity SAE 15W/40 to API SF/CC	Duckhams Hypergrade
4 Brake hydraulic system	Hydraulic fluid to SAE J1703 or DOT 3	Duckhams Universal Brake and Clutch Fluid
5 Clutch hydraulic system	Hydraulic fluid to SAE J1703 or DOT 3	Duckhams Universal Brake and Clutch Fluid
6 Cooling system	Ethylene glycol based antifreeze (9730.70)	Duckhams Universal Antifreeze and Summer Coolant
Wheel bearings	Multi-purpose grease	Duckhams LB 10
Manual steering rack	Molybdenum disulphide grease	Duckhams LBM 10
Power steering system	Dexron type automatic transmission fluid	Duckhams D-Matic

Fault diagnosis

Introduction

The vehicle owner who does his or her own maintenance according to the recommended schedules should not have to use this section of the manual very often. Modern component reliability is such that, provided those items subject to wear or deterioration are inspected or renewed at the specified intervals, sudden failure is comparatively rare. Faults do not usually just happen as a result of sudden failure, but develop over a period of time. Major mechanical failures in particular are usually preceded by characteristic symptoms over hundreds or even thousands of miles. Those components which do occasionally fail without warning are often small and easily carried in the vehicle.

With any fault finding, the first step is to decide where to begin investigations. Sometimes this is obvious, but on other occasions a little detective work will be necessary. The owner who makes half a dozen haphazard adjustments or replacements may be successful in curing a fault (or its symptoms), but he will be none the wiser if the fault recurs and he may well have spent more time and money than was necessary. A calm and logical approach will be found to be more satisfactory in the long run. Always take into account any warning signs or abnormalities that may have been noticed in the period preceding the fault – power loss, high or low gauge readings, unusual noises or smells, etc – and remember that failure of components such as fuses may only be pointers to some underlying fault.

The pages which follow here are intended to help in cases of failure to start or breakdown on the road. There is also a Fault Diagnosis Section at the end of each Chapter which should be consulted if the preliminary checks prove unfruitful. Whatever the fault, certain basic principles apply. These are as follows:

Verify the fault. This is simply a matter of being sure that you know what the symptoms are before starting work. This is particularly important if you are investigating a fault for someone else who may not have described it very accurately.

Don't overlook the obvious. For example, if the vehicle won't start, is there fuel in the tank? (Don't take anyone else's word on this particular point, and don't trust the fuel gauge either!) If an electrical fault is indicated, look for loose or broken wires before digging out the test gear.

Cure the disease, not the symptom. Substituting a flat battery with a fully charged one will get you off the hard shoulder, but if the underlying cause is not attended to, the new battery will go the same way.

Don't take anything for granted. Particularly, don't forget that a 'new' component may itself be defective (especially if it's been rattling round in the boot for months), and don't leave components out of a fault diagnosis sequence just because they are new or recently fitted. When you do finally diagnose a difficult fault, you'll probably realise that all the evidence was there from the start.

Electrical faults

Electrical faults can be more puzzling than straightforward mechanical failures, but they are no less susceptible to logical analysis if the basic principles of operation are understood. Vehicle electrical wiring exists in extremely unfavourable conditions – heat, vibration and chemical attack – and the first things to look for are loose or corroded connections and broken or chafed wires, especially where the wires pass through holes in the bodywork or are subject to vibration.

All metal-bodied vehicles in current production have one pole of the battery 'earthed', ie connected to the vehicle bodywork, and in nearly all modern vehicles it is the negative (–) terminal. The various electrical components – motors, bulb holders etc – are also connected to earth, either by means of a lead or directly by their mountings. Electric current flows through the component and then back to the battery via the bodywork. If the component mounting is loose or corroded, or if a good path back to the battery is not available, the circuit will be incomplete and malfunction will result. The engine and/or gearbox are also earthed by means of flexible metal straps to the body or subframe; if these straps are loose or missing, starter motor, generator and ignition trouble may result.

Assuming the earth return to be satisfactory, electrical faults will be due either to component malfunction or to defects in the current supply. If supply wires are broken or cracked internally this results in an open-circuit, and the easiest way to check for this is to bypass the suspect wire temporarily with a length of wire having a crocodile clip or suitable connector at each end. Alternatively, a 12V test lamp can be used to verify the presence of supply voltage at various points along the wire and the break can be thus isolated.

If a bare portion of a live wire touches the bodywork or other earthed metal part, the electricity will take the low-resistance path thus formed back to the battery: this is known as a short-circuit. Hopefully a short-circuit will blow a fuse, but otherwise it may cause burning of the insulation (and possibly further short-circuits) or even a fire. This is why it is inadvisable to bypass persistently blowing fuses with silver foil or wire.

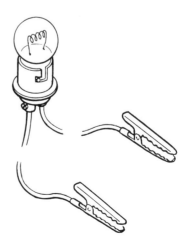

A simple test lamp is useful for tracing electrical faults

Spares and tool kit

Most vehicles are supplied only with sufficient tools for wheel changing; the *Maintenance and minor repair* tool kit detailed in *Tools and working facilities*, with the addition of a hammer, is probably sufficient for those repairs that most motorists would consider attempting at the roadside. In addition a few items which can be fitted without too much trouble in the event of a breakdown should be carried. Experience and available space will modify the list below, but the following may save having to call on professional assistance:

Drivebelt(s) – emergency type may suffice
Spare fuses
Set of principal light bulbs
Tin of radiator sealer and hose bandage
Exhaust bandage
Roll of insulating tape
Length of soft iron wire
Length of electrical flex
Torch or inspection lamp (can double as test lamp)
Battery jump leads
Tow-rope
Litre of engine oil
Sealed can of hydraulic fluid
Emergency windscreen
Worm drive clips
Tube of filler paste

If spare fuel is carried, a can designed for the purpose should be used to minimise risks of leakage and collision damage. A first aid kit and a warning triangle, whilst not at present compulsory in the UK, are obviously sensible items to carry in addition to the above.

When touring abroad it may be advisable to carry additional spares which, even if you cannot fit them yourself, could save having to wait while parts are obtained. The items below may be worth considering:

Clutch and throttle cables
Cylinder head gasket
Alternator brushes
Fuel injector(s) and fire seal washer(s)
Tyre valve core

One of the motoring organisations will be able to advise on availability of fuel etc in foreign countries.

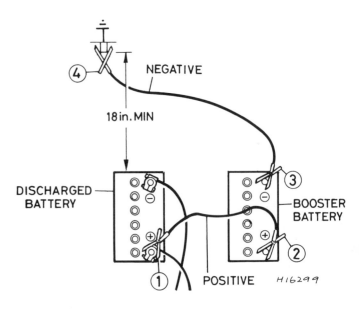

Jump start lead connections for negative earth vehicles – connect leads in order shown

Engine will not start

Engine fails to turn when starter operated
Flat battery (recharge, use jump leads, or push start)
Battery terminals loose or corroded
Battery earth to body defective
Engine earth strap loose or broken
Starter motor (or solenoid) wiring loose or broken
Ignition/starter switch faulty
Major mechanical failure (seizure)
Starter or solenoid internal fault (see Chapter 7)

Starter motor turns engine slowly
Partially discharged battery (recharge, use jump leads, or push start)
Battery terminals loose or corroded
Battery earth to body defective
Engine earth strap loose
Starter motor (or solenoid) wiring loose
Starter motor internal fault (see Chapter 7)

Starter motor spins without turning engine
Starter motor reduction gears stripped (where applicable)
Starter motor mounting bolts loose

Engine turns normally but fails to start
No fuel in tank
Wax formed in fuel (in very cold weather)
Poor compression

Fuel system or preheater fault (see Chapter 3)
Major mechanical failure

Engine fires but will not run
Preheater fault (see Chapter 3)
Wax formed in fuel (in very cold weather)
Other fuel system fault (see Chapter 3)

Engine cuts out and will not restart

Engine misfires before cutting out – fuel fault
Fuel tank empty
Fuel filter blocked (check for delivery)
Fuel tank filler vent blocked (suction will be evident on releasing cap)
Other fuel system fault (see Chapter 3)

Engine cuts out – other causes
Serious overheating
Major mechanical failure (eg camshaft drive)

Engine overheats

Coolant loss due to internal or external leakage (see Chapter 2)
Thermostat defective
Low oil level
Brakes binding
Radiator clogged externally or internally
Electric cooling fan not operating correctly
Engine waterways clogged

Note: *Do not add cold water to an overheated engine or damage may result*

Low engine oil pressure

Gauge reads low or warning light illuminated with engine running
> Oil level low or incorrect grade
> Defective gauge or sender unit
> Wire to sender unit earthed
> Engine overheating
> Oil filter clogged or bypass valve defective
> Oil pressure relief valve defective
> Oil pick-up strainer clogged
> Oil pump worn or mountings loose
> Worn main or big-end bearings

Note: *Low oil pressure in a high-mileage engine at tickover is not necessarily a cause for concern. Sudden pressure loss at speed is far more significant. In any event, check the gauge or warning light sender before condemning the engine.*

Engine noises

To inexperienced ears, the diesel engine sounds alarming even when there is nothing wrong with it, so it may be prudent to have an unusual noise expertly diagnosed before making renewals or repairs.

Whistling or wheezing noises
> Leaking vacuum hose
> Leaking manifold gasket
> Blowing head gasket

Tapping or rattling
> Incorrect valve clearances
> Worn valve gear
> Worn oil pump chain
> Broken piston ring (ticking noise)

Knocking or thumping
> Unintentional mechanical contact (eg fan blades)
> Worn drivebelt
> Peripheral component fault (alternator, water pump etc)
> Fuel injector(s) leaking or sticking (see Chapter 3)
> Worn big-end bearings (regular heavy knocking, perhaps less under load)
> Worn main bearings (rumbling and knocking, perhaps worsening under load)
> Piston slap (most noticeable when cold)

Chapter 1 Engine

Contents

Specifications

General

Type	Four-cylinder, in-line, four-stroke, overhead camshaft, compression-ignition, mounted transversely and inclined 30° to rear. Transmission mounted on left-hand end of engine.

Designation:
205 and 305 1.7	XUD 7 – 161A
305, 309 and Horizon 1.9	XUD 9 – 162
Number of cylinders	4

Bore and stroke:
    1.7 .... 80.0 x 88.0 mm (3.150 x 3.465 in)
    1.9 .... 83.0 x 88.0 mm (3.268 x 3.465 in)

Compression ratio:
    1.7 .... 23.0 : 1
    1.9 .... 23.5 : 1

Compression pressures (engine hot, cranking speed):
    Minimum .... 18 bar (261 lbf/in²)
    Normal .... 25 to 30 bar (363 to 435 lbf/in²)
    Maximum difference between any two cylinders .... 5 bar (73 lbf/in²)

Cubic capacity:
    1.7 .... 1769 cc (107.9 cu in)
    1.9 .... 1905 cc (116.2 cu in)

Maximum torque (ISO):
    1.7 .... 110 Nm (81 lbf ft) at 2200 rpm
    1.9 .... 118 Nm (87 lbf ft) at 2000 rpm

Maximum power (ISO):
    1.7 .... 43.5 kW at 4600 rpm
    1.9 .... 47.0 kW at 4600 rpm

Maximum speed:
    No load .... 5100 rpm
    Laden .... 4600 rpm
Firing order .... 1-3-4-2 (No 1 at flywheel end)

Cylinder block

Cylinder bore diameter:
    1.7 .... 80.000 to 80.018 mm (3.1496 to 3.1503 in) or
                                                       80.030 to 80.048 mm (3.1508 to 3.1515 in)
    1.9 .... 83.000 to 83.018 mm (3.2677 to 3.2684 in) or
                                                       83.030 to 83.048 mm (3.2689 to 3.2696 in)

Pistons and piston rings

Piston diameter:
    1.7 .... 79.93 ± 0.008 mm (3.1468 ± 0.0003 in) or
                                                       79.96 ± 0.008 mm (3.1480 ± 0.0003 in)
    1.9 .... 82.930 ± 0.009 mm (3.2650 ± 0.0004 in) or
                                                       82.960 ± 0.009 mm (3.2661 ± 0.0004 in)

Piston ring end gaps (fitted):
    Top compression .... 0.20 to 0.40 mm (0.008 to 0.016 in)
    2nd compression .... 0.15 to 0.35 mm (0.006 to 0.014 in)
    Oil scraper .... 0.10 to 0.30 mm (0.004 to 0.012 in)
Connecting rod small-end bush inner diameter .... 25.007 to 25.020 mm (0.9845 to 0.9850 in)
Maximum weight difference between any two pistons .... 2.5 g (0.09 oz)
Maximum piston protrusion difference between any two pistons .... 0.12 mm (0.0047 in)

Crankshaft

Endfloat .... 0.07 to 0.32 mm (0.003 to 0.013 in)
Main bearing journal diameter:

    Standard .... $60.0 \, {}^{+0}_{-0.019}$ mm $\quad (2.3622 \, {}^{+0}_{-0.0008}$ in$)$
    Undersize .... -0.3 mm (0.0118 in)

Crankpin diameter:

    Standard .... $50.0 \, {}^{+0}_{-0.016}$ mm $\quad (1.9685 \, {}^{+0}_{-0.0006}$ in$)$
    Undersize .... -0.3 mm (0.0118 in)

Maximum journal/crankpin out-of-round .... 0.007 mm (0.0003 in)

Cylinder head

Maximum warp:
    1.7 .... 0.03 mm (0.0012 in)
    1.9 .... 0.05 mm (0.0020 in)
Swirl chamber protrusion .... 0 to 0.03 mm (0 to 0.001 in)

Valves

Seat angle (inclusive):
    Inlet .... 120°
    Exhaust .... 90°

Valve recess below cylinder head:
    Inlet .... 0.90 to 1.45 mm (0.0354 to 0.0571 in)
    Exhaust .... 0.50 to 1.05 mm (0.0197 to 0.0413 in)
Valve clearances (cold):
    Inlet .... 0.15 ± 0.08 mm (0.006 ± 0.003 in)
    Exhaust .... 0.30 ± 0.08 mm (0.012 ± 0.003 in)
Valve timing (at 1.0 mm clearance):
    Inlet opens .... 8° BTDC
    Inlet closes .... 40° ABDC
    Exhaust opens .... 56° BBDC
    Exhaust closes .... 12° ATDC

Camshaft
Endfloat .... 0.07 to 0.16 mm (0.003 to 0.006 in)

Lubrication system
Lubricant type/specification .... Multigrade engine oil, viscosity SAE 15W/40 to API SE/CD (Duckhams Hypergrade)
Oil capacity (drain and refill) .... 4.5 litres (7.9 pints)
Dipstick minimum to maximum marks .... 1.5 litres (2.6 pints)
Oil pressure (at engine temperature of 80°C/176°F):
    Minimum .... 2.0 bar (29.0 lbf/in²) at 800 rpm
    Maximum .... 3.5 to 5.0 bar (51 to 73 lbf/in²) at 4000 rpm
Oil pressure switch operating pressures:
    On .... 0.58 to 0.44 bar (8.4 to 6.4 lbf/in²)
    Off .... 0.8 bar (11.6 lbf/in²) maximum

Oil pump
Type .... Two gear
Pressure relief valve opens .... 4.0 bar (58 lbf/in²)
Gear endfloat .... 0.12 mm (0.005 in)
Clearance between gear lobes and housing .... 0.064 mm (0.0025 in)

Torque wrench settings

	Nm	lbf ft
Camshaft bearing cap	18	13
Big-end bearing cap	50	37
Oil gallery plug	28	21
Main bearing cap	70	52
Front housing	11	8
Oil pump cover	9	7
Oil pump mounting	13	10
Sump	19	14
Flywheel	50	37
Cylinder head bolts (up to 1987):		
Stage 1	30	22
Stage 2	60	44
Stage 3 Loosen 1/4 turn then	60	44
Stage 4 (after 10 mins at 3000 rpm). Loosen 1/4 turn then	65	48
Cylinder head bolts (1987 on):		
Stage 1	30	22
Stage 2	70	52
Stage 3	Tighten a further 120°	
Injection pump bracket	20	15
Camshaft sprocket	35	26
Bottom timing cover	12	9
Crankshaft pulley bolt:		
Stage 1	40	30
Stage 2	plus 60° or to 150	plus 60° or to 111
Oil pressure switch	30	22
Valve cover	2	1.5
Pump pulley to camshaft	35	26
Oil cooler	68	50
Sump oil drain bracket	3	2.2
Oil filter	14	10
Left-hand engine mounting:		
Centre nut	35	26
Small nuts	18	13
Centre stud to transmission	50	37
Right-hand lower engine mounting bracket	18	13
Right-hand upper engine mounting bracket:		
To engine	35	26
To mounting rubber	28	21
Lower link mounting	35	26
Timing belt tensioner	18	13
Timing belt intermediate roller	18	13

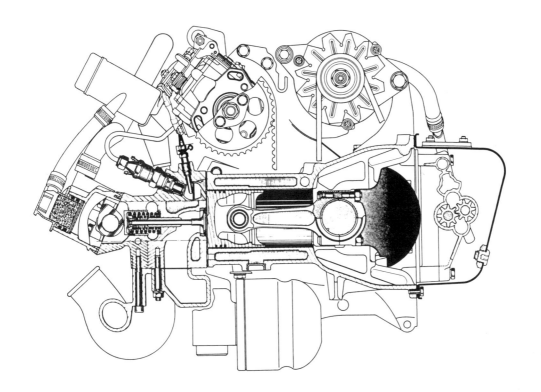

Fig. 1.2 Engine side cross-section (Sec 1)

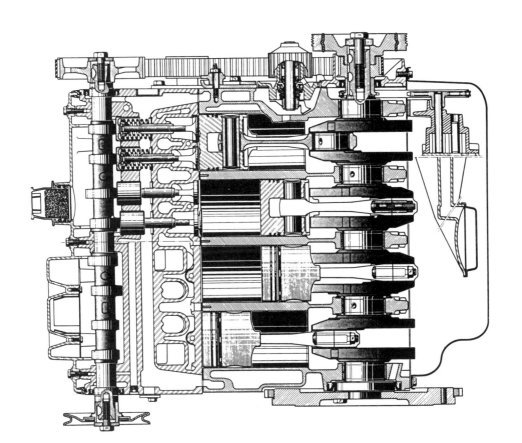

Fig. 1.1 Engine longitudinal cross-section (Sec 1)

1 General description

The engine is of four-cylinder overhead camshaft design, mounted transversely and inclined 30° to the rear, with the transmission mounted on the left-hand side. Both the block and the cylinder head are of cast iron.

A toothed timing belt drives the camshaft, injection pump and water pump. Bucket tappets are fitted between the camshaft and valves, and valve clearance adjustment is by means of selective shims. The camshaft is supported by three bearings machined directly in the cylinder head.

The crankshaft runs in five main bearings of the usual shell type. Endfloat is controlled by thrust washers either side of No 2 main bearing.

The pistons are selected to be of matching weight, and incorporate fully floating gudgeon pins retained by circlips.

The oil pump is chain driven from the front of the crankshaft. An oil cooler is fitted to some 1.9 engines.

2 Routine maintenance

Carry out the following procedures at the intervals given in *Routine Maintenance* at the beginning of the manual.

Check engine oil level
1 The vehicle must be parked on level ground and the engine must have been stopped for approximately 10 minutes to allow oil in circulation to return to the sump.

2 Withdraw the dipstick from its tube, wipe the end with a piece of clean rag, re-insert it fully and then withdraw it again. Read the oil level on the end of the dipstick; it should be between the two cut-outs which represent the maximum and minimum oil levels (photos).

3 It is not strictly necessary to top up the engine oil until it reaches the minimum cut-out, but on no account allow the level to fall any lower. The amount of oil needed to top up from minimum to maximum is 1 litre (1.8 pints) for 1.7 models and approximately 1.5 litres (2.6 pints) for 1.9 models.

2.2A Withdrawing the engine oil dipstick (1.7 engine)

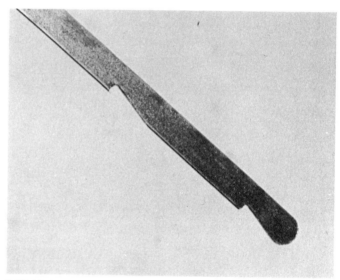

2.2B Minimum and maximum level cut-outs on the engine oil dipstick

2.4 Topping up the engine oil level

2.7 Engine oil drain plug

4 When topping-up is necessary, use clean engine oil of the specified type, preferably of the same make and grade as that already in the engine. Top up by removing the filler cap from the valve cover or filler tube as applicable (photo). Allow time for the oil to run down to the sump before rechecking the level on the dipstick. Refit the filler cap and dipstick on completion.

5 All engines use some oil, depending on the degree of wear and the pattern of use. Oil which is not being lost through external leaks is entering the cylinders and being burnt, however, the diesel engine is not so prone to this problem as its petrol counterpart since there is no inlet vacuum to suck oil past piston rings and inlet valve stems.

Drain engine oil and renew oil filter
6 The engine oil should be drained when hot (ie just after a run) with the vehicle parked on level ground.

7 Position a drain pan of adequate capacity beneath the sump. Wipe clean around the drain plug then unscrew it using a hexagon key and allow the oil to drain (photo). If the oil is very hot take precautions to avoid scalding.

8 Remove the oil filler cap and allow the oil to drain for at least 15 minutes.

2.10 Unscrewing the oil filter with a strap wrench

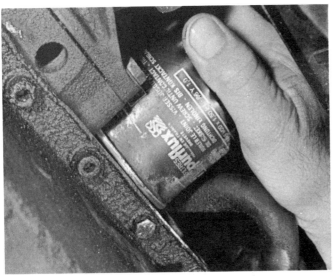

2.11 Tighten the oil filter by hand only

9 Check and if necessary renew the drain plug washer then wipe the sump, refit the drain plug and tighten it.

10 Position the drain pan beneath the oil filter on the front of the cylinder block. Using a strap wrench, unscrew the filter and remove it (photo). If a strap wrench is not available a screwdriver can be driven through the filter and used as a lever to remove it.

11 Wipe clean the filter seat on the cylinder block or oil cooler (as applicable). Smear a little engine oil on the new oil filter's sealing ring then screw on the filter until it just touches the seat. Hand tighten the oil filter by a further two-thirds of a turn (photo).

12 Fill the engine with the correct grade and quantity of oil as previously described.

13 Start the engine and allow it to idle. Check that the oil pressure warning light goes out and also check that there is no oil leakage from the oil filter.

14 Switch off the engine and recheck the oil level.

15 Put the old oil into a sealed container and dispose of it safely.

Clean oil filler cap (where applicable)
16 Pull the oil filler cap from the top of the valve cover then loosen the clip and disconnect the crankcase ventilation hose.

17 Clean the wire mesh filter in paraffin and allow to dry. If it is blocked with sludge, however, renew the cap complete.

18 Refit the hose to the filler cap and fit the cap to the valve cover.

Renew the timing belt
19 Refer to Section 4.

---

3 Major operations possible with the engine in the vehicle

The following operations can be carried out without having to remove the engine from the car:

  (a) Timing belt – removal and refitting
  (b) Camshaft – removal and refitting
  (c) Cylinder head – removal and refitting
  (d) Camshaft oil seals – renewal
  (e) Crankshaft oil seals – renewal
  (f) Sump – removal and refitting
  (g) Oil pump – removal and refitting
  (h) Pistons and connecting rods – removal and refitting
  (i) Flywheel – removal and refitting

---

4 Timing belt – inspection, removal, refitting and tensioning

---

1 The timing belt drives the camshaft, injection pump, and water pump from a toothed sprocket on the front of the crankshaft. If it breaks in service the pistons are likely to hit the valve heads and result in an expensive repair.

2 The timing belt should be renewed at 50 000 mile (75 000 km) intervals, however, if it is contaminated with oil or if it is at all noisy in operation (a 'scraping' noise due to uneven wear) it should be renewed earlier. Where a Bosch injection pump is fitted, excessive play in the front bearing can cause wear to the sides of the timing belt.

3 Apply the handbrake then jack up the front right-hand corner of the vehicle until the wheel is just clear of the ground. Support the vehicle on an axle stand and engage 4th or 5th gear. This will enable the engine to be turned easily by turning the right-hand wheel.

4 Remove the engine splash guard from under the right-hand front wheel arch. For extra working room on 205, 305 and 309 models drain the cooling system (Chapter 2) and disconnect the bottom hose from the water pump inlet. On 205 and 309 models also remove the intermediate metal tube after removing the cross head screws.

5 Disconnect the battery negative lead.

6 Loosen the alternator pivot and adjustment bolts then unscrew the tension bolt until it is possible to slip the drivebelt from the pulleys.

7 With 4th or 5th gear selected, have an assistant depress the footbrake pedal, then unscrew the crankshaft pulley bolt. Alternatively the crankshaft can be locked by unbolting the gearbox cover plate and using a wide-bladed screwdriver to lock the starter ring gear.

8 Slide the pulley from the front of the crankshaft.

9 Unbolt the bottom timing cover.

10 Support the weight of the engine using a hoist or trolley jack.

11 Unscrew the nuts and remove the right-hand engine mounting bracket. On Horizon models it will first be necessary to remove the centre timing cover section.

12 Pull up the front clip, release the spring clips, and withdraw the two timing cover sections (photos). On Horizon models first push the engine as far forward as possible.

13 Turn the engine by means of the front right-hand wheel until the three bolt holes in the camshaft and injection pump sprockets are aligned with the corresponding holes in the engine front plate.

14 Insert an 8.0 mm diameter metal dowel rod or a drill through the special hole in the left-hand rear flange of the cylinder block by the starter motor, then carefully turn the engine either way until the rod enters the TDC hole in the flywheel (see photo 22.26).

15 Insert three M8 bolts through the holes in the camshaft and injection pump sprockets and screw them into the engine front plate fingertight (Fig. 1.4A).

16 Loosen the timing belt tensioner pivot nut and adjustment bolt, then turn the bracket anti-clockwise to release the tension and

retighten the adjustment bolt to hold the tensioner in the released position. If available use a ⅜ inch square drive extension in the hole provided to turn the bracket against the spring tension.

17 Mark the timing belt with an arrow to indicate its normal direction of turning then remove it from the camshaft, injection pump, water pump and crankshaft sprockets.

18 Inspect the belt for cracks, fraying, and damage to the teeth. Pay particular attention to the roots of the teeth. If any damage is evident or if the belt is contaminated with oil it must be renewed and any oil leak rectified.

19 Commence refitting by locating the timing belt on the crankshaft sprocket, making sure that, where applicable, the rotation arrow is facing the correct way.

20 Hold the timing belt engaged with the crankshaft sprocket then feed it over the roller and onto the injection pump, camshaft, and water pump sprockets and over the tensioner roller. To ensure correct engagement, locate only a half width on the injection pump sprocket before feeding the timing belt onto the camshaft sprocket keeping the belt taut and fully engaged with the crankshaft sprocket. Locate the timing belt fully onto the sprockets.

21 Loosen the tensioner adjustment bolt while holding the bracket against the spring tension, then slowly release the bracket until the roller presses against the timing belt. Retighten the adjustment bolt.

22 Remove the bolts from the camshaft and injection pump sprockets. Remove the metal dowel rod from the cylinder block.

23 Rotate the engine two complete turns in its normal direction. Do not rotate the engine backwards as the timing belt must be kept tight between the crankshaft, injection pump and camshaft sprockets.

24 Loosen the tensioner adjustment bolt to allow the tensioner spring to push the roller against the timing belt, then tighten both the adjustment bolt and pivot nut.

25 Recheck the engine timing as described in paragraphs 13 and 14 then remove the metal dowel rod.

26 Refit the timing cover sections and secure with the special clip and spring clips.

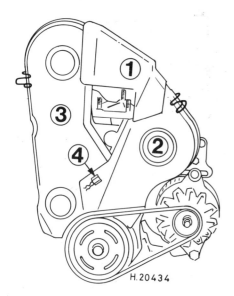

Fig. 1.3 Timing cover sections on Horizon models (Sec 4)

1   Centre section   3   Right-hand section
2   Left-hand section   4   Clip

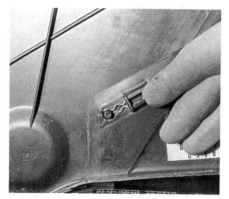

4.12A Timing cover front clip ...

4.12B ... and spring clips

27 Refit the right-hand engine mounting bracket and tighten the nuts. On Horizon models refit the centre timing cover section.

28 Remove the trolley jack or hoist.

29 Slide the pulley onto the front of the crankshaft.

30 Apply three drops of locking fluid on the threads of the crankshaft pulley bolt then insert it and tighten to the specified torque while holding the crankshaft stationary using the method described in paragraph 7.

31 Refit the alternator drivebelt and tension it as described in Chapter 7.

32 Reconnect the battery negative lead.

33 Refit the engine splash-guard under the right-hand front wheelarch.

34 Where applicable, reconnect the bottom hose and intermediate metal tube then refill the cooling system (Chapter 2).

35 Lower the vehicle to the ground.

5 Timing belt tensioner and right-hand engine mounting bracket – removal and refitting

1 Apply the handbrake then jack up the front right-hand corner of the vehicle until the wheel is just clear of the ground. Support the vehicle on an axle stand and engage 4th or 5th gear so that the engine may be rotated by turning the right-hand wheel.

2 Support the weight of the engine using a hoist or trolley jack.

3 Unscrew the nuts and remove the right-hand engine mounting bracket. On Horizon models it will first be necessary to remove the centre timing cover section.

4 Disconnect the battery negative lead.

5 Pull up the special clip, release the spring clips, and withdraw the two timing cover sections (see photos 4.12A and 4.12B). On Horizon models first push the engine as far forward as possible.

6 Turn the engine by means of the front right-hand wheel until the three bolt holes in the camshaft and injection pump sprockets are aligned with the corresponding holes in the engine front plate.

7 Insert an 8.0 mm diameter metal dowel rod or a drill through the special hole in the left-hand rear flange of the cylinder block by the starter motor, then carefully turn the engine either way until the rod enters the TDC hole in the flywheel (see photo 22.26).

8 Insert three M8 bolts through the holes in the camshaft and injection pump sprockets and screw them into the engine front plate fingertight (Fig. 1.4A).

9 Loosen the timing belt tensioner pivot nut and adjustment bolt, then turn the bracket anti-clockwise until the adjustment bolt is in the middle of the slot and retighten the bolt. If available use a ⅜ inch square drive extension in the hole provided to turn the bracket against the spring tension.

10 A tool must now be obtained in order to hold the tensioner plunger in the mounting bracket. The tool shown in Fig. 1.4B is designed to slide in the two lower bolt holes of the mounting bracket. The tool shown in Fig. 1.4B is designed to slide in the two lower bolt holes of the mounting bracket, and it should be quite easy to fabricate a similar tool out of sheet metal using long bolts instead of metal dowel rods.

11 Unscrew the two lower bolts then fit the special tool. Grease the inner surface of the tool to prevent any damage to the end of the tensioner plunger.

12 Unscrew the pivot nut a[...] tensioner bracket complete w[...]

13 Unbolt the engine moun[...] bolt is on the inside face of th[...] models).

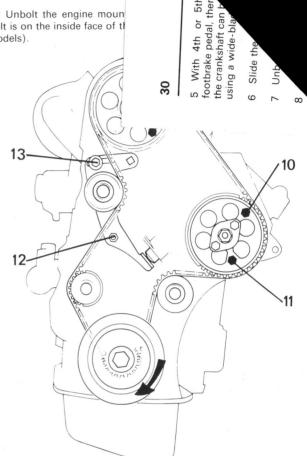

Fig. 1.4A Holding camshaft and injection pump sprockets in position using M8 bolts (Sec 4)

9, 10 and 11 M8 bolts   13 Tensioner adjustment bolt
12 Tensioner pivot nut

Fig. 1.4B Peugeot tool for holding the tensioner plunger (Sec 5)

14 Compress the tensioner plunger into the mounting bracket, remove the special tool then withdraw the plunger and spring.

15 Refitting is a reversal of removal, but refer to Section 4 paragraphs 21 to 25 for details of the timing belt adjustment procedure.

6 Timing belt intermediate roller – removal and refitting

1 Follow the procedure given in paragraphs 1 to 9 of Section 5.

2 Remove the engine splash guard from under the right-hand front wheel arch. For extra working room on 205, 305 and 309 models drain the cooling system (Chapter 2) and disconnect the bottom hose from the water pump inlet. On 205 and 309 models also remove the intermediate metal tube after removing the crosshead screws.

3 Disconnect the battery negative lead.

4 Loosen the alternator pivot and adjustment bolts then unscrew the tension bolt until it is possible to slip the drivebelt from the pulleys.

...ear selected have an assistant depress the
...unscrew the crankshaft pulley bolt. Alternatively
...e locked by unbolting the gearbox cover plate and
...ed screwdriver to lock the starter ring gear.

... pulley from the front of the crankshaft.

...olt the lower timing cover.

...Remove the spacer from the stud for the upper timing cover
...ections. Note the position of the stud then unscrew and remove it.

9 Unscrew the remaining bolts securing the intermediate roller
bracket to the cylinder block noting that the upper bolt also secures the
engine mounting bracket.

10 Slightly loosen the remaining engine mounting bracket bolts then
slide out the intermediate roller and bracket.

11 Refitting is a reversal of removal, but note the following additional
points:

   (a) Tighten all bolts to the specified torque
   (b) Apply three drops of locking fluid to the threads of the
        crankshaft pulley bolt before inserting it
   (c) Tension the alternator drivebelt as described in Chapter 7
   (d) Adjust the timing belt as described in Section 4, paragraphs
        21 to 25

7 Camshaft – removal and refitting

1 Follow the procedure given in paragraphs 1 to 9 of Section 5.

2 Remove the timing belt from the camshaft sprocket and tie it to one
side without bending it excessively.

3 Unscrew the M8 bolt holding the camshaft sprocket in the timing
position.

4 Remove the oil filler cap/breather and position it to one side.

5 Disconnect the battery negative lead. Also disconnect the air inlet
hose from the inlet manifold and air cleaner.

6 Loosen the pivot and adjustment bolts of the brake vacuum pump,
swivel the unit forwards, and disconnect the drivebelt from the pulleys.
Where applicable also disconnect the power steering pump drivebelt.

7 Disconnect the crankcase ventilation hose from the valve cover
(photo). Also disconnect the wiring for the diagnostic socket or oil
level sensor.

8 Unbolt and remove the valve cover. Remove the gasket (photos).

9 Hold the camshaft stationary with a spanner on the special lug
between the 3rd and 4th cams or by using a lever in the sprocket holes
then unscrew the camshaft sprocket bolt and withdraw the sprocket
(photos). Recover the Woodruff key if it is loose. Do not rotate the
camshaft otherwise the valves will strike the pistons of Nos 1 and 4
cylinders. If necessary turn the engine one quarter turn to position all
the pistons halfway down the cylinders in order to prevent any
damage, however, release the timing belt from the injection pump
sprocket first.

10 Mark the position of the camshaft bearing caps numbering them
from the flywheel end and making the marks on the manifold side.

11 Progressively unscrew the nuts then remove the bearing caps.

12 Lift the camshaft and withdraw it from the front engine plate.
Remove the oil seal from the timing end of the camshaft.

13 Hold the camshaft stationary with a spanner on the special lug
between the 3rd and 4th cams, then unscrew the bolt and remove the
pump pulley from the flywheel end of the camshaft. Use a puller if it is
tight (photo). Recover the Woodruff key if it is loose.

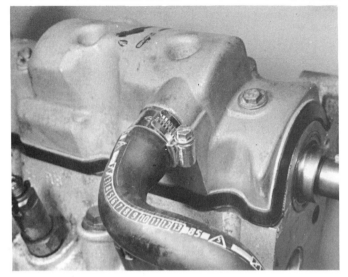

7.7 Crankcase ventilation hose

7.8A Unbolt the valve cover ...

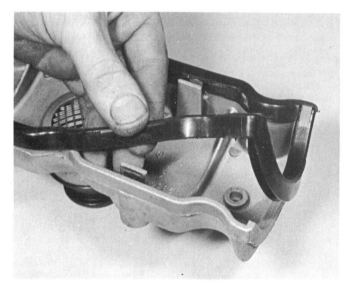

7.8B ... and remove the gasket

7.9A Special lug for holding the camshaft (arrowed)

7.9B Removing the camshaft sprocket

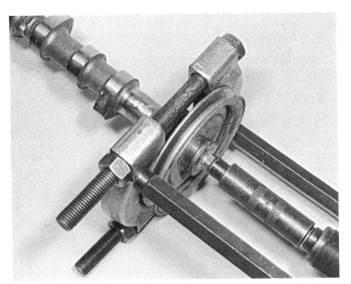

7.13 Using a puller to remove the pump pulley from the camshaft

7.17 The 'DIST' marking (arrowed) must be at the timing belt end

14 Remove the oil seal from the flywheel end of the camshaft.

15 Clean all the components including the bearing surfaces in the cylinder head. Examine the components carefully for wear and damage, in particular check the surface of the cams for scoring and pitting. Renew components as necessary and obtain new oil seals.

16 Commence reassembly by lubricating the cams and bearing journals with engine oil.

17 Locate the camshaft on the cylinder head, passing it through the

engine front plate, with the tips of the cams 4 and 6 facing downwards and resting on the bucket tappets. The cast DIST marking on the camshaft should be at the timing belt end of the cylinder head (photo) and the key slot for the camshaft sprocket should be facing upwards.

18 Fit the centre bearing cap the correct way round as previously noted then screw on the nuts and tighten them two or three turns.

19 Apply sealing compound to the end bearing caps on the areas shown in Fig. 1.5. Fit them in the correct positions and tighten the nuts two or three turns (photo).

7.19 Fitting a camshaft end bearing cap

7.20A Tightening the camshaft bearing cap nuts

20 Tighten all the nuts progressively to the specified torque making sure that cams 4 and 6 remain facing downwards (photo). Check that the camshaft endfloat is as given in the Specifications using feeler blades (photo). If not, the only course of action is to renew the cylinder head.

21 If the original camshaft is being refitted and it is known that the valve clearances are correct, proceed to paragraph 22, otherwise check and adjust the valve clearances as described in Section 8. Note that as the timing belt is disconnected at this stage, the crankshaft must be turned one quarter turn either way from the TDC position so that all the pistons are halfway down the cylinders. This will prevent the valves striking the pistons when the camshaft is rotated. Release the timing belt from the injection pump sprocket while turning the engine as the timing bolts are still in position.

22 Smear the lips of the oil seals with oil then fit them over each end of the camshaft, open end first, and press them in until flush with the end faces of the end caps. Use an M10 bolt, washers and a suitable socket to press in the oil seals (photo).

23 Fit the Woodruff key and pump pulley to the flywheel end of the camshaft, insert the bolt and tighten it while holding the camshaft stationary.

24 Fit the Woodruff key and camshaft sprocket to the timing end of the camshaft. Apply locking fluid to the threads then insert the bolt and tighten it to the specified torque while holding the camshaft stationary.

25 Refit the valve cover, together with a new gasket, and tighten the bolts. Reconnect the wiring.

26 Refit the crankcase ventilation hose.

27 Locate the drivebelt on the camshaft and and vacuum pump pulleys. Press the pump rearwards until the deflection of the belt midway between the two pulleys is approximately 5.0 mm (0.2 in) under firm thumb pressure. Tighten the adjustment bolt followed by the pivot bolt. Similarly refit the power steering pump drivebelt where applicable.

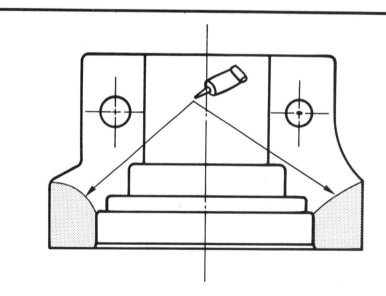

Fig. 1.5 Areas on camshaft end bearing caps to apply
sealing compound (Sec 7)

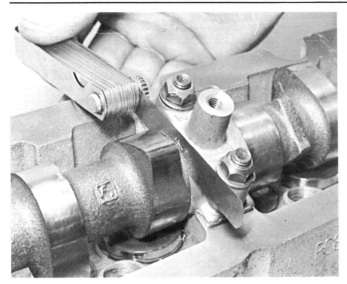

7.20B Checking the camshaft endfloat

7.22 Using a socket and bolt to fit a camshaft oil seal

28 Reconnect the battery negative lead and the air inlet hose.

29 Refit the oil filler cap/breather.

30 Align the holes and refit the M8 timing bolt to the camshaft sprocket.

31 If the crankshaft was turned a quarter turn from TDC as in paragraphs 9 and 21, turn the crankshaft back the quarter turn so that pistons 1 and 4 are again at TDC. Do not turn the engine more than a quarter turn otherwise pistons 2 and 3 will pass their TDC positions and will strike valves 4 and 6.

32 Refit the TDC dowel rod to the flywheel.

33 Refit and adjust the timing belt with reference to Section 4, paragraphs 20 to 25. The remaining procedure is a reversal of removal.

8 Valve clearances – checking and adjustment

Checking
1 Apply the handbrake then jack up the front right-hand corner of the vehicle until the wheel is just clear of the ground.

2 Support the vehicle on an axle stand and engage 4th or 5th gear so that the engine may be rotated by turning the right-hand wheel.

3 Disconnect the battery negative lead.

4 Remove the oil filler cap/breather and position it to one side.

5 Disconnect the air inlet hose from the inlet manifold and air cleaner.

6 Disconnect the crankcase ventilation hose from the valve cover. Also disconnect the wiring for the diagnostic socket or oil level sensor.

7 Unbolt and remove the valve cover. Remove the gasket.

8 On a piece of paper draw the outline of the engine with the cylinders numbered from the flywheel end and also showing the position of each valve, together with the specified valve clearance. Above each valve draw two lines for noting (1) the actual clearance and (2) the amount of adjustment required (see Fig. 1.6).

9 Turn the engine until the inlet valve of No 1 cylinder (nearest the flywheel) is fully closed and the apex of the cam is facing directly away from the bucket tappet.

10 Using feeler gauges measure the clearance between the base of the cam and the bucket tappet (photo). Record the clearance on line (1).

11 Repeat the measurement for the other seven valves, turning the engine as necessary so that the cam lobe in question is always facing directly away from the particular bucket tappet.

12 Calculate the difference between each measured clearance and the desired value and record it on line (2). Since the clearance is different for inlet and exhaust valves make sure that you are aware which valve you are dealing with. The valve sequence from either end of the engine is:

Inlet – Exhaust – Exhaust – Inlet – Inlet – Exhaust – Exhaust – Inlet

13 If all the clearances are within tolerance, refit the valve cover using a new gasket if necessary. If any clearance measured is outside the specified tolerance, adjustment must be carried out as described below.

8.10 Checking the valve clearances with feeler gauges

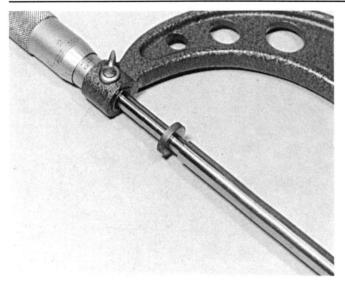

8.15 Checking the shim thickness with a micrometer

Adjustment

14 Remove the camshaft as described in Section 7.

15 Withdraw the first bucket tappet and its shim. Be careful that the shim does not fall out of the tappet. Clean the shim and measure its thickness with a micrometer (photo).

16 Refer to the clearance recorded for the valve concerned. If the clearance was more than the amount required the shim thickness must be increased by the difference recorded (2), if too small the thickness must be decreased.

17 Draw three more lines beneath each valve on the calculation paper as shown in Fig. 1.6. On line (4) note the measured thickness of the shim then add or deduct the difference from line (2) to give the final shim thickness required on line (5).

18 Shims are available in thicknesses between 2.425 mm and 3.550 mm in steps of 0.075 mm. Clean new shims before measuring or fitting them.

19 Repeat the procedure given in paragraphs 15 to 17 on the remaining valves keeping each tappet identified for position.

20 When reassembling, oil the shim and fit it on the valve stem first with the size marking facing downwards then oil the bucket tappet and lower it onto the shim. Do not raise the tappet after fitting as the shim may become dislodged.

21 When all the tappets are in position with their shims, refit the camshaft with reference to Section 7, but recheck the clearances to make sure they are correct.

9 Cylinder head – removal and refitting

1   Follow the procedure given in paragraphs 1 to 9 of Section 5.

2   Remove the timing belt from the camshaft sprocket and tie it to one side without bending it excessively.

3   Drain the cooling system as described in Chapter 2. On Horizon models remove the expansion tank.

4   Remove the air cleaner as described in Chapter 3.

5   Unscrew the M8 bolt holding the camshaft sprocket in the timing position. Also unscrew the tensioner adjustment bolt and the one or two upper bolts from the engine mounting bracket. On Horizon models unscrew the rear bolt securing the front plate.

6   At this stage the right-hand engine mounting bracket may be temporarily refitted and the hoist or trolley jack removed.

7   Disconnect the heater hose from the flywheel end of the cylinder head.

8   Disconnect the two small hoses from the thermostat housing then unbolt the housing from the cylinder head and position it to one side.

9   Remove the oil filler cap/breather and position it to one side.

10 Disconnect the air inlet hose from the inlet manifold.

11 Remove the brake vacuum pump as described in Chapter 5. Where applicable also disconnect the power steering pump drivebelt.

12 Disconnect the crankcase ventilation hose from the valve cover. Also disconnect the wiring for the diagnostic socket or oil level sensor.

13 Unbolt and remove the valve cover. Remove the gasket.

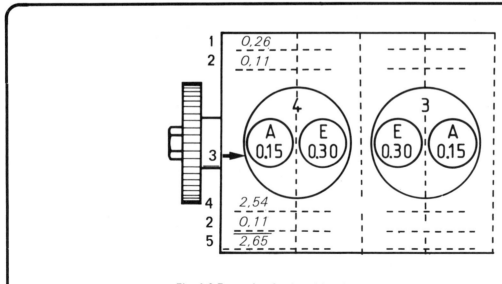

Fig. 1.6 Example of valve shim thickness calculation (Sec 8)

14 Unscrew the union nuts securing the injection pipes to the injectors and fuel injection pump, and remove the pipes as two assemblies.

15 Unbolt the left-hand engine lifting bracket.

16 Disconnect the wiring from the glow plugs.

17 Disconnect the fuel leak off pipe from the injection pump.

18 Hold the camshaft stationary with a spanner on the special lug between the 3rd and 4th cams or by using a lever in the sprocket holes, then unscrew the camshaft sprocket bolt and withdraw the sprocket. Recover the Woodruff key if it is loose. Do not rotate the camshaft otherwise the valves will strike the pistons of Nos 1 and 4 cylinders. If necessary release the timing belt from the injection pump sprocket and turn the engine one quarter turn in either direction to position all the pistons halfway down the cylinders in order to prevent any damage.

19 Unscrew the exhaust manifold to downpipe bolts. Recover the springs and collars.

20 Progressively unscrew the cylinder head bolts in the reverse order to that shown in Fig. 1.9. Remove the washers.

21 Release the cylinder head from the cylinder block and location dowel by rocking it. The Peugeot tool for doing this consists simply of two metal dowel rods with 90° angled ends (Fig. 1.7).

22 Lift the cylinder head from the block and remove the gasket.

23 Do not dispose of the old gasket until a new one has been obtained. The correct thickness of gasket is determined after measuring the protrusion of the pistons at TDC.

24 Clean the gasket faces of the cylinder head and cylinder block, preferably using a soft blunt instrument to prevent damage to the mating surfaces. Clean the threads of the cylinder head bolts and the corresponding holes in the cylinder block.

25 Check that the timing belt is clear of the injection pump sprocket, then turn the engine until pistons 1 and 4 are at TDC. Position a dial test indicator (DTI) on the cylinder block and zero it on the block face. Transfer the probe to the centre of piston 1 then slowly turn the crankshaft back and forth past TDC noting the highest reading on the indicator (photo). Record this reading.

26 Repeat this measurement procedure on piston 4 then turn the crankshaft half a turn (180°) and repeat the procedure on pistons 2 and 3.

27 If a dial test indicator is not available, piston protrusion may be measured using a straight-edge and feeler blades or vernier calipers, however, these methods are inevitably less accurate and cannot therefore be recommended.

28 Ascertain the greatest piston protrusion measurement and use this to determine the correct cylinder head gasket from the following chart:

Piston protrusion	Gasket identification
0.54 to 0.65 mm (0.021 to 0.026 in)	1 notch or 1 hole (for factory fitment only – use next thickness as replacement)
0.65 to 0.77 mm (0.026 to 0.030 in)	2 notches or 2 holes
0.77 to 0.82 mm (0.030 to 0.032 in)	3 notches or 3 holes

Note that the notch or hole on the centre line of the gasket (Fig. 1.8) identifies the gasket for use only on the 1.7 engine (type XUD 7) and has no significance for the gasket thickness.

29 Turn the crankshaft clockwise until pistons 1 and 4 pass bottom dead centre (BDC) and commence to rise, then position them halfway up their bores. Pistons 2 and 3 will also be at their mid-way positions, but descending their bores.

Fig. 1.7 Removing the cylinder head using angled dowel rods (Sec 9)

9.25 Checking the piston protrusion

30 Fit the correct gasket the right way round on the cylinder block with the identification notches or holes at the flywheel end (photo). Make sure that the location dowel is in place at the timing end of the block.

Models up to 1987

31 Lower the cylinder head onto the block.

32 Grease the threads and contact faces of the cylinder head bolts, then insert them, together with their washers (convex sides uppermost) and tighten them in the sequence shown in Fig. 1.9A in three stages as given in Specifications.

Models from 1987 on

33 Carefully clean the cylinder head threads using a suitable tap.

34 Lower the cylinder head onto the block.

35 Using new bolts, coat the threads and contact faces with thread-locking compound and fit new washers. Insert the bolts and tighten them in the order shown in Fig. 1.9B in three stages as given in Specifications.

All models

36 Recheck the valve clearances with reference to Section 8 and

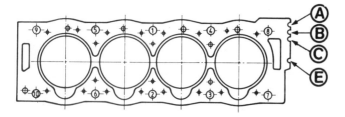

Fig. 1.8 Head gasket thickness identification notches
(Sec 9)

A = 1.49 mm (0.059 in)   A + B + C = 1.73 mm (0.068 in)
A + B = 1.61 mm (0.063 in)   E = 1.7 engine identification

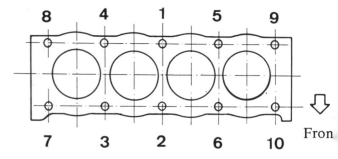

Fig. 1.9B Cylinder head bolt tightening sequence – models
from 1987 on (Sec 9)

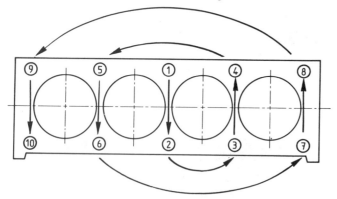

Fig. 1.9A Cylinder head bolt tightening sequence – models
up to 1987 (Sec 9)

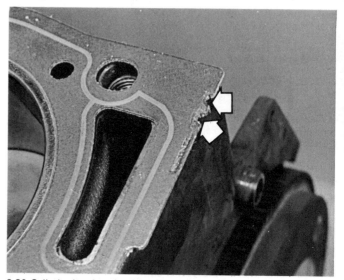

9.30 Cylinder head gasket identification notches (arrowed)

adjust them as necessary. Do this even if the clearances have been adjusted with the cylinder head removed, as there may be minor differences.

37 Lubricate the exhaust manifold-to-downpipe contact surfaces with heat resistant grease, then reconnect them and fit the bolts, together with the springs, cups and self-locking nuts. On 1.9 engines the bolts incorporate a shoulder to ensure that the springs are compressed correctly, however, on 1.7 engines, tighten the nuts progressively until approximately four threads are visible and the springs are compressed to 23.5 mm (0.925 in) in length.

38 Check that the Woodruff key is in place on the camshaft then fit the camshaft sprocket and bolt. Tighten the bolt to the specified torque while holding the camshaft stationary with a spanner on the special lug between the 3rd and 4th cams.

39 Turn the camshaft until the tips of cams 4 and 6 (counting from the flywheel end) are facing downwards.

40 Turn the crankshaft a quarter turn clockwise until pistons 1 and 4 are at TDC, and fit the TDC dowel rod to the flywheel. Do not turn the crankshaft anti-clockwise otherwise pistons 2 and 3 will pass their TDC positions and will strike valves 4 and 6.

41 Align the holes and refit the M8 timing bolt to the camshaft sprocket.

42 Refit the valve cover, together with a new gasket.

43 Apply locking fluid to the threads then refit and tighten the one or two upper bolts to the right-hand engine mounting bracket. Also refit the tensioner adjustment bolt and tighten it. Loosen the tensioner pivot nut.

44 Refit and adjust the timing belt with reference to Section 4, paragraphs 20 to 25.

45 Reconnect the fuel leak-off pipe to the injection pump.

46 Reconnect the glow plug wiring.

47 Refit the left-hand engine lifting bracket.

48 Refit the injection pipes and tighten the union nuts.

49 Reconnect the crankcase ventilation hose to the valve cover. Also reconnect the wiring for the diagnostic socket or oil level sensor.

50 Refit the brake vacuum pump as described in Chapter 5. Where applicable also reconnect and adjust the power steering pump drivebelt.

51 Reconnect the air inlet hose to the inlet manifold.

52 Refit the oil filter cap/breather.

53 Clean the thermostat housing mating faces then refit it together with a new gasket and tighten the bolts. Refit the two small hoses.

54 Reconnect the heater hose to the cylinder head.

55 Refit the timing cover sections. On Horizon models insert and tighten the front plate bolt.

56 Refit the right-hand engine mounting bracket and tighten the nuts. Remove the hoist or trolley jack.

57 Refit the air cleaner (Chapter 3).

58 Reconnect the battery negative lead.

59 On Horizon models refit the cooling system expansion tank.

60 Refill the cooling system (Chapter 2).

61 Lower the vehicle to the ground.

Models up to 1987

62 Run the engine at 3000 rpm for 10 minutes then switch off the ignition and let the engine cool for at least 3½ hours.

63 Remove the filler cap from the cooling system expansion tank to release any remaining pressure, then refit it.

64 Working on each cylinder head bolt in turn in the correct sequence first loosen the bolt 90° then retighten to the final torque given in the Specifications (photo).

9.64 Retightening the cylinder head bolts

10.2 Removing the bucket tappets

10 Cylinder head – dismantling, overhaul and reassembly

1 With the head removed as described in the previous Section remove the camshaft with reference to Section 7.

2 Withdraw the bucket tappets, together with their respective shims, keeping them all identified for location (photo).

3 Disconnect the remaining leak off pipes and unscrew the injectors. Remove the special washers.

4 Disconnect the wiring and unscrew the glow plugs.

5 Unscrew the nuts and bolts, and remove the inlet and exhaust manifolds from the cylinder head. Remove the exhaust manifold gaskets.

6 Using a valve spring compressor, depress one valve spring retainer to gain access to the collets. The valves are deeply recessed, so the end of the compressor may need to be extended with a tube or box section with a 'window' for access. Remove the collets and release the compressor. Recover the retainer, large and small valve springs, and the spring seat, then withdraw the valve from the cylinder head. (photos). Repeat the procedure to remove the other seven valves, keeping each valve and components identified for position. Remove the timing probe blank if necessary.

7 Dismantling of the cylinder head is now complete. Refer to Section 11 for decarbonisation procedures.

10.6A Depress the retainer with a valve spring compressor and remove the collets, retainer ...

10.6B ... large valve spring ...

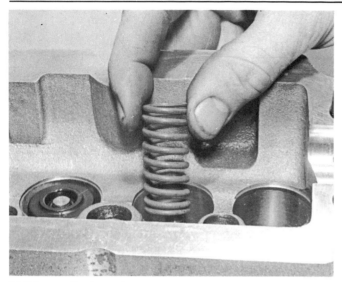

10.6C ... small valve spring ...

10.6D ... spring seat ...

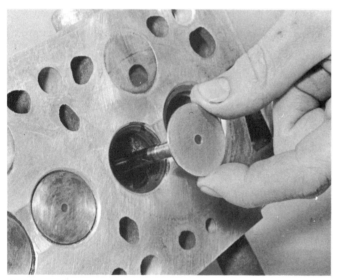

10.6E ... and valve

Fig. 1.10 Checking the cylinder head for distortion (Sec 10)

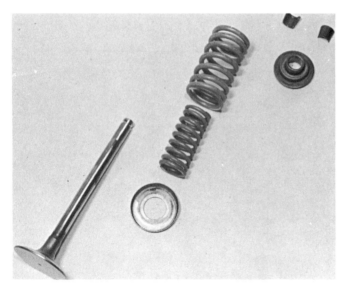

10.6F Valve components

8   Clean all the components and examine them for wear. Obtain new gaskets for the cylinder head, manifolds, valve cover and thermostat housing. Inspect the head for cracks or other damage.

9   Check the head gasket face for distortion (warp) using a straight-edge and feeler blades (photo). Any distortion in excess of the specified amount measured diagonally or along the edges (see Fig. 1.10) is unacceptable and the only course of action is to renew the cylinder head. Note that machining of the cylinder head is not permitted. When using the straight-edge do not position it over the swirl chambers as these may be proud of the cylinder head face resulting in an inaccurate reading.

10 Inspect the valve seats and swirl chambers for burning or cracks (photo). Both can be renewed but the work should be entrusted to a specialist.

11 Using a dial test indicator check that the swirl chamber protrusion is within the limits given in the Specifications (photos).

12 Check each valve for straightness, freedom from burning or cracks, and for an acceptable fit in its guide. Excessive play in the guide may be caused by wear in either component; measure the valve stem with a micrometer, or try the fit of a new valve, if available, to establish whether it is the valve or the guide which is worn.

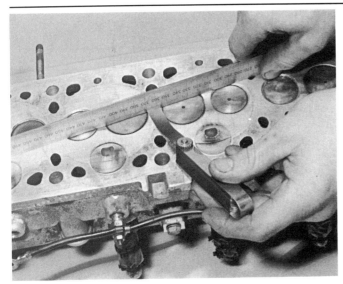

10.9 Checking the cylinder head for distortion

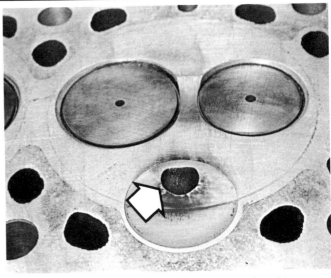

10.10 This swirl chamber is showing the first signs of cracking (arrowed)

10.11A Zero the dial test indicator on the cylinder head ...

13 The valve guides can be renewed but this involves the use of a press and a special reamer so this work is best entrusted to a Peugeot garage or specialist engineering works.

14 Slight marking of the sealing area on the valve head may be removed by grinding. Any more severe damage means that the valve must be refaced, if possible, or renewed. The amount of grinding needed to remove large burn marks, besides being tedious, may cause the valve to sit unacceptably deeply in its seat. After grinding use a dial test indicator to check that the valve heads are within the recess limits given in the Specifications (photo).

15 New or refaced valves and seats should be ground together as follows (the coarse paste may be omitted if the fit is already good).

16 Invert the head and support it securely. Smear a little coarse grinding paste round the sealing area of the valve head. Insert the valve in its guide and grind it to the seat with a to-and-fro motion. The customary tool for this operation is a stick with a rubber sucker on the end (photo). Lift the valve occasionally to redistribute the grinding paste.

10.11B ... then check the swirl chamber protrusion

10.14 Checking the valve head depth

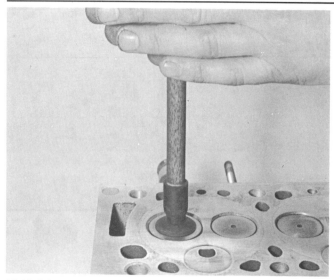

10.16 Grinding in a valve

17 When an unbroken ring is present on the valve head and seat, wipe them clean, then repeat the operation with fine grinding paste.

18 When all the valves have been ground in clean away all traces of grinding paste, first with a paraffin-soaked rag then with clean dry rags, finally with compressed air if available. Do not overlook the valve guides. It will be obvious that even a small quantity of grinding paste remaining in the engine could cause extremely rapid wear.

19 Examine the valve springs for signs of fatigue and if possible compare their length with a new spring. It is worth renewing all the springs if the engine has completed a high mileage.

20 Examine the tappets and their bores for scoring or other damage.

21 Examine the camshaft bearing surfaces in the cylinder head and bearing caps. Also examine the camshaft with reference to Section 7.

22 Inspect the studs for the manifolds and camshaft bearing caps. Renew them if necessary by using a proprietary stud extractor, or lock two nuts together on the exposed threads. Studs which have come out by mistake should be cleaned up and refitted using thread locking fluid.

23 Commence reassembly by oiling a valve stem and inserting it into its guide. With the cylinder head on its side, fit the spring seat followed by the two springs (either way up) and the retainer.

24 Compress the springs with the compressor and fit the collets. A smear of grease on the collets will hold them in place on the valve stem groove. Carefully release the compressor and remove it.

25 Repeat the procedure to fit the other seven valves. Refit the timing probe blank if removed.

26 Refit the inlet and exhaust manifolds with new gaskets and progressively tighten the nuts.

27 Insert and tighten the heater plugs to the specified torque (Chapter 3). Reconnect the wiring.

28 Insert and tighten the injectors with their washers to the specified torque (Chapter 3). Reconnect the leak-off pipes.

29 Oil and insert the bucket tappets, together with their respective shims, making sure that they are fitted in the correct locations, and with the size markings downwards. Make a note of the shim thickness fitted at each position, if not already done, for reference when checking the valve clearances.

30 Refit the camshaft with reference to Section 7.

11 Cylinder head and pistons – decarbonisation

1 With the cylinder head removed as described in Section 9, the carbon deposits should be removed from the valve heads and surrounding surface of the head. Use a blunt scraper or wire brush and take care not to damage the valve heads.

2 Where a more thorough job is to be carried out, the cylinder head should be dismantled as described in the previous Section so that the valves may be ground in and the parts cleaned, brushed and blown out after the manifolds have been removed. Also clean the manifolds, particularly the exhaust manifold where an accumulation of carbon is most likely.

3 Before grinding-in a valve, remove the carbon and deposits completely from its head and stem. With an inlet valve this is usually simply a matter of scraping off the carbon with a blunt knife and finishing with a wire brush. With an exhaust valve the deposits are much harder to remove. One method of cleaning valves quickly is to mount them in the chuck of an electric drill using a piece of card or foil to protect the surface of the stem. A scraper or wire brush may then be used carefully to remove the carbon.

4 An important part of the decarbonising operation is to remove the carbon deposits from the piston crowns. To do this, turn the crankshaft so that two pistons are at the top of their stroke and press some grease between these pistons and the cylinder walls. This will prevent carbon particles falling down into the piston ring grooves. Cover the other two bores and the cylinder block internal oil and water channels with newspaper taped down securely.

5 Using a blunt scraper remove all the carbon from the piston crowns, taking care not to score the soft alloy. Thoroughly clean the combustion spaces which are recessed in the piston crowns.

6 Remove the newspaper then rotate the crankshaft half a turn and repeat the cleaning operation on the remaining two pistons after wiping away the grease from the top of the bores.

7 Finally clean the top surface of the cylinder block.

12 Oil seals – renewal

Note: *The procedures described here are for renewal with the engine in the vehicle – with the engine removed, the steps taken to gain access may be ignored.*

Camshaft (Timing belt end)

1 Follow the procedure given in paragraphs 1 to 12 of Section 5.

2 Remove the timing belt from the camshaft sprocket and tie it to one side without bending it excessively.

3 Unscrew the M8 bolt holding the camshaft sprocket in the timing position.

4 Hold the camshaft sprocket stationary using a suitable tool through two of the holes (Fig. 1.11). A tool may be made out of flat metal bar and two long bolts. Alternatively a strap wrench as used for removing oil filters may be used to hold the sprocket.

5 Unscrew the bolt and withdraw the sprocket from the camshaft. Do not rotate the camshaft otherwise the valves will strike the pistons of Nos 1 and 4 cylinders. Recover the Woodruff key if it is loose.

6 Pull out the oil seal using a hooked instrument.

7 Clean the oil seal seating.

8 Smear the lip of the new oil seal with oil then fit it over the end of the camshaft, open end first, and press it in until flush with the end face

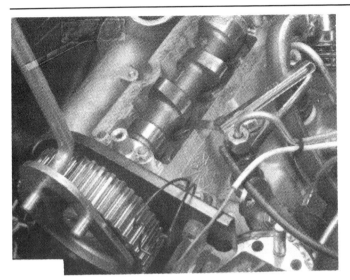

Fig. 1.11 Holding the camshaft sprocket stationary with the special tool (Sec 12)

12.8 Using a socket and bolt to fit a camshaft oil seal

16 Pull out the oil seal using a hooked instrument.

17 Clean the oil seal seating.

18 Smear the lip of the new oil seal with oil then fit it over the end of the camshaft, open end first, and press it in until flush with the end face of the cylinder head (photo). Use a bolt, washers and a suitable socket to press it in.

19 Refit the Woodruff key (if removed) and the pump pulley to the camshaft and tighten the centre bolt.

20 Locate the drivebelt on the camshaft and vacuum pump pulleys then press the pump rearwards until the deflection of the belt midway between the two pulleys is approximately 5.0 mm (0.2 in) under firm thumb pressure. Tighten the adjustment bolt followed by the pivot bolt. Similarly refit the power steering pump drivebelt where applicable.

21 Refit the air cleaner.

22 Refit the inlet ducting.

12.18 Camshaft oil seal (flywheel end)

of the cylinder head. Use an M10 bolt, washers and a suitable socket to press it in (photo).

9 Fit the Woodruff key (if removed) and the camshaft sprocket to the camshaft, insert the bolt and tighten it while holding the camshaft stationary.

10 Refit the M8 timing bolt to the camshaft sprocket.

11 Refit and adjust the timing belt with reference to Section 4, paragraphs 20 to 25. The remaining procedure is a reversal of removal.

Camshaft (flywheel end)
12 Remove the air cleaner.

13 Remove the inlet ducting as necessary.

14 Loosen the pivot and adjustment bolts of the brake vacuum pump, swivel the unit forwards, and disconnect the drivebelt from the pulleys. Where applicable also disconnect the power steering pump drivebelt.

15 Unscrew the centre bolt and remove the pump pulley from the camshaft. If the centre bolt is very tight it will be necessary to remove the timing covers and hold the camshaft sprocket stationary while the bolt is loosened (to prevent damage to the timing belt). Recover the Woodruff key if it is loose.

Crankshaft (timing belt end)
23 Remove the timing belt as described in Section 4.

24 Slide the timing belt sprocket from the crankshaft and recover the Woodruff key if it is loose.

25 Note the fitted depth then pull the oil seal from the housing using a hooked instrument. Alternatively drill a small hole in the oil seal and use a self-tapping screw to remove it.

26 Clean the housing and crankshaft then dip the new oil seal in engine oil and press it in (open end first) to the previously noted depth. A piece of thin plastic is useful to prevent damage to the oil seal (photo).

27 Refit the Woodruff key and timing belt sprocket.

28 Refit the timing belt with reference to Section 4.

Crankshaft (flywheel end)
29 Remove the flywheel as described in Section 16.

30 Using vernier calipers measure the fitted depth of the oil seal and record it.

31 Pull out the oil seal using a hooked instrument. Alternatively drill a small hole in the oil seal and use a self-tapping screw to remove it.

12.26 Fitting the crankshaft oil seal (timing belt end)

12.33 Fitting the flywheel end oil seal to the crankshaft using a plastic protector

2   Position a suitable container beneath the engine. Unscrew the drain plug and allow the oil to drain from the sump.

3   Wipe clean the drain plug, then refit and tighten it.

4   Note the location of the sump bolts (see Fig. 1.17) then unscrew them.

5   Remove the sump and gasket (photo). The sump will probably be stuck in position, in which case it will be necessary to cut it free using a thin knife.

6   Clean the remains of gasket from the sump and block and wipe dry.

7   Apply a little sealing compound where the front housing abuts the block on both sides.

8   Position a new gasket on the sump then lift the sump into position and insert the bolts in their correct locations.

9   Tighten the bolts evenly to the specified torque.

10 Lower the vehicle to the ground and refill the engine with the correct quantity and grade of oil.

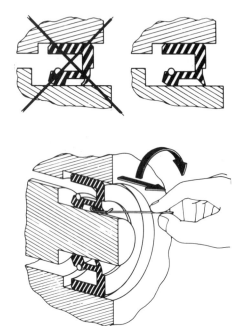

Fig. 1.12 Correct fitting of the crankshaft flywheel end oil seal (Sec 12)

32 Clean the oil seal seating and crankshaft flange.

33 Dip the new oil seal in engine oil, locate it on the crankshaft open end first, and press it in squarely to the previously noted depth using a suitable metal tube. A piece of thin plastic is useful to prevent damage to the oil seal (photo). When fitted note that the outer lip of the oil seal must point outwards; if it is pointing inwards use a piece of bent wire to pull it out (Fig. 1.12).

34 Refit the flywheel with reference to Section 16.

13 Sump – removal and refitting

1   Apply the handbrake then jack up the front of the vehicle and support on axle stands.

13.5 Removing the sump

14 Oil pump – removal, inspection and refitting

1   Remove the timing belt as described in Section 4.

2   Slide the timing belt sprocket from the crankshaft and recover the Woodruff key if it is loose.

3   Remove the sump as described in Section 13.

4   Unscrew the bolts and remove the front oil seal housing. Remove the gasket.

5   Unscrew the three bolts securing the oil pump to the crankcase. Identify them for position as all three are of different lengths.

6   Withdraw the L-shaped spacer from beneath the oil pump.

7   Remove the location dowel and disengage the oil pump sprocket from the chain. Withdraw the oil pump.

8   Remove the chain and sprocket from the nose of the crankshaft and recover the Woodruff key if it is loose.

9   Remove the six bolts which hold the two halves of the oil pump together. Separate the halves, being prepared for the release of the relief valve spring and plungers (photos).

10 If necessary remove the strainer by prising off the cap, then clean all components (photos).

11 Inspect the gears and the housings for wear and damage. Check the endfloat of the gears using a straight-edge and feeler blades, also check the clearance between the tip of the gear lobes and the housing (photos). If any of these clearances exceeds the specified limit, renew the pump. Note that with the exception of the relief valve spring and plunger, individual components are not available.

12 If the pump is to be renewed it is wise to renew the chain and the crankshaft sprocket also.

13 Lubricate the gears with engine oil then reassemble the oil pump in reverse order and tighten the six bolts evenly to the specified torque.

14 Locate the Woodruff key on the nose of the crankshaft and refit the sprocket, teeth end first. Engage the chain with the sprocket.

14.9A Unscrew the oil pump bolts ...

14.9B ... separate the halves ...

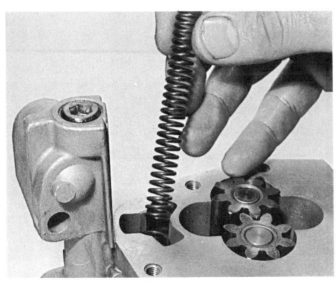

14.9C ... and remove the relief valve spring ...

14.9D ... and plunger

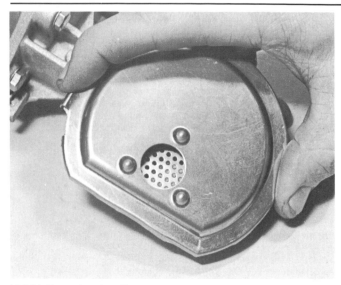

14.10A Removing the oil pump cap ...

14.10B ... and strainer

14.11A Oil pump rotors and housing

14.11B Checking the rotor endfloat

14.11C Checking the rotor side clearance

15 Prise the oil seal from the front housing. Refit the housing to the cylinder block, together with a new gasket, and tighten the bolts evenly to the specified torque.

16 Fit a new oil seal to the housing with reference to Section 12.

17 Check that the location dowel is fitted to the block. Engage the oil pump sprocket with the chain and slide the L-shaped spacer into position, making sure that its open end engages the dowel.

18 Insert the bolts in their correct locations (Fig. 1.13), the longest bolt through the dowel and the next longest by the oil return hole. Tighten the bolts evenly to the specified torque (photo).

19 Refit the sump with reference to Section 13.

20 Refit the Woodruff key and timing belt sprocket.

21 Refit the timing belt with reference to Section 4.

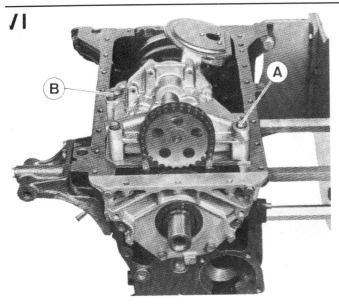

Fig. 1.13 Oil pump mounting bolt locations (Sec 14)

A   Longest bolt   B   Next longest bolt

14.18 Tightening the oil pump mounting bolts

15 Pistons and connecting rods – removal and refitting

1   Remove the cylinder head as described in Section 9.

2   Remove the oil pump as described in Section 14.

3   If there is a pronounced wear ridge at the top of any bore, it may be necessary to remove it with a scraper or ridge reamer to avoid piston damage during removal. Such a ridge may indicate that reboring is necessary, which will entail new pistons in any case.

4   Check that each connecting rod and cap is marked for position and, if not, mark them with a centre punch on the oil filter side, number one at the flywheel end.

5   Turn the crankshaft to bring pistons 1 and 4 to BDC (bottom dead centre). Unscrew the nuts from No 1 piston big-end bearing cap, then take off the cap and recover the bottom half bearing shell (photo).

6   Using a hammer handle push the piston up through the bore and remove it from the block. Loosely refit the shell bearings and cap to ensure correct reassembly.

7   Remove No 4 piston in the same manner then turn the crankshaft 180° to bring pistons 2 and 3 to BDC (bottom dead centre) and remove them.

8   If new piston rings are to be fitted to old bores, the bores must be deglazed to allow the new rings to bed-in properly. Protect the big-end journals by wrapping them in masking tape, then use a piece of coarse emery paper to produce a cross-hatch pattern in each bore. A flap wheel in an electric drill may be used, but beware of spreading abrasive dust. When deglazing is complete wash away all abrasive particles and unwrap the big-end journals.

9   Commence refitting by laying out the assembled pistons and rods in order, with the bearing shells, connecting rod caps and nuts.

10   Arrange the piston ring gaps 120° from each other.

11   Clean the bearing shells, caps and rods then press the shells into position so that the locating tangs engge in the grooves.

12   Oil the bores, pistons, crankpins and shells. Fit a piston ring compressor to No 1 piston. With Nos 1 and 4 crankpins at BDC, insert

15.5 Removing a big-end bearing cap

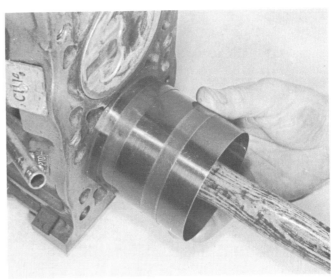

15.13 Using a hammer handle to tap the piston through the ring compressor

No 1 piston in the bore at the flywheel end, making sure that the clover leaf cut-out on the piston crown is towards the oil filter side of the engine.

13 Using a hammer handle, tap the piston though the ring compressor and into the bore (photo). Guide the connecting rod into the crankpin and fit the cap, together with its shell bearing, making sure it is the correct way round.

14 Fit the nuts and tighten them to the specified torque (photo). Turn the crankshaft to check for free movement.

15 Repeat the procedure to fit the other three pistons.

16 Refit the oil pump as described in Section 14.

17 Refit the cylinder head as described in Section 9.

16 Flywheel – removal and refitting

1   Either remove the engine and gearbox and separate them (Sections 19 and 20), or remove the gearbox alone as described in the appropriate manual for petrol-engined vehicles.

2   Make alignment marks then slacken the clutch pressure plate bolts progressively and remove the pressure plate and driven plate (photo).

3   Hold the flywheel stationary with a screwdriver or suitable bar inserted between the teeth of the starter ring gear and the transmission location dowel, then unscrew and remove the bolts and lift the flywheel from the crankshaft. Alignment marks are not required as there is a location dowel on the crankshaft flange. Obtain new bolts for reassembly.

4   Commence refitting by cleaning the mating surfaces of the crankshaft and flywheel.

5   Locate the flywheel on the crankshaft dowel.

6   Apply locking fluid to the threads of the bolts, insert them, and tighten them to the specified torque while holding the flywheel stationary (photos).

7   Refit the clutch driven and pressure plates.

8   Refit the gearbox, and the engine if removed.

15.14 Tightening the big-end bearing cap nuts

16.2 Removing the clutch pressure plate and driven plate

16.6A Apply locking fluid to the flywheel bolts ...

16.6B ... then insert and tighten them

17 Engine/gearbox mountings – removal and refitting

Right-hand mounting

1 Support the engine with a hoist or with a trolley jack and block of wood beneath the sump.

2 Unscrew the nuts and remove the right-hand mounting bracket (photo). On Horizon models first remove the centre timing cover.

3 On non-Horizon models unscrew the lower mounting nut from under the right-hand front wing. Also unscrew the rubber stop nuts and remove the stops noting the location of any shims. On Horizon models unbolt the mounting from the body.

4 Refitting is a reversal of removal, but tighten all nuts to the specified torque. On non-Horizon models with the weight of the engine on the mounting, the clearance between the mounting bracket and each rubber stop should be 1.0 ± 0.7 mm (0.04 ± 0.03 in). If necessary adjust the clearance by means of shims positioned under the stops.

Left-hand mounting

5 Support the transmission with a hoist or with a trolley jack and block of wood.

6 Remove the air cleaner and trunking.

7 Remove the battery and battery tray.

8 Unscrew the nut/bolt and remove the rubber mounting. On Horizon models first knock back the locking tab. Also unscrew the nuts or bolts and remove the mounting bracket.

9 If necessary unscrew the mounting stud from the transmission casing where applicable.

10 Refitting is a reversal of removal, but before fitting the mounting stud, clean the threads and apply a little locking fluid. Tighten the nuts and bolts to the specified torque. On Horizon models lock the bolt by bending the lock tab.

Lower mounting

11 Jack up the front of the car and support on axle stands.

12 Unscrew and remove both bolts from the torque link and withdraw the link.

13 Drive or press the mounting from the housing.

14 Drive or press the new mounting into position then refit the torque link and tighten the bolts to the specified torque.

15 Lower the car to the ground.

18 Engine – method of removal

1 The engine is removed, together with the gearbox, by lowering from the engine compartment.

2 It is possible to remove the gearbox alone from under the vehicle, after which it would in theory be possible to lower the engine separately. However, this method is not recommended as it involves the extra work of disconnecting the gearbox which, if required, is best carried out with the engine and gearbox removed from the vehicle.

19 Engine and gearbox – removal

1 Either remove the bonnet or raise it to the highest position. On 205 models unbolt the strut from the right-hand suspension tower, raise the bonnet, and retain it by inserting U-bolts through the special holes in the bonnet hinges.

2 If available, on 309 models, fit Peugeot special cables No 0903 to

the front suspension struts as described in the petrol engine manual. Loosen the strut mounting nuts.

3 Apply the handbrake then jack up the front of the vehicle and support on axle stands. Allow at least 2 feet (60 cm) between the bumper and the ground for removing the engine and gearbox. Remove both front wheels.

4 Drain the cooling system.

5 Using a hexagon key unscrew the drain plug and drain the gearbox oil into a suitable container (photo). On completion refit and tighten the drain plug.

6 If necessary drain the engine oil.

7 Remove the air cleaner (Chapter 3).

8 Disconnect the battery leads then unscrew the clamp bolt and remove the battery and tray (photo).

9 Remove the radiator (Chapter 2).

10 Disconnect the top hose from the thermostat housing and the expansion hose(s) from the expansion tank and thermostat housing (photos).

19.5 Using a hexagon key to unscrew the gearbox oil drain plug

19.8 Battery clamp (205 models)

19.10A Disconnect the expansion hose from the expansion tank ...

19.10B ... and thermostat housing ...

19.10C ... and release it from the clip

19.11 Heater hose location on the bulkhead (205 models)

19.13A Front disc pad warning system wiring connector (205 models)

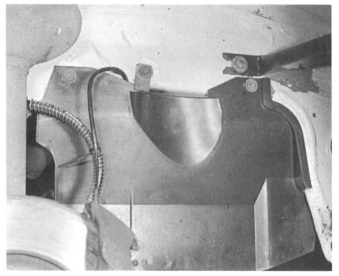

19.13B Engine shield ...

19.13C ... and mounting bolt removal (205 models)

19.13D Engine shield side mounting bolt (arrowed)

19.13E ... front mounting bolt (arrowed) ...

19.13F ... and rear mounting bolt (arrowed) (Horizon models)

19.14 Coolant intermediate metal pipe (205 models)

19.15 Heater supply hose on rear of cylinder head

11 Disconnect the heater hoses at the bulkhead (photo).

12 Where applicable remove the power steering pump without disconnecting the hoses and position it to one side.

13 Working under the right-hand wheel arch, remove the engine shield. Where applicable disconnect the wiring for the front disc pad warning system (photos).

14 Disconnect the bottom hose from the block and, where fitted, remove the metal pipe from the right-hand inner wing panel (photos).

15 Disconnect the heater supply hose from the rear of the cylinder head (photo).

16 Unclip and disconnect the bypass hose from the water pump inlet and front of the cylinder head (photos).

17 On Horizon models unbolt and remove the coolant expansion tank (photo). The expansion tank may also be removed on other models to provide extra working room.

18 Disconnect the engine wiring harness by the battery location, and release the securing clip on the gearbox (photos).

19 Disconnect the wiring from the following:
  (a) Starter motor
  (b) Alternator
  (c) Water temperature switch (photos)
  (d) Oil level switch (photo)
  (e) Oil pressure switch (photo)
  (f) Reversing lamp switch (photo)
  (g) Heater plugs
  (h) Stop solenoid on the injection pump
  (i) Diagnostic socket (photo)

19.16A Bypass hose on the water pump inlet (arrowed)

19.16B Bypass hose retaining clips (arrowed)

19.16C Disconnecting the bypass hose from the cylinder head

19.17 Coolant expansion tank on Horizon models

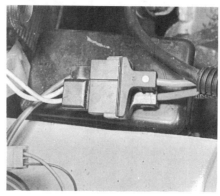
19.18A Engine wiring harness connector ...

19.18B ... and harness clip (205 models)

19.19A Water temperature switch (arrowed) ...

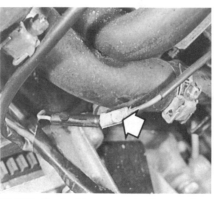
19.19B ... and wiring connector (arrowed)

19.19C Oil level switch (205 models)

19.19D Oil pressure switch

19.19E Reversing lamp switch

19.19F Diagnostic socket – arrowed (Horizon models)

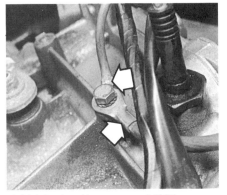

19.20A Earth cables – arrowed (205 models)

19.20B Earth cable – arrowed (Horizon models)

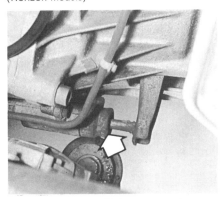

19.21 Clutch slave cylinder – arrowed (Horizon models)

19.22 Clutch cable – arrowed (non-Horizon models)

19.27A Unscrew the nut (arrowed) ...

19.27B ... and remove the reverse gear stop cable

20 Unbolt the earth cables(s) from the gearbox (photos).

21 On Horizon models unbolt the clutch slave cylinder and position it to one side (photo).

22 On non-Horizon models disconnect the clutch cable and recover the pushrod (photo).

23 Disconnect the speedometer cable from the gearbox.

24 Disconnect the accelerator cable from the injection pump and position it to one side.

25 Disconnect the vacuum hose from the vacuum pump and brake servo unit. Also disconnect the discharge hose from the pump and inlet manifold.

26 Disconnect the fuel supply and return hoses from the injection pump (photo).

27 Where fitted unscrew the nut and remove the reverse gear stop cable from the top of the gearbox (photos). Position the cable to one side.

28 Disconnect the gearchange control rods at the gearbox end. A small open-ended spanner will be found helpful to prise off the rods (photos).

29 Unscrew and remove the exhaust manifold-to-downpipe bolts, together with the springs and collars (photos).

30 Unscrew the bolts/nuts securing the front lower suspension arms to the hub carriers (photo). Unbolt the anti-roll bar links on 305 models.

31 On non-Horizon models use a lever to move the suspension arms down in turn so that the balljoints are removed from the bottom of the hub carriers. Recover the balljoint protectors if fitted.

19.28A Disconnecting the gearchange engagement rod (205 models)

19.28B Disconnecting the gearchange selection rod (205 models)

19.28C Gearchange control rods on Horizon models

19.29A Exhaust manifold-to-downpipe bolts

19.29B Exhaust manifold-to-downpipe bolt components

19.30 Lower suspension arm-to-hub carrier bolt (arrowed)

19.33 Removing the left-hand driveshaft

19.35A Right-hand driveshaft intermediate bearing bolts – arrowed (non-Horizon models)

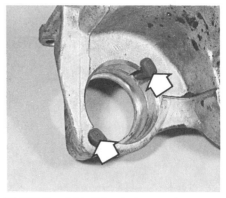

19.35B Special bolt heads (arrowed) on the right-hand driveshaft intermediate bearing (non-Horizon models)

19.36 Right-hand driveshaft intermediate bearing on Horizon models (arrowed)

19.37 Removing the right-hand driveshaft

19.38A Lower engine mounting (non-Horizon models)

32 On Horizon models use a balljoint separator tool to release the balljoints, but leave them in the suspension arms at this stage.

33 Have an assistant pull the left-hand hub carrier outwards while the left-hand driveshaft is levered from the differential side gear (photo). Use a block of wood to hold the hub carrier out.

34 On models manufactured before July 1984 the left-hand differential side gear must be supported using a suitable dowel, preferably wooden. If this precaution is not taken, the side gears may become misaligned when the right-hand driveshaft is removed.

35 On non-Horizon models loosen the two nuts retaining the right-hand driveshaft intermediate bearing in the lower engine mounting bracket bolted to the rear of the cylinder block and turn the bolt heads through 90° in order to release the bearing (photos).

36 On Horizon models unscrew the nuts and remove the clamp retaining the right-hand driveshaft intermediate bearing in the lower engine mounting bracket bolted to the rear of the cylinder block (photo).

37 Have an assistant pull the right-hand hub carrier outwards while the right-hand driveshaft is levered from the differential side gear (photo). Use a block of wood to hold the hub carrier out.

38 Unscrew the nuts from the lower engine mounting torque link bolts at the mounting and the crossmember, noting the location of any spacers (photos).

39 Unscrew the bolts and lever the lower engine mounting bracket from the dowels on the block (photo).

40 On non-Horizon models remove the bracket, swivel the right-hand driveshaft to the front and tie it to the front towing eye (photos).

41 On Horizon models tie the driveshaft to the rear.

19.38B Removing a spacer from the lower engine mounting

19.38C Removing the lower engine mounting torque link (non-Horizon models)

19.38D Lower engine mounting (Horizon models)

19.39 Removing the lower engine mounting bracket from the dowels (arrowed)

19.40A Remove the bracket ...

19.40B ... and tie the right-hand driveshaft to the front towing eye (non-Horizon models)

19.40C Lower engine mounting bracket removed

19.42 Right-hand engine lifting bracket (arrowed)

19.43A Unscrew the nuts (arrowed)

19.43B ... and remove the right-hand engine mounting bracket

19.43C Right-hand engine mounting bracket on Horizon models

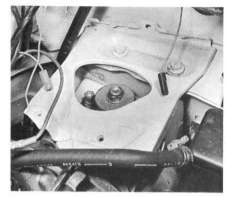
19.44A Left-hand engine mounting (non-Horizon models)

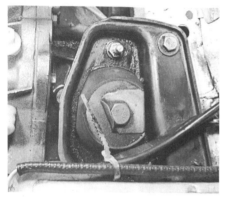
19.44B Left-hand engine mounting (Horizon models)

19.45A Lower the engine and gearbox to the ground ...

19.45B ... and remove from under the vehicle

20.2 Removing the TDC sensor

20.4 Gearbox bottom cover

42 Connect a hoist to the engine lifting brackets (photo) so that the engine and gearbox are supported in a horizontal position. Take the weight of the assembly.

43 Unscrew the nuts and remove the right-hand engine mounting bracket (photos). On Horizon models first remove the centre timing cover section.

44 Unscrew the nut/bolt from the left-hand engine mounting. On Horizon models first knock back the locking tab. Unscrew the nut(s) and remove the mounting rubber (photo).

45 Lower the engine and gearbox to the ground, taking care not to damage the surrounding components in the engine compartment (photos).

46 Withdraw the assembly from under the vehicle.

47 If the vehicle must be moved with the engine and gearbox out, reconnect the suspension arms to the hub carriers, refit the wheels, and support the driveshafts in their normal position with wire so that they can rotate without damage.

20 Engine and gearbox – separation

1 With the engine and gearbox removed from the vehicle clean away all external dirt.

2 Slacken the bolts and remove the TDC sensor (photo). Remove the bolts and withdraw the sensor holder.

3 Unbolt and remove the starter motor using a hexagon key.

4 Unbolt the bottom cover from the gearbox (photo).

5   Support the engine then unscrew the bolts and lift the gearbox directly from the engine.

21 Engine dismantling – general

1   Clean the engine thoroughly using a water-soluble grease solvent or similar product. Keep dirt and water out of vulnerable components such as the fuel injection pump and the alternator.

2   When possible the engine should be dismantled on a workbench or strong table. If an engine dismantling stand is available, so much the better. Avoid working directly on a concrete floor, as grit presents a serious problem. If there is no alternative to working on the floor, cover it with an old piece of lino or carpet.

3   As well as the usual selection of tools, have available some wooden blocks for propping up the engine. A notebook and pencil will be needed, as will a couple of segmented boxes or a good supply of plastic bags and labels.

4   A waterproof marker pen is useful for making alignment marks without recourse to punches or chisels, however, take care that the marks are not erased during cleaning.

5   Whenever possible, refit nuts, washers etc to the components from which they were removed. This makes reassembly much simpler.

6   Spills of oil, fuel and coolant are bound to occur during dismantling. Have rags and newspapers handy to mop up the mess.

7   Do not throw away old gaskets immediately, but save them for comparison with new ones or for use as patterns if new gaskets have to be made.

22 Engine – complete dismantling

1   If not already done, drain the engine oil.

2   Remove the brake vacuum pump as described in Chapter 5.

3   Pull up the special clip, release the spring clips, and withdraw the two timing cover sections (photos).

4   Unbolt and remove the diagnostic socket and bracket where fitted (photo).

5   Unscrew the bolt and withdraw the pump pulley from the flywheel end of the camshaft (photo). If it is tight due to corrosion, use a two or three-legged puller to remove it. Recover the Woodruff key.

6   Note the location of the fuel pipes from the injection pump to the injectors then unscrew the union nuts and remove the pipe assemblies. Cover the pipe ends, the injectors and the injection pump outlets to prevent entry of dust and dirt. Small plastic bags and elastic bands are ideal for this (photos).

7   Pull the leak-off hoses from the injectors.

8   Unbolt the engine lifting bracket from the cylinder head (photo).

9   Remove the alternator (Chapter 7) and bracket.

10 Unscrew the oil filter cartridge using a strap wrench if necessary.

11 Where fitted on the 1.9 engine disconnect the hoses from the oil cooler. Unscrew the centre stud and remove the oil cooler from the block. Disconnect the oil cooler hoses.

12 Disconnect the bottom hose from the water pump inlet if not already done.

22.3A Removing the left timing cover section ...

22.3B ... and the right timing cover section

22.4 Diagnostic socket and mounting bolt

22.5 Removing the pump pulley from the flywheel end of the camshaft

22.6A Fuel pipe locations (arrowed)

22.6B Small plastic bags can be used to protect the injectors from dust and dirt

22.8 Engine lifting bracket

22.13 Sump inlet and crankcase ventilation hose

22.18A Oil level sensor location in the cylinder block

13 Disconnect the crankcase ventilation hoses from the valve cover and sump inlet (photo). Remove the clip and slide the oil separator from the dipstick tube.

14 Remove the oil filler cap and ventilation hose if fitted.

15 Unscrew the bolts and remove the inlet manifold from the cylinder head. There are no gaskets.

16 Unscrew the nuts and withdraw the exhaust manifold and gaskets from the studs.

17 Slacken the bolt and remove the clamp from the end of the fast idle cable. Unscrew the locknut and remove the fast idle outer cable from the bracket on the injection pump.

18 Unscrew and remove the oil level sensor from the cylinder block if fitted (photos).

19 Unscrew and remove the oil pressure switch (photo).

20 Unbolt the thermostat housing from the cylinder head, complete with the fast idle thermo-unit and temperature sensor(s) (photos).

22.18B Removing the oil level sensor

22.19 Removing the oil pressure switch

22.20A Unscrew the bolts ...

22.20B ... and remove the thermostat housing

22.21A Removing the water pump inlet

21 Unbolt the water pump inlet and remove the gasket. Also unbolt the coolant tube from the cylinder block (photos).

22 Where applicable unscrew the nuts securing the inlet bracket to the sump. Remove the bracket and gasket (photos).

23 Have an assistant hold the flywheel stationary with a screwdriver or suitable bar inserted between the teeth of the starter ring gear and the transmission location dowel, then unscrew the crankshaft pulley bolt. Slide the pulley from the front of the crankshaft (photo).

24 Unbolt the bottom timing cover (photo).

25 Turn the engine by the flywheel until the three bolt holes in the camshaft and injection pump sprockets are aligned with the corresponding holes in the engine front plate.

26 Insert an 8.0 to 8.5 mm diameter metal dowel rod or twist drill through the special hole in the left-hand rear flange of the cylinder block then carefully turn the engine either way until the rod enters the TDC hole in the flywheel (photo).

27 Insert three M8 bolts through the holes in the camshaft and injection pump sprockets and screw them into the engine front plate finger tight.

22.21B Coolant tube mounting on the rear of the cylinder block

22.21C Coolant tube mounting on the front of the cylinder block

22.22A Unscrew the nuts ...

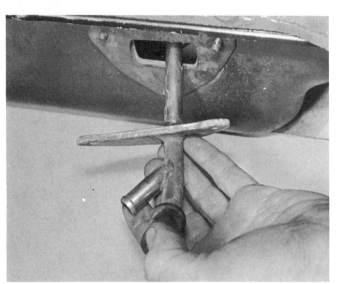

22.22B ... and remove the inlet bracket ...

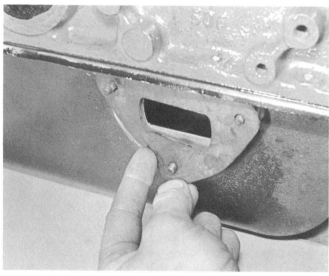

22.22C ... and gasket

22.23 Removing the crankshaft pulley

22.24 Bottom timing cover (arrowed)

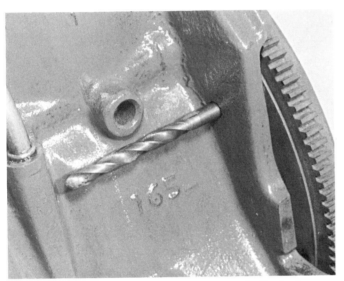

22.26 Using a twist drill to enter the TDC hole in the flywheel

22.31A Unscrew the nut ...

22.31B ... and remove the injection pump sprocket

22.36 Injection pump mounting bracket

28 Loosen the timing belt tensioner pivot nut and adjustment bolt, then turn the bracket anti-clockwise to release the tension and retighten the adjustment bolt to hold the tensioner in the released position.

29 Mark the timing belt with an arrow to indicate its normal direction of turning then remove it from the camshaft, injection pump, water pump, and crankshaft sprockets.

30 Unbolt and remove the valve cover. Remove the gasket.

31 With the injection pump sprocket held stationary by the timing bolts, unscrew the central nut to release the sprocket from the pump shaft taper. Remove the timing bolts and the pump sprocket with its nut and puller, and recover the Woodruff key if it is loose (photos). The puller is incorporated in the sprocket by means of the plate bolted over the nut, and the nut has an outer shoulder which bears against the plate.

32 Similarly unscrew the bolt from the camshaft sprocket and withdraw the sprocket.

33 Slide the sprocket from the crankshaft and recover the Woodruff key if it is loose.

34 Unscrew the bolts and remove the water pump from the cylinder block. Remove the gasket.

35 Mark the injection pump in relation to the mounting bracket. Unscrew the nuts and bolt and withdraw the injection pump.

36 Unbolt and remove the mounting bracket (photo).

37 Unscrew the timing belt tensioner adjustment bolt and pivot nut. A tool may now be used to hold the tensioner plunger as described in Section 5 while the tensioner arm and roller is removed. However, it is possible to remove the arm and roller by keeping the arm pressed against the plunger (photo).

38 Remove the plunger and spring (photo).

39 Unscrew the bolts and remove the engine mounting bracket and the timing belt intermediate roller and bracket as applicable (photos).

40 Unbolt the engine front plate (photo).

41 Progressively unscrew the cylinder head bolts in the reverse order to that shown in Fig. 1.9. Remove the washers.

42 Release the cylinder head from the cylinder block and location dowel by rocking it. Lift the head from the block and remove the gasket.

43 Remove the clutch then hold the engine stationary with a screwdriver or suitable bar inserted between the teeth of the starter ring gear and the transmission location dowel, then unscrew and remove the bolts and lift the flywheel from the crankshaft.

44 Invert the engine and unbolt the sump. Remove the gasket.

45 Unscrew the three bolts securing the oil pump to the crankcase. Identify them for position as all three are of different lengths.

46 Withdraw the L-shaped spacer from beneath the oil pump (photo).

47 Remove the location dowel and disengage the oil pump sprocket from the chain. Withdraw the oil pump (photo).

48 Unscrew the bolts and remove the front oil seal housing (photo). Remove the gasket.

49 Remove the oil pump chain followed by the sprocket. Recover the Woodruff key if it is loose (photos).

50 Check that each connecting rod and cap is marked for position and, if not, mark them with a centre punch on the oil filter side, number one at the flywheel end.

22.37 Removing the tensioner arm and roller

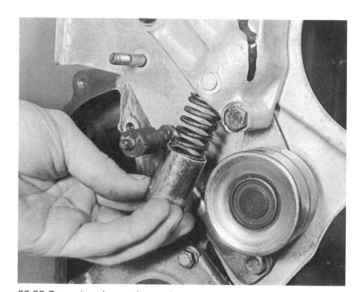

22.38 Removing the tensioner plunger and spring

22.39A Right-hand engine mounting bracket (non-Horizon models)

22.39B Timing belt intermediate roller and bracket

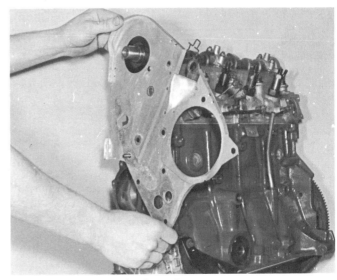

22.40 Removing the engine front plate

22.46 Withdrawing the oil pump spacer

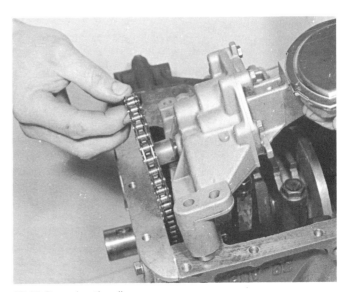

22.47 Removing the oil pump

22.48 Removing the crankshaft front oil seal housing

22.49A Slide off the oil pump sprocket ...

22.49B ... and remove the Woodruff key

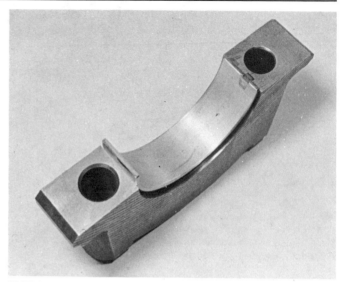

22.56 Main bearing cap and lower half bearing shell

22.57A Lift out the crankshaft ...

22.57B ... and remove the upper half bearing shells

51 Position the cylinder block either on its side or on the flywheel end.

52 Turn the crankshaft to bring pistons 1 and 4 to BDC (bottom dead centre). Unscrew the nuts from No 1 piston big-end bearing cap, then take off the cap and recover the bottom half bearing shell.

53 Using a hammer handle push the piston up through the bore and remove it from the block. Loosely refit the shell bearings and cap to ensure correct reassembly.

54 Remove No 4 piston in the same manner then turn the crankshaft 180° to bring pistons 2 and 3 to BDC and remove them.

55 The main bearing caps should be numbered 1 to 5 from the flywheel end. If not mark them accordingly. Also note the fitted depth of the rear oil seal.

56 Invert the engine then unbolt and remove the main bearing caps. Recover the lower half bearing shells keeping them with their respective caps (photo). Also recover the thrust washers.

57 Lift out the crankshaft. Discard the rear oil seal. Recover the upper half bearing shells and keep them together with their respective caps, however, identify them as the upper shells (photos). Also recover and identify the upper thrust washers.

23 Examination and renovation – general

1   With the engine completely dismantled, all components should be cleaned and examined as detailed in the appropriate Sections of this Chapter.

2   Most components can be cleaned with rags, a soft brush and paraffin, or some other solvent. Do not immerse parts with oilways in solvent since it can be very difficult to remove and if left will contaminate the oil. Clean oilways and water channels with a piece of wire and blow through with compressed air if available.

3 When faced with a borderline decision as to whether to renew a particular part, take into consideration the expected future life of the engine and the degree of trouble or expense which will be caused if the part fails before the next overhaul.

4 If extensive overhauling is required, estimate the likely cost and compare it with the cost of a complete reconditioned engine. The difference may not be great, and the reconditioned engine will have a guarantee.

24 Engine components – examination and renovation

Cylinder block and bores

1 Check the cylinder block casting for any damage or cracking.

2 If necessary unscrew the two plugs from the rear of the block and from the flange beneath the oil filter location, and clean the oil gallery. Refit and tighten the plugs on completion. The water channels may be cleaned by removing the inspection plate from the rear of the block.

3 Check the core plugs for signs of leakage and if necessary renew them. It may be possible to remove the old plugs by drilling a small hole and using a self-tapping screw to pull them out. Alternatively, use a hammer to drive a chisel through the old plugs and prise them out. Clean the seating then apply a little sealing compound and tap the new plug into position with the flat face of a hammer. Spread the core plug by striking the centre with a ball face hammer.

4 If cracks in the block are suspected it may be necessary to have it crack-tested professionally. There are various ways of doing this, some involving special dyes and chemicals, some using ultrasonic or electromagnetic radiation.

5 Bore wear is indicated by a wear ridge at the top of the bore. For accurate assessment a bore micrometer is required, however, a rough measurement can be made by inserting feeler gauges between a piston (without rings) and the bore wall. Compare the clearance at the bottom of the bore, which should be unworn, with that just below the wear ridge. No wear limits are specified, but out-of-round or taper in excess of 0.1 mm (0.004 in) would normally be considered grounds for a rebore. Scuffs, scores and scratches must also be taken into account.

6 If reboring is undertaken the machine shop will normally obtain the oversize pistons and rings at the same time.

7 Where the degree of wear does not justify a rebore, the fitting of proprietary oil control rings may be considered.

Crankshaft and bearings

8 Check the crankshaft for damage or excessive wear.

9 Examine the bearing shells for wear and scratches on the working surfaces. New shells should be fitted in any case, unless the old ones are obviously in perfect condition and are known to have covered only a nominal mileage (photo). Refitting used shells is false economy.

10 Examine the bearing journals on the crankshaft for scoring or other damage, which if present will probably mean that regrinding or renewal is necessary. If a micrometer is available, measure the journals in several places to check for out-of-round and taper. No limits are specified but typically 0.025 mm (0.001 in) is the maximum acceptable.

11 Note that the crankshaft may already have been reground, and that the makers only specify one stage of regrinding.

12 Main and big-end bearing clearances can be measured using Plastigage thread. The journal and bearing shell are wiped dry before placing the thread across the journal. After tightening the bearing cap onto the Plastigage it is removed and a special gauge used to determine the running clearance. The makers do not specify any clearances but typically it would be between 0.025 and 0.050 mm (0.001 and 0.002 in).

24.9 Big-end bearing shell

24.13 Checking the crankshaft endfloat

24.14 Removing the piston rings with an old feeler blade

19.13C ... and mounting bolt removal (205 models)

19.13D Engine shield side mounting bolt (arrowed) ...

19.13E ... front mounting bolt (arrowed) ...

19.13F ... and rear mounting bolt (arrowed) (Horizon models)

19.14 Coolant intermediate metal pipe (205 models)

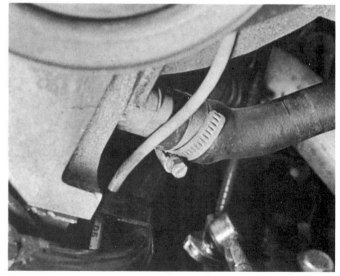

19.15 Heater supply hose on rear of cylinder head

17 If the rings are renewed the bores must be deglazed as described in Section 15.

18 Examine the pistons for damage, in particular for burning on the crown and for scores or other signs of 'picking-up' on the skirts and piston ring lands. Scorch marks on the sides show that blow-by has occurred.

19 If the pistons pass this preliminary inspection clean all the carbon out of the ring grooves using a piece of old piston ring. Protect your fingers – piston rings are sharp. Do not remove any metal from the ring grooves.

20 Roll each ring around its groove to check for tight spots. Any excessive clearance not due to worn rings must be due to piston wear and, unless the piston can be machined to accept special rings, renewal is required.

21 If renewing pistons without reboring make sure that the correct size is obtained. Piston class is denoted by either an 'A1' mark or no mark at all on the centre of the crown. The identical code appears also on the corner of the cylinder block at the timing belt end. The piston weight class is stamped on the crown and must be identical on all pistons in the same engine.

22 To separate a piston from its connecting rod, prise out the circlips and push out the gudgeon pin (photos). Hand pressure is sufficient to remove the pin. Identify the piston and rod to ensure correct reassembly.

23 Wear between the gudgeon pin and the connecting rod small-end bush can be cured by renewing both the pin and bush. Bush renewal, however, is a specialist job because press facilities are required and the new bush must be reamed accurately.

24 New gudgeon pins and circlips are supplied when purchasing new pistons. The connecting rods themselves should not be in need of renewal unless seizure or some other major mechanical failure has occurred.

25 Reassemble the pistons and rods. Make sure that the pistons are fitted the right way round – the clover leaf cut-out on the crown must

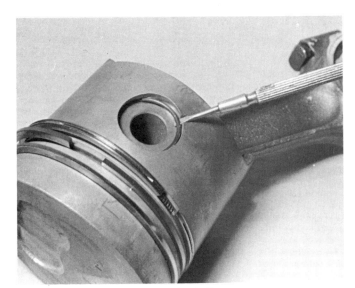

24.22A Prising out the gudgeon pin circlip

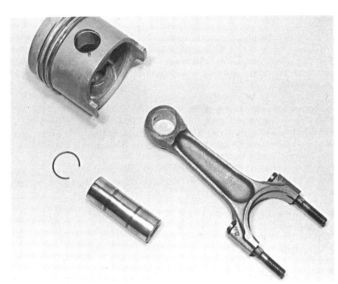

24.22B Piston and connecting rod components

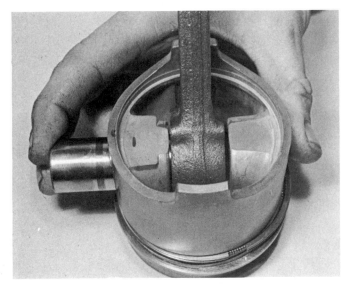

24.25A Pushing the gudgeon pin into the piston

24.25B Clover leaf cut-out on the piston crown

face the same way as the shell bearing cut-out in the connecting rod. Oil the gudgeon pins before fitting them (photos). When assembled, the piston should pivot freely on the rod.

26 Fit the piston rings using the same technique as for removal. Fit the bottom ring first and work up. When fitting the oil control ring first insert the expander then fit the ring with its gap positioned 180° from the expander's gap. Arrange the gaps of the upper two rings 120° either side of the oil control ring gap. Make sure that No 2 ring is fitted the correct way round (Fig. 1.15).

Oil pump
27 Refer to Section 14.

Timing belt and sprockets
28 Refer to Section 4 and also examine the sprockets for wear and damage.

Camshaft
   Refer to Section 7.

Cylinder head
30 Refer to Section 10.

Flywheel
31 Examine the clutch mating surface of the flywheel for scoring or cracks. Light grooving or scoring may be ignored. Surface cracks or deep grooving can sometimes be removed by specialist machining, provided not too much metal is taken off, otherwise the flywheel must be renewed.

32 Inspect the starter ring gear for damaged or missing teeth. The ring gear can be renewed separately to the flywheel as follows. Drill through the width of the ring gear then split it with a cold chisel and remove it. The new ring gear must be heated then quickly tapped onto the flywheel and allowed to cool naturally. The temperature to which the ring gear must be heated is critical – too little heat and the ring gear may not fit or may even jam halfway on, too much heat and the temper of the metal may be lost causing it to wear rapidly in use. The correct temperature is normally attached to the new ring gear, however, the average DIY mechanic may prefer to leave the job to a garage or engineering works.

Miscellaneous
33 The makers recommend that the flywheel bolts only are renewed at overhaul, however, it would be prudent to also renew the cylinder head bolts especially if they have been tightened more than once.

25 Engine reassembly – general

1 Before commencing reassembly, make sure that all parts are clean and that the new components required have been obtained. A full set of oil seals and gaskets must be purchased – refer to Section 9 for selection of the correct head gasket.

2 Renew any nuts, bolts or studs with damaged threads.

3 A dial test indicator and stand (preferably magnetic) will be needed, also an oil can filled with clean engine oil to lubricate working parts as they are assembled.

4 Small quantities of grease, thread locking compound, anti-seize compound and various types of sealant will be called for.

5 Have available a good quantity of lint-free rags for wiping excess oil off hands and engine parts.

26 Engine – complete reassembly

1 Position the block upside down on the bench. Wipe clean the main bearing shell seats in the block and caps.

2 Wipe any protective coating from the new bearing shells. Fit the top half main bearing shells (with the oil grooves) to their seats in the block. Make sure that the locating tangs on the shells engage with the recesses in the seats.

3 Fit the thrust washers on each side of No 2 main bearing, grooved side outwards. Use a smear of grease to hold them in position (photo).

4 Lubricate the top half shells and lower the crankshaft into position (photo).

5 Fit the plain bottom half main bearing shells to their caps, making sure that the locating tangs engage with the recesses. Oil the shells.

6 Fit the thrust washers on each side of No 2 main bearing cap using a smear of grease to hold them in position.

7 Before fitting the caps check that the crankshaft endfloat is within the specified limits using a dial test indicator on the crankshaft nose.

8 Fit the main bearing caps Nos 2 to 5 to their correct locations (photo) and the right way round (the bearing shell tang locations in the block and caps must be on the same side). Insert the bolts loosely.

9 Apply a small amount of thread locking fluid to the No 1 main bearing cap face on the block around the sealing strip holes (photo).

10 Press the sealing strips in the grooves on each side of No 1 main bearing cap (photo). It is now necessary to obtain two thin metal strips of 0.25 mm (0.010 in) thickness or less in order to prevent the strips moving when the cap is being fitted. Peugeot garages use the tool shown in Fig. 1.16 which acts as a clamp, however, metal strips can be used provided all burrs which may damage the sealing strips are first removed.

11 Oil both sides of the metal strips and hold them on the sealing strips. Fit the No 1 main bearing cap, insert the bolts loosely, then carefully pull out the metal strips with a pair of pliers in a horizontal direction (photos).

12 Tighten the main bearing bolts evenly to the specified torque (photo).

13 Check that the crankshaft rotates freely – there must be no tight spots or binding.

14 Dip the new rear oil seal in engine oil, locate it on the crankshaft open end first, and press it squarely to the previously noted depth

26.3 No 2 main bearing and thrust washers

26.4 Oiling the main bearing shells

26.8 Fitting No 5 main bearing cap

26.9 Applying thread locking fluid to the No 1 main bearing cap joint face

26.10 Sealing strips fitted to No 1 main bearing cap

Fig. 1.16 Using the special tool to fit No 1 main bearing cap (Sec 26)

26.11A Slide the No 1 main bearing cap and metal strips into position ...

26.11B ... insert the bolts ...

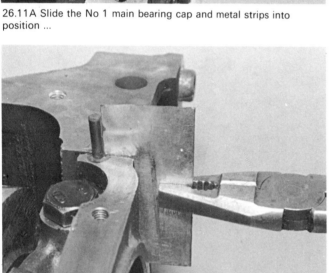

26.11C ... then carefully pull out the metal strips

26.12 Tightening the main bearing bolts

26.14 Fitting the crankshaft rear oil seal with a plastic protector

using a metal tube slightly less than 102 mm (4.0 in) in diameter. A piece of thin plastic is useful to prevent damage to the oil seal (photo). Make sure that the outer lip of the oil seal points outwards and if necessary use a piece of bent wire to pull it out.

15 Position the cylinder block either on its side or on the flywheel end.

16 Lay out the assembled pistons and rods in order with the bearing shells, connecting rod caps and nuts.

17 Check that the piston ring gaps are arranged 120° from each other.

18 Clean the bearing shells, caps and rods then press the shells into position so that the locating tangs engage in the grooves.

19 Oil the bores, pistons, crankpins and shells. Fit a piston ring compressor to No 1 piston. With Nos 1 and 4 crankpins at BDC insert No 1 piston in the bore at the flywheel end, making sure that the clover leaf cut-out on the piston crown is towards the oil filter side of the engine.

20 Using a hammer handle tap the piston through the ring compressor and into the bore. Guide the connecting rod onto the crankpin and fit the cap, together with its shell bearing, making sure it is the correct way round.

21 Fit the nuts and tighten them to the specified torque. Turn the crankshaft to check for free movement.

22 Repeat the procedure to fit the other three pistons.

23 Temporarily refit the pulley bolt to the nose of the crankshaft then, using a torque wrench, check that the torque required to turn the crankshaft does not exceed 41 Nm (30 lbf ft) (photo). Any excessive tightness must be investigated before proceeding.

24 Using feeler blades and a knife, cut the sealing strips on No 1 main bearing cap to 1.0 mm (0.040 in) above the sump gasket mating surface (photo).

25 Fit the Woodruff key to the groove in the crankshaft and refit the oil pump sprocket, teeth end first. Engage the chain with the sprocket and tie it up or to one side so that it remains engaged (photo).

26 Prise the oil seal from the front housing. Check that the two dowels are located in the front of the cylinder block then refit the front housing, together with a new gasket, and tighten the bolts evenly to the specified torque (photo).

27 Check that the dowel is fitted to the bottom of the block. Engage the oil pump sprocket with the chain and slide the L-shaped spacer under the pump, making sure that its open end engages the dowel.

28 Insert the oil pump bolts in their correct location, the longest bolt through the dowel and the next longest by the oil return hole. Tighten the bolts evenly to the specified torque.

29 Dip the front oil seal in engine oil then press it into the front housing until flush with the outer face.

30 Apply a little sealing compound where the front housing abuts the block on both sides. Position a new gasket on the block and refit the sump (photos). Note the correct location of the bolts as shown in Fig. 1.17. Tighten the bolts evenly to the specified torque. Remove the sump drain plug, renew the washer, then refit and tighten the plug.

31 Locate the flywheel on the crankshaft dowel.

32 Apply locking fluid to the threads of the bolts, insert them, and tighten them to the specified torque while holding the flywheel stationary with a screwdriver or suitable bar inserted between the teeth of the starter ring gear and the gearbox location dowel.

33 Position the cylinder block upright on the bench.

34 Check that the cylinder head bolt holes in the block are clear preferably using a 12 x 150 tap (photo).

35 Locate the correct cylinder head gasket (see Section 9) in the block the right way round with the identification notches or holes at the flywheel end. Check that the location dowel is fitted (photo).

36 Turn the crankshaft clockwise (from timing belt end) until pistons 1 and 4 pass BDC and commence to rise, then position them halfway up their bores. Pistons 2 and 3 will also be at their mid-way positions, but descending their bores. The Woodruff key groove on the nose of the crankshaft will be at the 9 o'clock position.

37 Check that the camshaft is set to TDC with the Woodruff key position facing upwards and the tips of cams 4 and 6 resting on the bucket tappets.

38 Lower the cylinder head onto the block (photo).

39 Grease the threads and contact faces of the cylinder head bolts, then insert them and tighten them in the sequence shown in Fig. 1.9 in three stages as given in Specifications (photos).

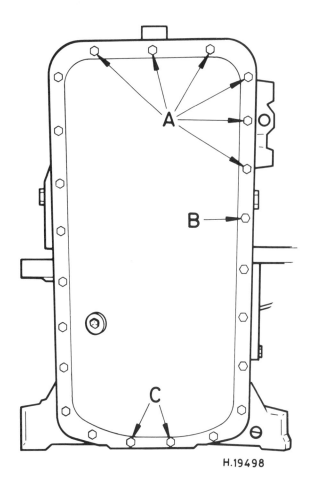

H.19498

Fig. 1.17 Sump bolt locations (Sec 26)

A 6 socket-head bolts
B 15 bolts (16 mm length)
C 2 bolts (14 mm length)

26.23 Checking the crankshaft turning torque

26.24 Cutting the sealing strips on No 1 main bearing cap

26.25 Fitting the chain to the oil pump sprocket

26.26 Tightening the front oil seal housing bolts

26.30A Apply sealing compound here (arrowed) ...

26.30B ... then fit the new sump gasket

26.34 Cleaning the cylinder head bolt holes with a tap

26.35 Head gasket fitted to cylinder block with location dowel arrowed

26.38 Lowering the cylinder head onto the block

40 Recheck the valve clearances with reference to Section 8 and adjust them if necessary. Do this even if the clearances have been adjusted with the cylinder head removed as there may be minor differences.

41 Refit the engine front plate followed by the timing belt intermediate roller and bracket, and the engine mounting bracket. Tighten all the bolts. On non-Horizon models do not forget the mounting bracket bolt on the inside face of the engine front plate (photo).

42 Insert the timing belt tensioner spring and plunger in the mounting bracket. Press the tensioner arm against the plunger and refit the bracket and roller onto the pivot stud. Alternatively compress the plunger with the tool described in Section 5. Fit the adjustment bolt and pivot nut, and tighten the bolt with the tensioner in the released position (ie spring compressed) (photos).

43 Refit the injection pump mounting bracket and tighten the bolts.

44 Refit the injection pump, align the previously made marks then tighten the nuts followed by the bolt.

45 Refit the water pump together with a new gasket and tighten the bolts to the specified torque (Chapter 2).

46 Locate the Woodruff key in the groove then refit the timing belt sprocket to the crankshaft (photo).

26.39A Insert the cylinder head bolts ...

47 Fit the camshaft sprocket to the timing end of the camshaft. Apply locking fluid to the threads then insert the bolt and tighten it to the specified torque while holding the camshaft sprocket stationary. A tool made out of metal bar and two bolts may be used to hold the sprocket, or alternatively the timing bolt may be screwed into the head (photo).

48 Unbolt the special puller from the injection pump sprocket. Refit the Woodruff key then fit the sprocket to the injection pump shaft. Refit the nut and tighten it while holding the sprocket stationary using either method described in paragraph 47 (photo).

49 Refit the special puller to the sprocket then insert and tighten the bolts (photo).

50 Refit the valve cover, together with a new gasket, and tighten the bolts.

51 Check that the camshaft and injection pump sprockets are at their TDC positions with the three timing bolts inserted in the front plate.

52 Insert an 8.0 mm diameter metal dowel rod through the special hole in the left-hand rear flange of the cylinder block then carefully turn the engine clockwise (from the timing belt end) until the rod

26.39B ... and tighten them to the specified torque

26.41 Inner bolt location for the engine mounting bracket (arrowed) (non-Horizon models)

26.42A Turn the tensioner bracket anti-clockwise ...

26.42B ... and tighten the bolt to hold the tensioner in the released position

26.46 Fitting the sprocket to the crankshaft

26.47 Tightening the camshaft sprocket bolt with the timing bolt in position

26.48 Tightening the injection pump sprocket bolt with the timing bolts in position

26.49 Tightening the special puller to the injection pump sprocket

26.54A Fitting the timing belt over the injection pump sprocket ...

26.54B ... the camshaft sprocket ...

enters the TDC hole in the flywheel. It is only necessary to turn the crankshaft a quarter turn as Nos 1 and 4 pistons are already halfway up their bores. Do not turn the crankshaft more than this otherwise pistons 2 and 3 will strike valves 4 and 6.

53 Locate the timing belt on the crankshaft sprocket making sure where applicable that the rotation arrow is facing the correct way.

54 Hold the timing belt engaged with the crankshaft sprocket then feed it over the roller and onto the injection pump, camshaft, and water pump sprockets and over the tensioner roller. To ensure correct engagement locate only a half width on the injection pump sprocket before feeding the timing belt onto the camshaft sprocket, keeping the belt taut and fully engaged with the crankshaft sprocket (photos). Locate the timing belt fully onto the sprockets.

55 With the pivot nut loose, slacken the tensioner adjustment bolt while holding the bracket against the spring tension, then slowly release the bracket until the roller presses against the timing belt. Retighten the adjustment bolt (photo).

56 Remove the bolts from the camshaft and injection pump sprockets. Remove the metal dowel rod from the cylinder block.

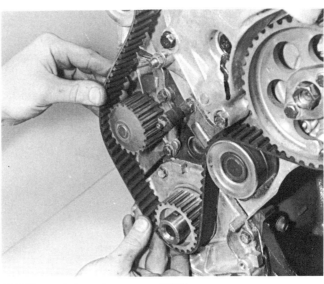

26.54C ... and the water pump sprocket

57 Rotate the engine two complete turns in its normal direction. Do not rotate the engine backwards as the timing belt must be kept tight between the crankshaft, injection pump and camshaft sprockets.

58 Loosen the tensioner adjustment bolt to allow the tensioner spring to push the roller against the timing belt, then tighten both the adjustment bolt and pivot nut.

59 Recheck the engine timing by turning the engine until the sprocket bolt holes are aligned, and check that the metal dowel rod can be inserted into the flywheel.

60 Refit the bottom timing cover and tighten the bolts (photo).

61 Fit the pulley to the front of the crankshaft over the Woodruff key.

62 Apply locking fluid to the threads of the pulley bolt then insert it and tighten to the specified torque while an assistant holds the flywheel stationary with a screwdriver inserted between the teeth of the starter ring gear and the transmission location dowel. Note that after tightening to the initial torque, the bolt must be angle tightened a further 60° which is the equivalent of one flat on the bolt head. Alternatively mark the flat extremities on the socket together with a starting datum on the pulley (photos).

63 Where applicable, locate a new gasket on the side of the sump, refit the inlet bracket, and tighten the nuts.

64 Refit the water pump inlet together with a new gasket and tighten the bolts.

65 Bolt the coolant tube to the cylinder block and fit the hoses.

66 Refit the thermostat housing, together with a new gasket, and tighten the bolts.

67 Insert the oil pressure switch in the block and tighten.

68 Where applicable insert the oil level sensor and tighten.

69 Refit the fast idle cable to the injection pump with reference to Chapter 3.

70 Refit the exhaust manifold, together with new gaskets, and tighten the nuts evenly.

71 Refit the inlet manifold and tighten the bolts evenly. There are no gaskets.

72 Refit the oil filler cap and ventilation hose if fitted.

73 Slide the oil separator onto the dipstick tube (photo) and secure with the clip. Reconnect the crankcase ventilation hoses to the valve cover and sump inlet.

74 Reconnect the bottom hose to the water pump inlet.

75 Where fitted on the 1.9 engine reconnect the oil cooler hoses and refit the oil cooler, tightening the centre stud to the specified torque (photos).

76 Smear a little engine oil on the sealing ring of the oil filter cartridge then refit it and tighten by hand only.

77 Refit the alternator (Chapter 7).

78 Refit the engine lifting bracket to the cylinder head.

79 Reconnect the leak off hoses to the injectors.

80 Refit the fuel pipe assemblies to the injectors and injection pump and tighten the union nuts to the specified torque (Chapter 3).

81 Slide the pump pulley onto the flywheel end of the camshaft. Insert the bolt and tighten it to the specified torque (photo).

26.55 Tightening the tensioner adjustment bolt

26.60 Bottom timing cover fitted

26.62A Apply locking fluid to the crankshaft pulley bolt before fitting it

26.62B Tightening the crankshaft pulley bolt

26.62C Markings necessary in order to angle-tighten the crankshaft pulley bolt by 60°

26.73 Oil separator located on the dipstick tube (where applicable)

26.75A Oil cooler ...

26.75B ... and coolant hose connections

26.81 Tightening the pump pulley bolt on the camshaft

82 Where applicable refit the diagnostic socket and bracket and tighten the bolt.

83 Refit the two timing cover sections and press down the special clip to secure.

84 Refit the brake vacuum pump as described in Chapter 5.

85 Refit the clutch.

27 Engine and gearbox – reconnection

1 Support the engine then lift the gearbox into position. It may be necessary to turn the gearbox slightly one way or the other to enable the splined input shaft to enter the clutch driven plate.

2 Push the gearbox onto the location dowels, insert the bolts and tighten them.

Models up to 1987

3 Refit the bottom cover and tighten the bolts.

4 Refit the starter motor and tighten the bolts.

5 Refit the TDC sensor and holder and tighten the bolts. When the TDC sensor is fitted new it incorporates three legs which are 1.0 mm (0.04 in) long and these automatically set the sensor 1.0 mm from the flywheel. When fitting an old sensor the legs should be filed off – the unit can then be fully inserted until it touches the flywheel and then withdrawn by 1.0 mm (0.04 in) before tightening the bolts.

28 Engine and gearbox – refitting

1 Reverse the procedure given in Section 19 but note the following additional points:

  (a) *Use a final drive oil seal protector (Chapter 4) when inserting the right-hand driveshaft. Remove the protector when the driveshaft is fitted*
  (b) *Refill the gearbox and engine with oil*
  (c) *Adjust the accelerator and fast idle cables with reference to Chapter 3*
  (d) *On 1.7 engines tighten the exhaust manifold-to-downpipe bolts with reference to Section 9 paragraph 34*
  (e) *Refit the engine/gearbox mountings with reference to Section 17*

  (f) *On non-Horizon models adjust the clutch cable*
  (g) *Refill the cooling system (Chapter 2)*
  (h) *Check the injection pump timing if necessary*

29 Engine – initial start-up after overhaul

1 Check that the oil, coolant and fuel have all been replenished and that the battery is well charged.

2 On early models fitted with a Roto-Diesel fuel filter unscrew the pump plunger.

3 Switch on the ignition to energize the stop solenoid then actuate the pump on the fuel filter until resistance is felt. Retighten the plunger where necessary.

4 Fully depress the accelerator pedal, turn the ignition key to position 'M' and wait for the preheating warning light to go out.

5 Start the engine. Additional cranking may be necessary to bleed the fuel system before the engine starts.

6 Once started keep the engine running at a fast tickover. Check that the oil pressure light goes out, then check for leaks of oil, fuel and coolant.

Models up to 1987

7 If all is well, continue to run the engine at 3000 rpm for 10 minutes then switch off the ignition and let the engine cool for at least $3^1/_2$ hours.

8 Remove the filler cap from the cooling system expansion tank to release any remaining pressure, then refit it.

9 Working on each cylinder head bolt in turn in the correct sequence first loosen the bolt 90° then retighten to the final torque given in the Specifications.

All models

10 If many new parts have been fitted, the engine should be treated as new and run in at reduced speeds and loads for the first 600 miles (1000 km) or so. After this mileage it is beneficial to change the engine oil and oil filter.

11 Have the injection pump timing and idling speed checked and adjusted as described in Chapter 3.

30 Fault diagnosis – engine

Faults in the fuel injection system can produce noises suggesting bearing failure. To locate such a fault, slacken each injector union in turn with the engine running. The noise will disappear when the union on the faulty injector is slackened, however, to prove conclusively that the injector is faulty, fit it to another cylinder and carry out the test again. Air or other contaminants in the fuel can also cause knocking noises.

Symptom	Reason(s)
Engine will not turn over when starter switch is operated	Flat battery Battery connections corroded or loose Starter solenoid connections loose Engine/gearbox earth cable loose or broken Starter motor defective
Engine turns normally, but will not start	Incorrect starting procedure Injection pump stop solenoid faulty or wire disconnected Wax in fuel (very cold conditions only) Timing belt broken Fuel system fault Poor compression (see below) Injection pump timing incorrect
Engine idles unevenly	Fuel system fault Incorrect valve clearance Burnt out valves Blown head gasket
Poor compression	Burnt out valves Valve clearances too small Blown head gasket Worn piston rings/cylinder bores Cylinder head or block cracked
Lack of power	Poor compression (see above) Injection pump timing incorrect Worn or dirty injectors Air cleaner clogged
Excessive oil consumption	Oil leaks from crankshaft or camshaft oil seals Worn piston rings/cylinder bores (smoky exhaust is an indication) External leakage
Unusual noises	Peripheral component fault (eg water pump or alternator) Worn or damaged timing belt or alternator drivebelt Piston ring(s) broken Big-end bearings worn (worst when off load) Main bearings worn (worst when on load) Injector or injection pump fault (see Chapter 3)
Excessive smoke in exhaust	Oil being burnt (blue smoke) Fuel system fault (white or black smoke) – see Chapter 3

Chapter 2 Cooling system

Contents

Specifications

General

System type .... Pressurised, front-mounted radiator, remote expansion tank, coolant pump and thermostat. Electric cooling fan(s)

Capacity:
    205 .... 8.3 litres (14.6 pints)
    305 .... 9.5 litres (16.7 pints)
    309 .... 8.5 litres (15.0 pints)
    Horizon .... 6.2 litres (10.9 pints)
Antifreeze type/specification .... Ethylene glycol based [9730.70] (Duckhams Universal Antifreeze and Summer Coolant)

Thermostat:
    Starts to open at .... 81°C (178°F)
    Fully open at .... 93°C (199°F)
    Minimum travel .... 7.5 mm (0.295 in)
Expansion tank cap pressure .... 1 bar (14.5 lbf/in²)
Temperature warning switch operating temperature .... 103 to 107°C (217 to 225°F)
Electric cooling fans:
    Cut-in temperature:
        1st speed .... 84 to 88°C (183 to 190°F)
        2nd speed .... 88 to 92°C (190 to 198°F)
    Cut-out temperature:
        1st speed .... 75 to 83°C (167 to 181°F)
        2nd speed .... 83 to 87°C (181 to 189°F)

Torque wrench setting	Nm	lbf ft
Water pump	12	9

1 General description

The cooling system is pressurised, with a front-mounted radiator and a water pump driven by the engine timing belt. The thermostat is located on the flywheel end of the cylinder head, and enables the engine to achieve a fast warm-up period by initially restricting the coolant flow within the engine and heater circuits. Thereafter the coolant flows through the radiator to provide additional cooling. The main engine temperature control is provided by one or two electric cooling fans mounted either in front of or behind the radiator, according to model. A twin-action sensor in the radiator activates the fan(s) according to the coolant temperature.

Essential to the operation of the system is the expansion tank which provides a reservoir to allow for expansion and contraction of the coolant with changes in temperature. It also incorporates a filler/pressure relief valve cap.

The radiator is of the crossflow type, with plastic or metal side tanks. A temperature warning switch is provided on the water outlet from the cylinder head to warn the driver of excessive temperature.

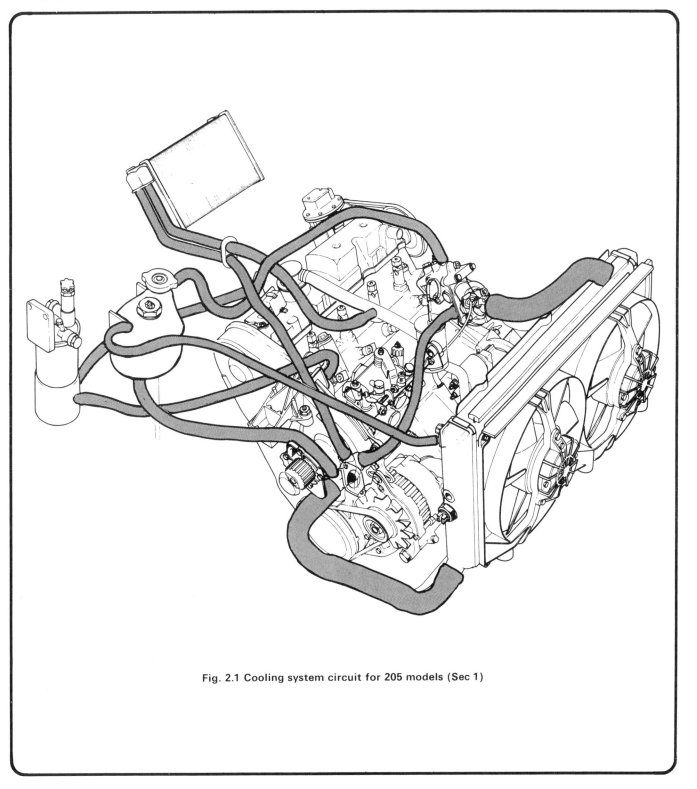

Fig. 2.1 Cooling system circuit for 205 models (Sec 1)

Fig. 2.2 Cutaway view of the expansion tank on Horizon models (Sec 2)

a   Maximum level   b   Minimum level

2   Routine maintenance

Carry out the following procedures at the intervals given in *Routine Maintenance* at the beginning of the manual.

Check coolant level

1   This check should be carried out with the engine cold.

2   Where marked on the outside of the expansion tank, check that the coolant is at or near the maximum level mark.

3   Where there are no external marks on the expansion tank, depress the filler cap and turn it anti-clockwise to remove it. Inside the filler neck there is either a level plate or tube incorporating both minimum and maximum levels. Check that the coolant is at or near the maximum level.

4   If necessary, top up the coolant to the maximum level then refit the filler cap.

Renew the coolant mixture

5   Drain and flush the cooling system as described in Sections 4 and 5.

6   Fill the system with the recommended coolant as described in Section 6.

3   Cooling system – pressure test

1   In cases where leakage is difficult to trace a pressure test can prove helpful. The test involves pressurising the system by means of a hand pump and an adaptor which is fitted to the expansion tank in place of the filler cap. The resourceful home mechanic may be able to improvise the apparatus using an old filler cap and a tyre valve, alternatively the test can be performed by a Peugeot/Talbot garage.

2   Fit the test equipment to the expansion tank then run the engine to normal operating temperature and switch it off.

3   Apply 1.4 bar (20.3 lbf/in²) pressure and check that this pressure is held for at least 10 seconds. If the pressure drops prematurely there is a leak in the cooling system which must be traced and rectified.

4   Besides leaks from hoses, pressure can also be lost through leaks in the radiator and heater matrix. A blown head gasket or a cracked head or block can cause an 'invisible' leak, but there are usually other clues to this condition such as poor engine performance, regular misfiring, or combustion gases entering the coolant.

5 After completing the test, allow the engine to cool then remove the test equipment.

6 The condition of the filler cap must not be overlooked. Normally it is tested with similar equipment to that used for the pressure test. The release pressure is given in the Specifications and is also usually stamped on the cap itself. Renew the cap if it is faulty.

4 Cooling system – draining

1 If the engine is hot allow it to cool for at least 10 minutes after switching off.

2 Depress the filler cap on the expansion tank and slowly turn it anti-clockwise until it can be removed. If the engine is hot cover the cap with a thick cloth before removing it as a precaution against scalding.

3 On Horizon models, position the heater control on maximum heat.

4 Place a suitable container beneath the left-hand side of the radiator, then unscrew the drain plug and allow the coolant to drain. If there is no drain plug fitted, disconnect the bottom hose from the right-hand side of the radiator.

5 When the radiator is completely drained, refit the drain plug or hose then drain the block by unscrewing the drain plug located on the rear of the engine at the flywheel end. Refit the drain plug on completion.

5 Cooling system – flushing

1 If the coolant is contaminated with rust and scale the complete system should be flushed as follows.

2 Drain the system as described in the previous Section.

3 Remove the thermostat as described in Section 8.

4 If not already done disconnect the bottom hose from the radiator.

5 Insert a garden hose into the thermostat housing so that the water runs through the engine in the reverse direction to normal flow and comes out of the bottom hose. Continue until the water emerges clean.

6 Run the water through the radiator in the normal direction of flow by inserting the garden hose in the top hose. In severe cases of contamination it may be helpful to remove the radiator and reverse-flush it.

7 Chemical descalers or flushing agents should only be used as a last resort, in which case follow the instructions given by the manufacturers.

8 When flushing is complete, refit the thermostat and reconnect the hoses.

6 Cooling system – filling

1 Make sure that the drain plugs are secure and that all hoses are in good condition and their clips tight.

2 Loosen or remove the bleed screws located on the thermostat housing cover and, where applicable, on the heater hose at the bulkhead (photos).

3 Fill slowly with coolant via the expansion tank and at the same time keep an eye on the bleed screw holes (photo). As soon as coolant free of air bubbles emerges refit and tighten the bleed screws.

4 Top up the expansion tank until it is full to the filler cap seating. There still remains air in the system which must be purged as follows.

6.2A Bleed screws on the thermostat housing cover (arrowed)

6.2B Bleed screw on the heater hose (arrowed)

5 Start the engine and run at a fast idle speed for several minutes. Stop the engine.

6 Top up the expansion tank to the maximum level. On some models this is marked on the outside of the expansion tank but on other models a level plate or tube is visible through the filler neck. Both minimum and maximum levels are indicated (photo).

7 Fit the filler cap.

8 Start the engine and run to normal operating temperature indicated by the electric cooling fan(s) cutting in then out after a few minutes.

9 Stop the engine and allow it to cool for at least 1 hour.

10 Recheck the coolant level as described in paragraph 6 and top up as necessary.

6.3 Filling the cooling system via the expansion tank

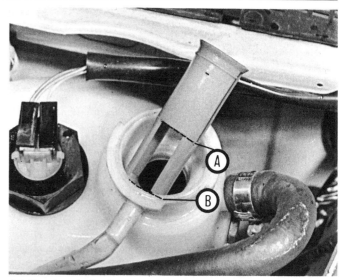

6.6 Showing the level tube removed from the expansion tank
A   Maximum level   B   Minimum level

7   Radiator (205 and Horizon models) – removal and refitting

1   Drain the cooling system as described in Section 4.

2   Remove the air cleaner as described in Chapter 3.

3   Loosen the clips and disconnect the top hose, bottom hose (photo) and vent hose from the radiator.

4   Disconnect the wiring from the thermal switch on the right-hand side of the radiator (photo).

205 models
5   Remove the radiator grille.

6   Unscrew the upper bolts, the cooling fan frame mounting bolts and the front side nuts so that the front crossmember, complete with bonnet lock and cable, can be positioned to the side of the engine compartment (photos).

7   Pull up the upper spring clips and move the top of the radiator clear (photo).

8   Carefully lift the radiator from the bottom mounting rubbers (photos).

Horizon models
9   Remove the electric cooling fans as described in Section 10.

10 With the upper mounting brackets removed, carefully lift the radiator from the bottom mounting rubbers.

All models
11 Check the radiator mounting rubbers for condition and renew them if necessary.

12 Refitting is a reversal of removal. Refill the system as described in Section 6.

8   Thermostat – removal, testing and refitting

1   Drain the cooling system as described in Section 4.

2   Remove the air cleaner as described in Chapter 3.

3   Loosen the clip and disconnect the top hose from the thermostat housing cover (photo).

4   Unscrew the four bolts and remove the thermostat housing cover from the cylinder head water outlet. There is no need to disconnect the fast idle cable. Remove the gasket (photos).

7.3 Bottom hose connection to radiator

7.4 Thermal switch and wiring

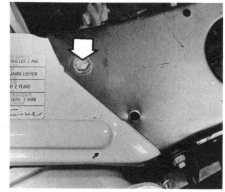

7.6A Front crossmember upper bolt – arrowed (205 models)

7.6B Front crossmember front side nut – arrowed (205 models)

7.7 Releasing the radiator upper spring clips (205 models)

7.8A Removing the radiator (205 models)

7.8B Radiator bottom mounting rubber (205 models)

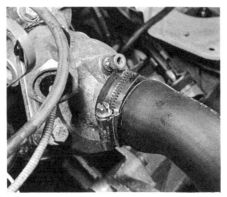

8.3 Top hose connection to thermostat housing cover

8.4A Unscrewing the thermostat housing cover bolts

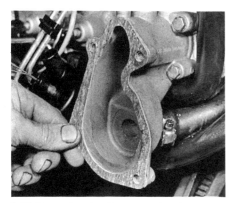

8.4B Removing the thermostat housing cover gasket

8.5 Thermostat and retaining circlip

8.6 Removing the rubber seal from the thermostat

5   Using circlip pliers, extract the circlip from the cover and lift out the thermostat (photo).

6   If necessary pull the rubber seal from the thermostat (photo).

7   To test the thermostat place it in a pan of cold water and check that it is initially closed. Heat the water and check that it commences to open at the temperature given in Specifications. Continue to heat the water and check the fully open temperature and minimum travel. Finally allow the water to cool and check that it fully closes. Discard it if it is faulty.

8   Refitting is a reversal of removal but when inserting the thermostat in the cover position the vent hole uppermost and also fit a new gasket. Refill the system as described in Section 6.

9   Water pump – removal and refitting

1   Remove the timing belt as described in Chapter 1, Section 4.

2   Drain the cooling system (Section 4 of this Chapter) then disconnect the bottom hose from the water pump inlet.

3   Unscrew the bolts and withdraw the water pump from the cylinder block (photos). Remove the gasket.

4   Clean the mating faces of the water pump and block.

5   Fit the water pump, together with a new gasket, insert the bolts, and tighten them evenly to the specified torque.

9.3A Unscrew the bolts ...

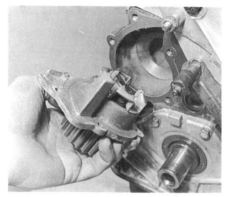

9.3B ... and withdraw the water pump

9.3C Water pump showing impeller vanes

10.4 Cooling fan frame mounting bolts (arrowed)

10.5 Radiator upper mounting bracket (Horizon models)

10.8 Cooling fan and retaining bolt (arrowed)

6   Refit the timing belt as described in Chapter 1, Section 4.

7   Refill the cooling system as described in Section 6 of this Chapter.

10 Electric cooling fans (205 and Horizon models) – removal and refitting

1   Disconnect the battery negative lead.

205 models
2   Remove the radiator grille.

3   Disconnect the wiring at the connector.

4   Unscrew the mounting bolts and withdraw the cooling fan frame assembly (photo).

Horizon models
5   Unbolt the radiator upper mounting brackets (photo).

6   Disconnect the wiring at the connector.

7   Move the top of the cooling fan frame assembly rearwards then lift the locating pegs from the lower mounting rubbers.

All models
8   If necessary unscrew the nuts and remove the fan motor(s) from the frame. The fan(s) may also be unbolted from the motor spindle(s) (photo).

9   Refitting is a reversal of removal. Should a fault develop in the electric cooling fans note that the control relays are located on the left-hand side of the engine compartment (photo).

10.9 Electric cooling fan control relays (205 models)

Chapter 3 Fuel and exhaust systems

Contents

Specifications

General

System type .... Rear-mounted fuel tank, injection pump with integral transfer pump, indirect injection

Firing order .... 1-3-4-2 (No 1 at flywheel end)

Fuel

Type .... Commercial diesel fuel for road vehicles (DERV)

Tank capacity:
    205 .... 50 litres (11.0 gallons)
    305 .... 43 litres (9.5 gallons)
    309 .... 55 litres (12.1 gallons)
    Horizon .... 45 litres (9.9 gallons)

Injection pump (Lucas CAV/Roto-Diesel)

Static advance .... 2.26 ± 0.05 mm (0.089 ± 0.002 in) BTDC
Dynamic advance:
    Except XUD9 pumps with code suffix 160A .... 14° BTDC at 800 rpm
    XUD9 pumps with code suffix 160A .... 17° BTDC at 800 rpm
Idle speed .... 800 rpm
Maximum engine speed (no load) .... 5100 ± 100 rpm
Rotation .... Clockwise from sprocket end

Injection pump (Bosch)

Static advance:
    1.7 .... 0.80 ± 0.03 mm (0.031 ± 0.001 in) BTDC
    1.9 .... 0.50 ± 0.03 mm (0.020 ± 0.001 in) BTDC
Dynamic advance:
    1.7 .... 14° BTDC at 800 rpm
    1.9 .... 13.5° BTDC at 800 rpm
Idle speed .... 800 rpm
Maximum engine speed (no load) .... 5100 ± 100 rpm
Rotation .... Clockwise from sprocket end

Injectors

Type .... Pintle
Opening pressure:
    Lucas CAV/Roto-Diesel .... 115 ± 5 bar (1668 ± 73 lbf/in²)
    Bosch .... 130 ± 5 bar (1885 ± 73 lbf/in²)

Heater plugs

Type .... Champion CH 68

Torque wrench settings

	Nm	lbf ft
Injector:		
Lucas CAV/Roto-Diesel	130	96
Bosch	90	66
Injector pipe union nuts	20	15
Heater plug	22	16
Injection pump	18	13
Cylinder head blanking plug	30	22
Injection pump (Bosch) blanking plug	20	15
Fuel filter through-bolt	10	7
Injection pump sprocket nut	50	37
Stop solenoid:		
Lucas CAV/Roto-Diesel	15	11
Bosch	20	15

1 General description

The fuel system consists of a rear-mounted fuel tank, a fuel filter, a fuel injection pump, injectors and associated components. The exhaust system is similar to that used on petrol-engined vehicles.

Fuel is drawn from the tank by a vane-type transfer pump incorporated in the delivery head of the injection pump. Before reaching the pump the fuel passes through a fuel filter where foreign matter and water are removed. The injection pump is driven at half crankshaft speed by the timing belt. The high pressure required to inject the fuel into the compressed air in the swirl chambers is achieved by two opposed pistons forced together by rollers running in a cam ring. The fuel passes through a central rotor with a single outlet drilling which aligns with ports leading to the injector pipes and injectors. Fuel metering is controlled by a centrifugal governor which reacts to

accelerator pedal position and engine speed. The governor is linked to the metering valve which moves the rotor sleeve to increase or decrease the amount of fuel transferred to the high pressure chamber. Injection timing is varied by turning the cam ring to suit the prevailing engine speed.

There are four precision-made injectors which inject a homogeneous spray of fuel into the swirl chambers located in the cylinder head. The injectors are calibrated to open and close at critical pressures to provide efficient and even combustion. The injector needle is lubricated by fuel which accumulates in the spring chamber and is channelled to the injection pump return hose by leak-off pipes.

Bosch or Lucas CAV/Roto-Diesel fuel system components may be fitted, depending on model. Components from the latter manufacturer are marked either 'Lucas CAV' or 'Roto-Diesel', depending on their date and place of manufacture.

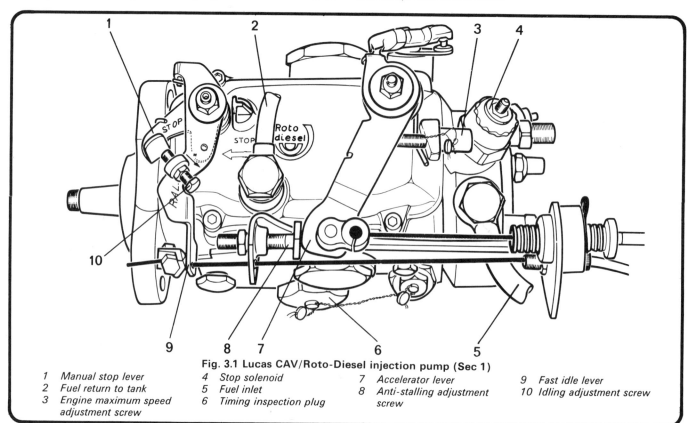

Fig. 3.1 Lucas CAV/Roto-Diesel injection pump (Sec 1)

1 Manual stop lever	4 Stop solenoid	7 Accelerator lever	9 Fast idle lever
2 Fuel return to tank	5 Fuel inlet	8 Anti-stalling adjustment	10 Idling adjustment screw
3 Engine maximum speed adjustment screw	6 Timing inspection plug	screw	

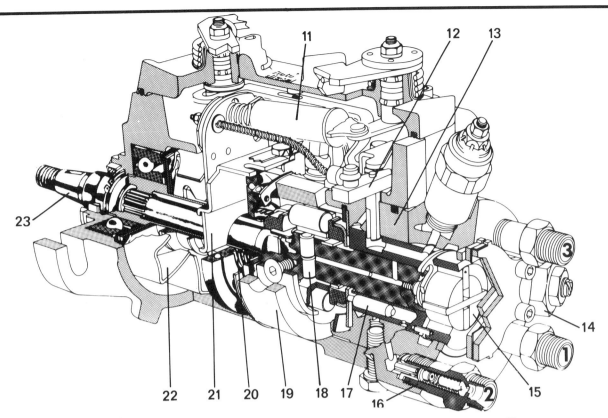

Fig. 3.2 Cutaway view of the Lucas CAV/Roto-Diesel injection pump (Sec 1)

11 MIN-MAX speed regulator
12 Fuel metering valve
13 Hydraulic head
14 Transfer pressure adjustment

15 Transfer pump
16 High pressure outlet and recirculation valve

17 Overload ram
18 Pistons
19 Cam ring

20 Overload springs
21 Control lever
22 Centrifugal governor
23 Driveshaft

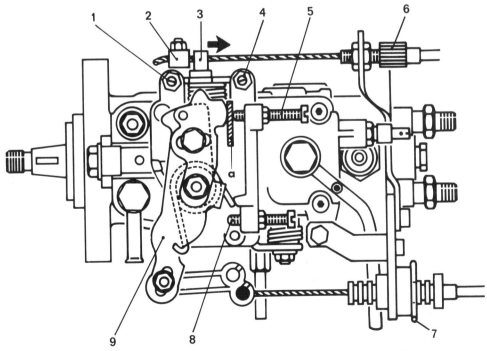

Fig. 3.3 Bosch injection pump – January 1984 on (Sec 1)

1 Fast idle adjustment screw
2 Cable end stop
3 Fast idle lever

4 Idling adjustment screw
5 Anti-stall adjustment screw
6 Fast idle cable adjustment ferrule

7 Accelerator cable adjustment ferrule
8 Engine maximum speed adjustment screw

9 Accelerator lever
a Shim for anti-stall adjustment

Preheater or 'glow' plugs are fitted to each swirl chamber to facilitate cold starting and, additionally, a thermostatic sensor in the cooling system operates a fast idle lever to increase the idling speed and supply additional fuel when the engine is cold.

A stop solenoid cuts the fuel supply to the injection pump rotor when the ignition is switched off, and there is also a hand-operated stop lever for use in an emergency.

Servicing of the injection pump and injectors is very limited for the home mechanic, and any dismantling other than that described in this Chapter must be entrusted to a Peugeot/Talbot dealer or fuel injection specialist.

2 Routine maintenance

Carry out the following procedures at the intervals given in *Routine Maintenance* at the beginning of the manual.

Renew the fuel filter
1   The fuel filter is located on the right-hand side of the engine compartment (photo), except for 305 models where it is on the left.

2   Place a suitable container beneath the filter. Drain the fuel from the filter by opening the water bleed screw on the bottom of the filter and (where fitted) the air bleed screw. When the fuel has drained, remove the container and place some rags below the filter to catch any further spillage.

3   Where applicable, disconnect the water detector wiring from the end cap or chamber (photo).

4   Unscrew the through-bolt from the top (Lucas CAV/Roto-Diesel) or bottom (Bosch) of the filter. On the Lucas CAV/Roto-Diesel version this will release the end cap and enable the cartridge and seals to be removed. On the Bosch version, remove the chamber, followed by the element and seals.

5   Clean the filter head and end cap or chamber.

6   Make sure that the old seals are removed, then locate the new seals in position and fit the new cartridge or element using a reversal of the removal procedure.

7   Finally prime the fuel injection system as described in Section 17.

Drain water from the fuel filter
8   Position a small container beneath the filter.

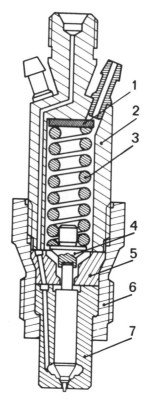 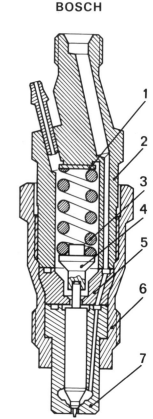

LUCAS CAV/ROTO-DIESEL   **BOSCH**

Fig. 3.4 Cross-section of the two injectors (Sec 1)

1	*Adjustment shim*	5	*Spacer*
2	*Upper body*	6	*Nut*
3	*Spring*	7	*Lower body and needle*
4	*Pushrod*		

9   Loosen the bleed screw on the bottom of the filter and allow any water to drain into the container. Where fitted, also loosen the air bleed screw on the filter head or inlet union bolt.

2.1 Fuel filter on a Horizon model

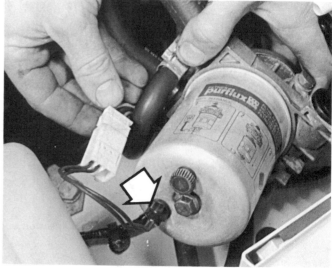

2.3 Water detector (arrowed) and wiring on the fuel filter

LUCAS CAV/ROTO-DIESEL   ## BOSCH

Fig. 3.5 Cross-section of the fuel filters (Sec 2)

1 Priming plunger	3 Seals	5 Through-bolt	7 Cartridge/element
2 Fuel bleed screw	4 Water bleed screw	6 Through-bolt seal	8 Air bleed screw

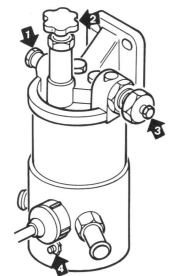

Fig. 3.6 Lucas CAV/Roto-Diesel fuel filter with coolant heated base (Sec 2)

1 Inlet union	3 Air bleed screw
2 Priming plunger	4 Water bleed screw

10 Tighten the lower bleed screw when fuel free of water flows. Retighten the air bleed screw where fitted.

11 Prime the fuel injection system as described in Section 17.

Renew the air cleaner element
12 Refer to Section 3.

3 Air cleaner and element – removal and refitting

1   On 205 and 309 models disconnect the air inlet duct from the tube on the front panel (photo).

2   On 305 models disconnect the air inlet and outlet ducts from the air cleaner.

3.1 Inlet duct connection to front panel tube

3   On Horizon models disconnect the outlet duct from the air cleaner cover.

4   Unscrew the nut or screw and lift off the cover (photo).

5   Remove the element and wipe clean the inside surfaces of the main body and cover (photo).

6   To remove the main body on non-Horizon models, disconnect the crankcase ventilation hose from the oil separator then unscrew the mounting bolt and withdraw the body from the mounting rubbers (photos). If necessary also disconnect the air duct from the cover.

7   On Horizon models disconnect the crankcase ventilation hose from the oil separator, and the inlet duct from the main body. Release the rubber band and lift the main body from its lower mounting rubber pad. If necessary also disconnect the air duct from the cover and inlet manifold noting the special spring clip (photos).

8   Refitting is a reversal of removal.

Fig. 3.7 Air cleaner element (1) removal on 305 models (Sec 3)

3.4 Air cleaner cover retaining screw (205 models)

3.5 Removing the air cleaner element (205 models)

3.6A Disconnect the crankcase ventilation hose from the oil separator ...

3.6B ... unscrew the mounting bolt ...

3.6C ... and withdraw the air cleaner body from the mounting rubbers (205 models)

3.7A Disconnect the crankcase ventilation hose from the oil separator ...

3.7B ... disconnect the inlet duct ...

3.7C ... release the rubber band ...

3.7D ... and lift out the air cleaner. Note the rubber mounting pad – arrowed (Horizon models)

3.7E Special spring clip on the air duct (Horizon models)

4 Fuel injection pump – removal and refitting

1 Disconnect the battery negative lead.

2 Cover the alternator with a plastic bag as a precaution against spillage of diesel fuel.

3 Remove the air cleaner and ducting with reference to Section 3.

4 Where necessary disconnect the crankcase ventilation hoses and remove the oil separator.

5 Apply the handbrake then jack up the front right-hand corner of the vehicle until the wheel is just clear of the ground. Support the vehicle on an axle stand and engage 4th or 5th gear. This will enable the engine to be turned easily by turning the right-hand wheel.

6 On Horizon models remove the centre timing cover section.

7 Pull up the special clip, release the spring clips and withdraw the front timing cover section.

8 Open the accelerator lever on the injection pump and disconnect the cable by passing it through the special slot (photo). Disconnect the cable adjustment ferrule from the bracket.

9 Note the position of the end stop on the fast idle cable then loosen the screw and disconnect the inner cable (photo). Unscrew the adjustment locknut and remove the cable and ferrule from the bracket.

10 Loosen the clip and disconnect the fuel supply hose (photo).

11 Disconnect the main fuel return pipe and the injector leak-off return pipe from the union tube (photo).

12 Disconnect the wire from the stop solenoid (photo).

13 Unscrew the union nuts securing the injector pipes to the injection pump (photo) and injectors. Remove the pipes complete.

14 Turn the engine by means of the front right-hand wheel until the two bolt holes in the injection pump sprocket are aligned with the corresponding holes in the engine front plate.

15 Insert two M8 bolts through the holes and hand tighten them. Note that the bolts must retain the sprocket while the injection pump is removed thereby making it unnecessary to remove the timing belt.

4.8A Accelerator cable connection – arrowed (205 models)

4.8B Accelerator cable connection – arrowed (Horizon models)

4.9 Fast idle cable and end stop – arrowed (Horizon models with early Bosch pump)

4.10 Fuel supply hose (A) and return pipe (B) (Horizon models with early Bosch pump)

4.11 Disconnecting the main fuel return pipe (205 models with Lucas CAV/Roto-Diesel pump)

4.12 Stop solenoid and wire (arrowed)

4.13 Injector pipe union nuts on the Lucas CAV/Roto-Diesel pump

4.16 Mark the injection pump in relation to the mounting bracket (arrow)

16 Mark the injection pump in relation to the mounting bracket using a scriber or felt tip pen (photo). This will ensure the correct timing when refitting. If a new pump is being fitted transfer the mark from the old pump to give an approximate setting.

17 Unscrew the three mounting nuts and remove the plates. Unscrew and remove the rear mounting bolt and support the injection pump on a block of wood (photos).

18 Unscrew the sprocket nut until the shaft taper is released from the sprocket. The nut acts as a puller, together with the plate bolted to the sprocket.

19 Continue to unscrew the sprocket nut and withdraw the injection pump from the mounting bracket (photo). Recover the Woodruff key from the shaft groove if it is loose.

20 Commence refitting the injection pump by fitting the Woodruff key to the shaft groove (if removed).

21 Unbolt the puller plate from the injection pump sprocket.

22 Insert the injection pump from behind the sprocket, making sure that the shaft key enters the groove in the sprocket. Screw on the nut and hand tighten it.

23 Fit the mounting nuts, together with their plates, and hand tighten the nuts.

24 Tighten the sprocket nut to the specified torque then refit the puller plate and tighten the bolts.

25 Unscrew and remove the two bolts from the injection pump sprocket.

26 If the original injection pump is being refitted, align the scribed marks and tighten the mounting nuts. If fitting a new pump, the timing must now be set as described in Sections 5 or 6.

27 Refit the rear mounting bolt and special nut, tightening the nut slowly to allow the bush to align itself as shown in Fig. 3.8.

28 Refit the injector pipes to the injection pump and injectors and tighten the union nuts.

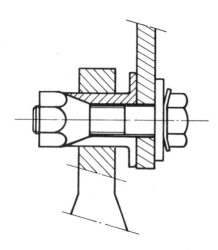

Fig. 3.8 Cross-section of injection pump rear mounting
(Sec 4)

4.17A Injection pump mounting nut and plate

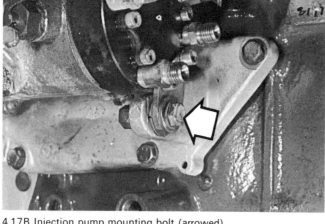

4.17B Injection pump mounting bolt (arrowed)

4.19 Removing the injection pump from its mounting bracket

29 Reconnect the wire to the stop solenoid.

30 Refit the fuel supply and return pipes.

31 Refit the fast idle cable and accelerator cable, and adjust them with reference to Sections 7 and 8.

32 Refit the timing cover sections and secure with the spring clips.

33 Lower the vehicle to the ground and apply the handbrake.

34 Remove the plastic bag from the alternator and reconnect the battery negative lead.

35 Where applicable refit the oil separator and crankcase ventilation hoses.

36 Refit the air cleaner and ducting.

37 Prime the fuel circuit by first switching on the ignition to energize the stop solenoid, then actuating the pump on the fuel filter until resistance is felt. On early models fitted with a Lucas CAV/Roto-Diesel

filter the pump plunger must first be unscrewed then retightened after priming.

38 Turn the ignition key to position 'M' and wait for the preheating warning light to go out. Start the engine and adjust the idling speed with reference to Section 9.

5   Fuel injection pump (Lucas CAV/Roto-Diesel) – checking and adjusting the static timing

Caution: *The maximum engine speed and transfer pressure settings, together with timing access plugs, are sealed by the manufacturers at the factory using locking wire and lead seals. Do not disturb the wire if the vehicle is still within the warranty period otherwise the warranty will be invalidated. Also do not attempt the timing procedure unless accurate instrumentation is available.*

1   Disconnect the battery negative lead.

2   Cover the alternator with a plastic bag as a precaution against spillage of diesel fuel.

3   Apply the handbrake then jack up the front right-hand corner of the vehicle until the wheel is just clear of the ground. Support the vehicle on an axle stand and engage 4th or 5th gear. This will enable the engine to be turned easily by turning the right-hand wheel.

4   Disconnect the wire and unscrew the heater plug from cylinder No 4 (timing belt end). Note that the engine is timed with **No 4** piston at TDC compression (ie No 1 piston at TDC with valves 'rocking').

5   Two dial test indicators are now necessary for checking the positions of the No 4 piston and the injection pump. Magnetic type stands will be found helpful or alternatively brackets may be made for fitting to appropriate positions on the engine.

6   Unscrew and remove the blanking plug from the cylinder head next to No 4 injector (photo).

7   Turn the engine forwards until pressure is felt in No 4 cylinder indicating that No 4 piston is commencing its compression stroke.

8   Position the dial test indicator over the blanking hole and fit the probe (photo).

9   Turn the engine forwards until the maximum lift of piston No 4 is registered on the dial test indicator. Turn the engine slightly back and forth to determine the exact point of maximum lift then zero the indicator.

10 Loosen the lower of the two large side plugs on the side of the injection pump. Position a small container beneath the plug then remove the plug and catch the escaping fuel in the container (photo).

11 Inside the plug aperture there is a probe guide. Insert the probe and connect it to the dial test indicator positioned directly over the hole (photo). Refer to Fig. 3.9 and note that the end of the probe must be pointed in order to fully engage the groove in the pump rotor.

5.6 Removing the blanking plug from No 4 cylinder

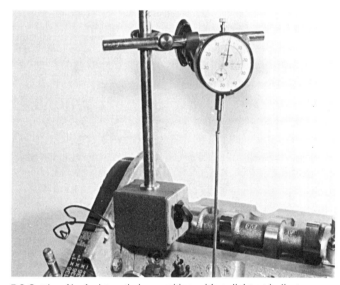
5.8 Setting No 4 piston timing position with a dial test indicator

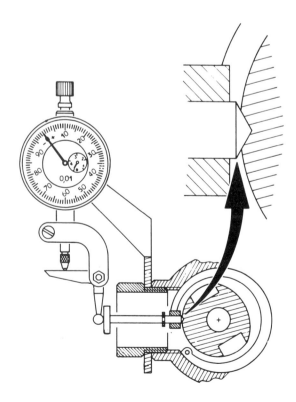
Fig. 3.9 Checking the timing on the Lucas CAV/Roto-Diesel fuel injection pump (Sec 5)

5.10 Lucas CAV/Roto-Diesel injection pump with the timing plug removed

5.11 Timing the Lucas CAV/Roto-Diesel injection pump with a dial test indicator

12 Turn the engine backwards approximately ⅛th of a turn or until the No 4 piston has moved 4.0 mm (0.158 in) down the cylinder. Now turn the engine slowly forwards while watching the dial test indicator on the injection pump. After the probe has reached the bottom of the timing groove then risen by 0.01 to 0.02 mm (0.0004 to 0.0008 in), check that the upper dial test indicator reads 2.26 ± 0.05 mm (0.089 ± 0.002 in) before TDC. If the timing is incorrect proceed as follows.

13 Check the zero setting of the upper dial test indicator by repeating the procedure given in paragraph 9.

14 Turn the engine backwards approximately ⅛th of a turn or until the No 4 piston has moved 4.0 mm (0.158 in) down the cylinder. Now turn the engine slowly forwards until No 4 piston is 2.26 ± 0.05 mm (0.089 ± 0.002 in) before TDC.

15 Unscrew the union nuts and disconnect the injector pipes from the injection pump. Loosen the injection pump mounting nuts and bolt.

16 Turn the pump body until the probe is at the bottom of the timing groove in the rotor. Zero the dial test indicator. Now turn the pump clockwise (from the injector pipe end) until the probe has risen by 0.01 to 0.02 mm (0.0004 to 0.0008 in).

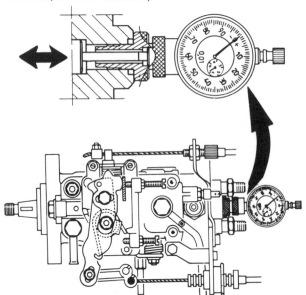

Fig. 3.10 Checking the timing on the Bosch fuel injection pump (Sec 6)

17 Tighten the mounting nuts and bolts making sure that there is no movement on the dial test indicator.

18 Recheck the timing as described in paragraph 12.

19 Remove the dial test indicators and refit the plugs. Reconnect the injector pipes and tighten the union nuts.

20 Refit the heater plug and connect the wire.

21 Lower the car to the ground and reconnect the battery negative lead. Remove the plastic bag from the alternator.

6 Fuel injection pump (Bosch) – checking and adjusting the static timing

Caution: *Some of the injection pump settings and access plugs may be sealed by the manufacturers at the factory using locking wire and lead seals. Do not disturb the wire if the vehicle is still within the warranty period otherwise the warranty will be invalidated. Also do not attempt the timing procedure unless accurate instrumentation is available.*

1 Disconnect the battery negative lead.

2 Cover the alternator with a plastic bag as a precaution against spillage of diesel fuel.

3 Apply the handbrake then jack up the front right-hand corner of the vehicle until the wheel is just clear of the ground. Support the vehicle on an axle stand and engage 4th or 5th gear. This will enable the engine to be turned easily by turning the right-hand wheel.

4 Disconnect the wire and unscrew the heater plug from cylinder No 4 (timing belt end). Note that the engine is timed with **No 4** piston at TDC compression (ie No 1 piston at TDC valves 'rocking').

5 Two dial test indicators are now necessary for checking the positions of the No 4 piston and the injection pump. Magnetic type stands will be found helpful or alternatively brackets may be made for fitting to appropriate positions on the engine.

6 Unscrew and remove the blanking plug from the cylinder head next to No 4 injector.

7 Turn the engine forwards until pressure is felt in No 4 cylinder indicating that No 4 piston is commencing its compression stroke.

8 Position the dial test indicator over the blanking hole and fit the probe.

9 Turn the engine forwards until the maximum lift of piston No 4 is registered on the dial test indicator. Turn the engine slightly to and fro to determine the exact point of maximum lift then zero the indicator.

10 Unscrew the union nuts and disconnect the injector pipes for cylinders 1 and 2 from the injection pump.

11 Unscrew the blanking plug from the end of the injection pump between the injector pipe connections. Be prepared for the loss of some fuel.

12 Insert the probe and connect it to the dial test indicator positioned directly over the hole. The fixture used by Peugeot technicians is shown in Fig. 3.10.

13 Turn the engine backwards approximately ⅛th of a turn or until the No 4 piston has moved 4.0 mm (0.157 in) down the cylinder.

14 Zero the dial test indicator on the injection pump.

15 Turn the engine slowly forwards until the dial test indicator on the injection pump reads 0.30 mm (0.012 in), then check that the upper dial test indicator reads 0.80 ± 0.03 mm (0.032 ± 0.001 in) before

TDC for 1.7 models or 0.50 ± 0.03 mm (0.020 ± 0.001 in) before TDC for 1.9 models. If the timing is incorrect proceed as follows.

16 Check the zero setting of the upper dial test indicator by repeating the procedure given in paragraph 9.

17 Turn the engine backwards approximately 1/8th of a turn or until the No 4 piston had moved 4.0 mm (0.158 in) down the cylinder bore. Now turn the engine slowly forwards until the upper dial test indicator reads 0.80 ± 0.03 mm (0.032 ± 0.001 in) before TDC for 1.7 models, or 0.50 ± 0.03 mm (0.020 ± 0.001 in) before TDC for 1.9 models.

18 Unscrew the union nuts and disconnect the remaining injector pipes from the injection pump. Loosen the injection pump mounting nuts and bolt.

19 Turn the pump body anti-clockwise (from the injector pipe end) and check that the dial test indicator is zeroed. Now turn the pump body slowly clockwise until the dial test indicator reads 0.30 mm (0.012 in).

20 Tighten the mounting nuts and bolts, making sure that there is no movement on the dial test indicator.

21 Recheck the timing as described in paragraphs 13 to 15.

22 Remove the dial test indicators and refit the plugs. Reconnect the injector pipes and tighten the union nuts.

23 Refit the heater plug and connect the wire.

24 Lower the vehicle to the ground and reconnect the battery negative lead. Remove the plastic bag from the alternator.

7 Fast idle control – removal, refitting and adjustment

1 Remove the air cleaner and ducting where necessary.

2 Drain the cooling system as described in Chapter 2.

3 Loosen the clamp screw or nut and remove the end fitting from the inner cable (photos).

4 Unscrew the locknut and remove the adjustment ferrule and outer cable from the bracket on the injection pump (photo).

5 Unscrew the thermostatic sensor from the thermostat housing cover and recover the washer.

6 Fit the new thermostatic sensor and washer and tighten it.

7 Insert the cable and ferrule in the bracket and screw on the locknut finger tight.

8 Insert the cable end through the lever and fit the end fitting loosely.

9 With the engine cold, push the fast idle lever or the knurled adjuster (pre January 1984 Bosch injection pumps) fully towards the flywheel end of the engine then tighten the clamp screw or nut with the end fitting touching the lever or adjuster.

10 Adjust the ferrule to ensure that the fast idle lever is touching its stop, or the adjuster is fully pushed in, then tighten the ferrule locknuts.

11 Measure the exposed length of the inner cable.

12 Refill the cooling system as described in Chapter 2, and run the engine to its normal operating temperature.

13 With the engine hot, check that the exposed length of the inner cable has increased by at least 6.0 mm (0.236 in) indicating that the thermostatic sensor is functioning correctly.

7.3A Fast idle cable end fitting (arrowed) on early Bosch pump

7.3B Fast idle cable end fitting (arrowed) on later Bosch pump

7.4 Fast idle cable adjustment ferrule (arrowed) on the Lucas CAV/Roto-Diesel pump

14 On pre January 1984 Bosch injection pumps check that there is a gap of 1.0 mm (0.04 in) between the cable end fitting and the end of the adjuster. If not, adjust the ferrule.

15 Check that the engine speed increases when the fast idle lever or adjuster is pushed towards the flywheel end of the engine. On the early Bosch pump the speed should increase by 200 ± 50 rpm, and on other models the fast idling speed should be 950 + 50 rpm. Turn the knurled adjuster or lever stop as necessary.

16 Switch off the engine.

8 Accelerator cable – removal, refitting and adjustment

1 Open the accelerator lever on the injection pump and disconnect the inner cable by passing it through the special slot (photos).

2 Disconnect the cable adjustment ferrule and outer cable from the bracket (photo).

3 Working inside the vehicle, remove the lower facia panel where necessary then release the inner cable end fitting from the top of the accelerator pedal.

4 Pull the spring shock absorber from the bulkhead and withdraw the accelerator cable from inside the engine compartment.

5 Refitting is a reversal of removal, but adjust the cable as follows. Have an assistant fully depress the accelerator pedal then check that the accelerator lever on the injection pump is touching the maximum speed adjustment screw. If not, pull the spring clip from the adjustment ferrule (photo), reposition the ferrule and fit the spring clip in the groove next to the metal washer. With the accelerator pedal fully released check that the accelerator lever is touching the anti-stall (or deceleration) adjustment screw. On the early Bosch pump note that the engine must be hot, otherwise the lever will be touching the fast idle knurled adjuster.

9 Idle speed – checking and adjustment

1 The usual type of tachometer (rev counter), which works from ignition system pulses, cannot be used on diesel engines. A diagnostic socket is provided for use of Peugeot test equipment, but this will not normally be available to the home mechanic. If it is not felt that adjusting the idle speed 'by ear' is satisfactory, one of the following

8.1A Accelerator cable on the Lucas CAV/Roto-Diesel pump

8.1B Accelerator cable attachment on the later Bosch pump

8.2 Accelerator cable adjustment ferrule on the later Bosch pump

8.5 Spring clip for adjusting accelerator cable (arrowed)

alternatives may be used:

    (a) *Purchase or hire of an appropriate tachometer*

    (b) *Delegation of the job to a Peugeot/Talbot dealer or other specialist*

    (c) *Timing light (strobe) operated by a petrol engine running at the desired speed. If the timing light is pointed at a mark on the camshaft pump pulley (photo) the mark will appear stationary when the two engines are running at the same speed (or multiples of that speed). The pulley will be rotating at half the crankshaft speed but this will not affect the adjustment (in practice it was found impossible to use this method on the crankshaft pulley due to the acute viewing angle)*

2 Before making adjustments warm up the engine to normal operating temperature.

3 Check that the engine idles at the specified speed.

4 If adjustment is necessary on the Lucas CAV/Roto-Diesel pump, loosen the locknut on the fast idle lever then turn the adjustment screw as required and retighten the locknut (photo).

5 If adjustment is necessary on the pre January 1984 Bosch pump, loosen the locknut and turn the stop screw as required (photo). Retighten the locknut on completion.

6 On the later Bosch pump first loosen the locknut and unscrew the anti-stall adjustment screw until it is clear of the accelerator lever. Loosen the locknut and turn the idle speed adjustment screw as required then retighten the locknut (see Fig. 3.3).

7 Adjust the anti-stall adjustment screw as described in Section 10 or 11 (not applicable to early Bosch pumps).

8 Stop the engine and disconnect the instrument as appropriate.

---

10 Fuel injection pump (Lucas CAV/Roto-Diesel) – anti-stall adjustment

---

Note: *This adjustment requires the use of a tachometer – refer to Section 9 for alternative methods.*

1 Run the engine to normal operating temperature then switch it off.

2 Insert a 3.0 mm (0.118 in) shim or feeler blade between the accelerator lever and the anti-stall adjustment screw.

3 Turn the stop lever clockwise until it is clear of the hole in the fast idle lever then insert a 3.0 mm (0.118 in) dowel rod or twist drill.

4 Start the engine and allow it to idle. The engine speed should be 900 ± 50 rpm.

5 If adjustment is necessary loosen the locknut, turn the anti-stall adjustment screw as required, then tighten the locknut (photo).

6 Remove the feeler blade and twist drill and adjust the idling speed as described in Section 9.

7 Turn the accelerator lever to increase the engine speed to 3000 rpm then quickly release the lever. If the deceleration is too fast and the engine stalls turn the anti-stall adjustment screw 1/4 turn anti-clockwise (viewed from flywheel end of engine). If the deceleration is too slow, resulting in poor engine braking, turn the screw 1/4 turn clockwise.

8 Retighten the locknut after making an adjustment then recheck the idling speed as described in Section 9.

9 With the engine idling check the operation of the manual stop control by turning the stop lever clockwise. The engine must stop instantly.

10 Switch off the ignition switch.

9.1 Mark on the camshaft pump pulley for checking the idle speed with a timing light operated by a petrol engine

9.4 Idle speed adjustment screw (arrowed) on the Lucas CAV/Roto-Diesel pump

9.5 Idle speed adjustment screw (arrowed) on the pre January 1984 Bosch pump

10.5 Anti-stall adjustment on the Lucas CAV/Roto-Diesel injection pump showing feeler blades (1) and twist drill (2)

12.3 Maximum engine speed adjustment screw on the Lucas CAV/Roto-Diesel pump

11 Fuel injection pump (Bosch – January 1984 on) – anti-stall adjustment

Note: *This adjustment requires the use of a tachometer – refer to Section 9 for alternative methods.*

1   Run the engine to normal operating temperature. Note the exact idling speed then switch off the engine.

2   Insert a 1.0 mm (0.039 in) shim or feeler blade between the accelerator lever and the anti-stall adjustment screw (see Fig. 3.3).

3   Start the engine and allow it to idle. The engine speed should exceed the normal idling speed by 50 rpm.

4   If adjustment is necessary loosen the locknut and turn the anti-stall adjustment screw as required. Retighten the locknut.

5   Remove the feeler blade and allow the engine to idle.

6   Move the fast idle lever fully towards the flywheel end of the engine and check that the engine speed increases to 950 ± 50 rpm. If necessary loosen the locknut and turn the stop adjusting screw as required, then retighten the locknut.

7   With the engine idling, check the operation of the manual stop control by turning the stop lever. The engine must stop instantly.

8   Switch off the ignition switch.

12 Maximum engine speed – checking and adjustment

Caution: *On Lucas CAV/Roto-Diesel injection pumps the maximum speed setting is sealed by the manufacturers at the factory using locking wire and a lead seal. Do not disturb the wire if the vehicle is still within the warranty period otherwise the warranty will be invalidated. This adjustment requires the use of a tachometer – refer to Section 9 for alternative methods.*

1   Run the engine to normal operating temperature.

2   Have an assistant fully depress the accelerator pedal and check that the maximum engine speed is as given in the Specifications. Do not keep the engine at maximum speed for more than two or three seconds.

3   If adjustment is necessary stop the engine then loosen the locknut, turn the maximum engine speed adjustment screw as necessary, and retighten the locknut (photo).

4   Repeat the procedure in paragraph 2 to check the adjustment.

5   Switch off the ignition switch.

13 Fuel injectors – removal, testing and refitting

1   Remove the air cleaner and ducting with reference to Section 3.

2   Clean around the injectors and injector pipe union nuts.

3   Pull the leak off pipes from the injectors (photo).

4   Loosen the injector pipe union nuts at the injection pump.

5   Unscrew the union nuts and disconnect the pipes from the injectors (photo). If required the injector pipes may be completely removed.

13.3 Disconnecting the leak off pipes from the injectors

6   Unscrew the injectors (27 mm across flats) and remove them from the cylinder head (photos).

7   Recover the copper washers, fire-seal washers, and sleeves from the cylinder head (photos).

8   Obtain new copper washers and fire-seal washers.

9   Take care not to drop the injectors or allow the needles at their tips to become damaged. The injectors are precision-made to fine limits and must not be handled roughly, in particular do not mount them in a bench vice.

10 Accurate testing and calibration of the injectors must be left to a specialist.

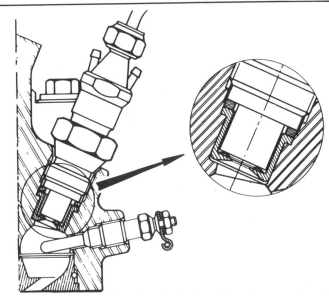

Fig. 3.11 Cross-section of cylinder head showing location of injector and heater plug (Sec 13)

Note fire seal washer position in inset

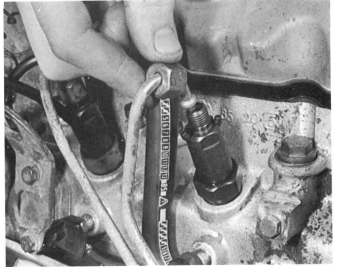

13.5 Disconnecting the injector pipes

13.6A Removing an injector

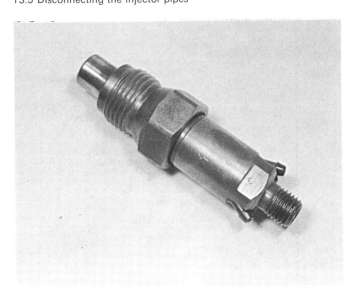

13.6B An injector

13.7A Removing an injector upper washer ...

13.7B ... fire-seal washer ...

13.7C ... and sleeve

13.12 Tightening an injector

13.14 A leak-off pipe connected between two injectors

11 Commence refitting by inserting the sleeves followed by the fire-seal washers (convex face uppermost), and copper washers.

12 Insert the injectors and tighten them to the specified torque (photo).

13 Refit the injector pipes and tighten the union nuts to the specified torque.

14 Reconnect the leak off pipes (photo).

15 Refit the air cleaner and ducting.

14 Preheater system – description and testing

1 Each swirl chamber has a preheater plug (commonly called a glow plug) screwed into it. The plugs are electrically operated before, during and immediately after starting a cold engine. Preheating is not required on a hot engine.

2 If the system malfunctions, testing is ultimately by substitution of

14.3 Heater plug terminal and main supply cable – arrowed (205 models)

known good units, but some preliminary checks may be made as follows.

3 Disconnect the main supply cable from the relevant heater plug terminal (photo).

4 Connect a voltmeter between the supply cable and earth making sure that the cable is kept clear of the engine and bodywork. Have an assistant switch on the preheater and check that there is a 12 volt supply for several seconds before the system cuts out. Typically there should be a 7 second supply at an ambient temperature of 20°C (68°F), but this will increase with colder temperatures and decrease with higher temperatures. If there is no supply, the relay or associated wiring is at fault. Switch off the ignition.

5 Connect an ammeter between the supply cable and the heater plug inter-connecting wire. Have the assistant switch on the preheater and check that the current draw after 20 seconds is 12 amps per working plug, ie 48 amps if all four plugs are working.

6 If one or more heater plugs appear not to be drawing the expected current, disconnect the inter-connecting wire and check them individually or use an ohmmeter to check them for continuity and equal resistance.

15.3 Plastic clips on heater plug terminals (arrowed)

15 Heater plugs and relay – removal and refitting

Heater plugs
1 Check that the ignition switch is off.

2 Remove the air cleaner and ducting with reference to Section 3.

3 Prise the plastic clips from the heater plugs (photo).

4 Unscrew the nuts from the heater plug terminals. Remove the main supply cable from the relevant heater plug then remove the inter-connecting wire from all the plugs (photo).

5 Unscrew the heater plugs and remove them from the cylinder head (photos).

6 Refitting is a reversal of removal but tighten the heater plugs to the specified torque (photo).

Relay
7 The relay is located on the left-hand side of the engine compartment near the battery (photo). First disconnect the battery negative lead.

15.4 Heater plug terminal and inter-connecting wire

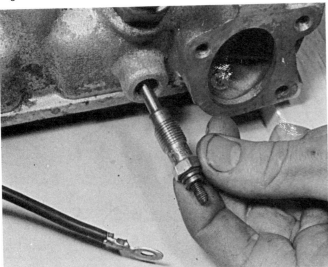

15.5A Removing a heater plug

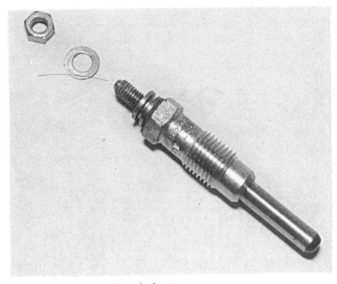

15.5B Heater plug and terminal nut

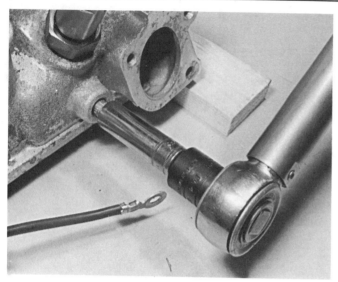

15.6 Tightening a heater plug

15.7 Heater plug control relay on 205 models

8   Unbolt the relay from the side panel and disconnect the wiring.

9   Refitting is a reversal of removal.

16 Stop solenoid – description, removal and refitting

1   The stop solenoid is located on the end of the injection pump by the injector pipes (photos). Its purpose is to cut the fuel supply when the ignition is switched off. If an open circuit occurs in the supply wiring it will be impossible to start the engine as the fuel will not reach the injectors.

2   With the ignition switched off unscrew the nut and disconnect the wire.

3   Unscrew and remove the stop solenoid and recover the washer or O-ring. On the Bosch pump, the fast idle cable support plate may be removed first.

4   Refitting is a reversal of removal.

17 Fuel injection system – priming

1   After disconnecting part of the fuel injection system or running out

of fuel it is necessary to carry out the priming procedure prior to starting the engine.

2   Loosen the bleed screw on the fuel filter head two or three turns. On the Lucas CAV/Roto-Diesel filter a plastic drain tube may be fitted to the bleed screw and a small container positioned to catch the fuel.

3   Actuate the plunger until fuel free from air bubbles flows from the bleed screw. On some Lucas CAV/Roto-Diesel filter heads the plunger must first be unscrewed (photo), and with this type the plunger may become detached from the internal piston. If this happens, unscrew the housing and press the piston back onto the plunger. Refit the housing and operate the plunger slowly.

4   Tighten the bleed screw.

5   Turn on the ignition so that the stop solenoid is energised then activate the plunger until resistance is felt.

6   Where applicable on Lucas CAV/Roto-Diesel filters retighten the plunger.

7   Turn the ignition switch to position 'M' and wait for the preheater warning light to go out.

8   Fully depress the accelerator pedal and start the engine. Additional cranking may be necessary to finally bleed the fuel system before the engine starts.

16.1A Stop solenoid (arrowed) on the Lucas CAV/Roto-Diesel pump

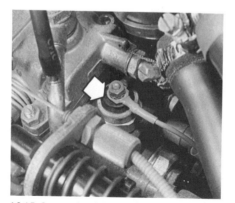

16.1B Stop solenoid (arrowed) on the early Bosch pump

17.3 Lucas CAV/Roto-Diesel fuel filter plunger

18 Manifolds – removal and refitting

Inlet

1 Disconnect the battery negative lead.

2 Remove the air cleaner as described in Section 3. Also disconnect the air duct from the inlet manifold (photos).

3 Remove the brake vacuum pump from the inlet manifold as described in Chapter 5. Also disconnect the pump outlet hose from the manifold (photo).

4 On Horizon models, unbolt the expansion tank from the bulkhead and position it over the engine. There is no need to drain the cooling system.

5 Using a hexagon key, unscrew the bolts and remove the inlet manifold from the cylinder head (photos). There are no gaskets.

6 Refitting is a reversal of removal but tighten the bolts evenly.

Exhaust

7 Apply the handbrake then jack up the front of the car and support on axle stands.

8 Unscrew and remove the exhaust manifold-to-downpipe bolts, together with the springs and collars. Tie the downpipe to one side.

9 Unscrew the nuts and withdraw the exhaust manifold from the studs in the cylinder head. Recover the gaskets (photos).

10 Where applicable unbolt the resonator from the manifold and remove the gasket.

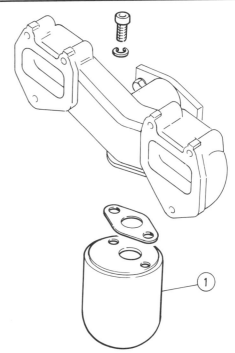

Fig. 3.12 Resonator (1) fitted to the exhaust manifold on some models (Sec 18)

11 Refitting is a reversal of removal, but clean the mating faces and fit new gaskets. Tighten the nuts evenly (photo).

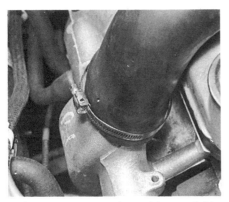

18.2A Air duct connection to inlet manifold (205 models)

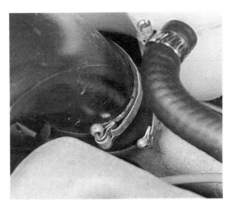

18.2B Air duct connection to inlet manifold (Horizon models)

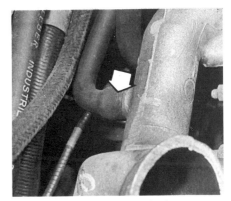

18.3 Brake vacuum pump outlet hose connection to the inlet manifold (arrowed)

18.5A Inlet manifold bolts (arrowed)

18.5B Removing the inlet manifold (engine removed from car)

18.9A Removing the exhaust manifold

18.9B Exhaust manifold gasket

18.11 Tightening the exhaust manifold nuts

19 Exhaust system – inspection, removal and refitting

1 Inspect the exhaust system periodically for leaks, corrosion and damage, and check the security and condition of the mountings. Small leaks are more easily detected if an assistant temporarily blocks the tailpipe with a wad of cloth whilst the engine is idling.

2 Proprietary pastes and bandages are available for the repair of holes and splits. They work well in the short term, but renewal of the section concerned will probably prove more satisfactory in the long run.

3 Check the rubber mountings for deterioration, and renew them if necessary.

4 The removal and refitting procedures are the same as for petrol versions as described in the appropriate Owners Workshop Manual.

20 Fault diagnosis – fuel injection system

Symptom	Reason(s)
Engine turns normally but will not start	Fuel tank empty
	Incorrect starting procedure
	Fuel filter blocked
	Wax in fuel (in very cold conditions)
	Stop solenoid disconnected or defective
	Preheater system faulty
	Fast idle cable broken or thermostatic sensor faulty
	Injection pump timing incorrect
	Injection pump defective
	Poor compression (see Chapter 1)
Erratic idling	Idle speed adjustment incorrect
	Injector(s) defective
Lack of power	Fuel filter blocked
	Air cleaner blocked
	Air or water in fuel
	Injection pump timing incorrect
	Injector(s) defective
Excessive fuel consumption	Fuel leakage
	Air cleaner blocked
	Injector(s) defective
	Injection pump timing incorrect
Excessive knocking	Injector(s) defective (sticking)
	Injection pump timing incorrect
	Excessive carbon deposit

Chapter 4 Clutch, transmission and driveshafts

Contents

Specifications

Clutch

Type .... Single dry plate with diaphragm spring. Cable-operated on non-Horizon models, hydraulically operated on Horizon models

Friction plate diameter .... 200 mm (7.87 in)
Lining thickness .... 7.7 ± 0.3 mm (0.303 ± 0.012 in)
Release bearing type .... Sealed ball
Pedal free play .... Nil
Pedal travel:
    205 and 309 .... 140.0 mm (5.5 in)
    305 .... 135.0 mm (5.3 in)
    Horizon .... Not adjustable

Manual transmission

Type .... Four or five forward speeds and one reverse, synchromesh on all forward gears

Code .... BE 1/4 (four-speed) or BE 1/5 (five-speed)
Oil capacity (all models) .... 2.0 litres (3.5 pints)
Lubricant type/specification:
    Models up to 1988 .... Multigrade oil, viscosity 15W/40 to API SF/CC (Duckhams Hypergrade)
    Models from 1988 .... Gear oil, viscosity SAE 75W/80W to API GL5 (Duckhams Hypoid PT 75W/80W)

Driveshafts

Type .... Solid shaft with inner 'tri-axe' joints and outer six-ball constant velocity joints

Grease capacity:
    Inner (tri-axe) joint .... 150 grams
    Outer (CV) joint .... 100 grams

Torque wrench settings

	Nm	lbf ft
Driveshaft nut:		
205	260	192
305	250	185
309	265	196
Horizon	195	144

1 General description

The clutch components are virtually identical to those used in petrol models, access being by removal of the gearbox.

Procedures for the BE1 type gearbox are to be found in the appropriate petrol model manual, but for 205 models fitted with a four-speed gearbox, the differences compared with the five-speed gearbox are described in Section 4.

The driveshafts are solid with inner 'tri-axe' joints and outer constant velocity joints.

2 Routine maintenance

Carry out the following procedures at the intervals given in *Routine Maintenance* at the beginning of the manual.

Check the clutch adjustment (not Horizon)
1   Refer to the relevant manual for petrol-engined models.

Renew the manual gearbox oil (models up to 1988)
2   Jack up the front of the vehicle and support on axle stands. Apply the handbrake.

3   Two drain plugs are provided on early models one for the gearbox and one for the differential (photo). On later models the gearbox drain plug is deleted and it is important not to confuse the reverse gear shaft clamping screw with a drain plug.

4   Unscrew the drain plug(s) and drain the oil into a suitable container. On completion refit and tighten the drain plug(s).

5   On models up to 1988 there is no provision for a level plug, so the correct quantity of oil must be measured before refilling the gearbox through the filler plug hole (photo).

6   Lower the vehicle to the ground.

Check manual gearbox oil level (models from 1988 on)
7   Check the oil level using the level plug provided.

Check the driveshaft rubber bellows
8   Jack up the front of the vehicle and support on axle stands. Apply the handbrake.

9   Thoroughly check the driveshaft rubber bellows for splits and damage by turning the appropriate front wheel slowly. It necessary renew the bellows.

10 Lower the vehicle to the ground.

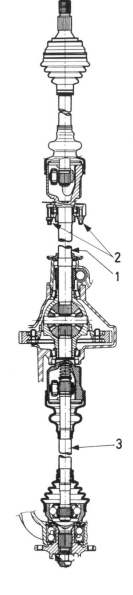

Fig. 4.1 Sectional view of the driveshaft (Sec 1)

1   *Right-hand driveshaft*
2   *Support bearing retaining bolts*
3   *Left-hand driveshaft*

2.2 Differential drain plug (arrowed)

2.4 Gearbox filler plug (arrowed)

3 Manual gearbox – removal and refitting

1   The procedure is basically as given for the relevant petrol engine model fitted with the BE1 gearbox. Where necessary the air cleaner and ducting must first be removed.

2   On all models, remove the starter motor.

3   Where applicable, on Horizon models, remove the power steering pump and position it to one side without disconnecting the hoses.

4   After tightening the mounting bolt on Horizon models, lock it by bending over the lock tab.

4 Manual gearbox (4-speed) – dismantling and reassembly

1   The four-speed and five-speed manual gearboxes differ only in respect of the 5th gear and its associated components.

2   To remove the components the input and output shafts must be locked before unscrewing the end nuts. The best way to do this is to engage a gear then immobilise the input shaft using an old clutch disc to which a metal bar has been welded. It is unwise to attempt to grip the input shaft splines with any other tool as damage may be caused.

3   With the input and output shaft nuts slackened proceed as described for the five-speed gearbox.

4   When reassembling the gearbox use the same method described in paragraph 2 to tighten the shaft nuts. Remember to stake the nuts after tightening them.

5 Driveshaft (Horizon models) – removal and refitting

1   The procedure is similar to that for petrol engine models with the following exceptions:

2   The right-hand driveshaft is supported by an intermediate bearing incorporated in the lower torque link mounting bracket. When removing the driveshaft unscrew the nuts and withdraw the bearing cap and retaining clips. Clean the bearing and seating before refitting the cap and tightening the nuts.

3   When inserting the right-hand driveshaft through the final drive oil seal it is important to protect the oil seal from the driveshaft splines. This is no problem when a new oil seal is being fitted, as a split protector is provided, as described in Section 7. A piece of thin plastic works just as effectively if it is first greased to prevent it being pushed into the final drive housing.

4   If both driveshafts are being removed on models manufactured before July 1984, remove the left-hand driveshaft first then support the left-hand differential side gear using a suitable dowel, preferably wooden. If this precaution is not taken, the side gears may become misaligned when the right-hand driveshaft is removed.

6 Driveshaft rubber bellows – renewal

1   With the driveshaft removed (refer to the relevant manual for petrol-engined models for removal procedure) loosen the clips on the outer rubber bellows. If plastic straps are fitted cut them free with snips (photo).

2   Prise the bellows large diameter from the outer joint housing (photo), then tap the centre hub outwards using a soft metal drift in order to release it from the retaining circlip. Slide the outer joint from the driveshaft splines.

3   Extract the circlip from the groove in the driveshaft (photo).

4   Prise off the rubber bellows. If necessary remove the plastic seating from the recess in the driveshaft (photos).

5   Loosen the clips on the inner rubber bellows. If plastic straps are fitted cut them free.

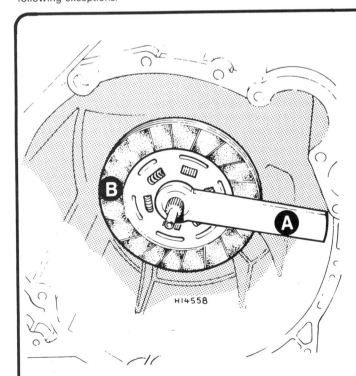

Fig. 4.2 Tool for locking the gearbox input shaft (Sec 4)

Lever (A) welded to old clutch driven plate (B)

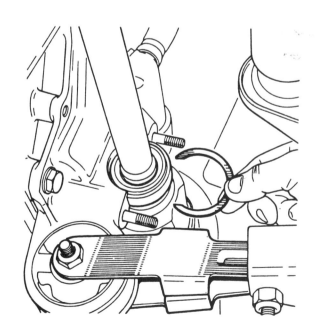

Fig. 4.3 Removing the retaining clips from the right-hand driveshaft intermediate bearing on Horizon models (Sec 5)

6.1 Plastic straps on the outer rubber bellows

6.2 Removing the rubber bellows from the outer joint housing

6.3 Driveshaft outer joint retaining circlip

6.4A Removing the outer rubber bellows from the driveshaft

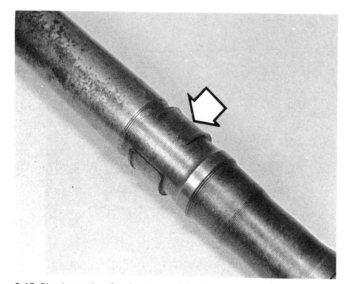

6.4B Plastic seating for the outer rubber bellows

6   Prise the bellows large diameter from the inner joint housing and slide the rubber bellows off the outer end of the driveshaft (photo).

7   Mark the driveshaft and inner joint housing in relation to each other then separate them, keeping the rollers engaged with their respective spigots (photo).

8   Clean away the grease then retain the rollers using adhesive tape (photo).

9   Remove the pressure pad and spring from inside the inner joint housing (photo).

10 Clean away the grease then commence reassembly by inserting the pressure pad and spring into the inner joint housing with the housing mounted upright in a soft-jawed vice.

11 Inject half the required amount of grease into the inner joint housing (photo).

12 Locate the new inner rubber bellows halfway along the driveshaft (photo).

6.6 Removing the inner rubber bellows

6.7 Separating the driveshaft and rollers from the inner joint housing

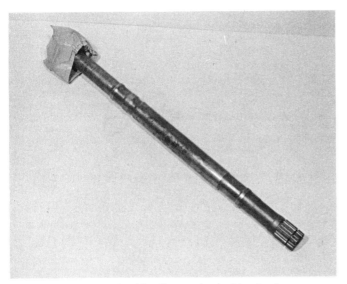

6.8 Left-hand driveshaft with rollers retained with adhesive tape

6.9 Removing the pressure pad and spring from the inner joint housing

6.11 Injecting grease into the inner joint housing

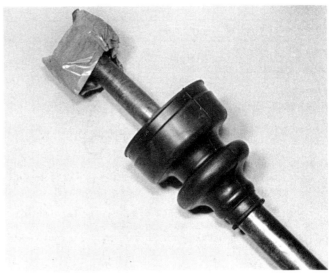

6.12 Inner rubber bellows located on the driveshaft

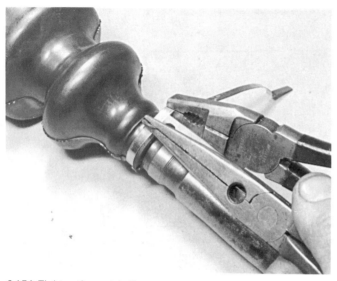

6.15A Tighten the metal clip ...

6.15B ... and bend it back under the buckle

13 Remove the adhesive tape and insert the driveshaft into the housing.

14 Inject the remaining amount of grease in the joint.

15 Keeping the driveshaft pressed against the internal spring, refit the rubber bellows and tighten the clips. Metal type clips can be tightened using two pliers, by holding the buckle and pulling the clip through. Cut off the excess and bend the clip back under the buckle (photos).

16 Fit the plastic seating in the driveshaft recess and refit the new rubber bellows small diameter on it.

17 Refit the circlip in the driveshaft groove.

18 Inject the required amount of grease in the outer joint then insert the driveshaft, engage the splines, and press in until the circlip snaps into the groove.

19 Ease the rubber bellows onto the outer joint, and fit the two clips, tightening them as previously described.

7 Driveshaft oil seals – renewal

1 Jack up the front of the vehicle and support on axle stands. Apply the handbrake.

2 Unscrew the drain plug(s) and drain the gearbox oil into a suitable container. On completion refit and tighten the plug(s).

3 Disconnect the front track control arms from the stub axle carriers (photo).

4 Have an assistant pull the left-hand wheel outwards while the left-hand driveshaft is levered from the differential side gear. Hold the strut/carrier outwards with a block of wood.

5 On models manufactured before July 1984 the left-hand differential side gear must be supported using a suitable dowel, preferably wooden. If this precaution is not taken, the side gears may become misaligned when the right-hand driveshaft is removed.

6 On Horizon models, unscrew the nuts and withdraw the bearing cap and retaining clip retaining the right-hand driveshaft intermediate bearing.

7 On non-Horizon models loosen the two nuts retaining the right-hand driveshaft intermediate bearing in the bracket on the block and turn the bolt heads through 90° in order to release the bearing.

8 Have an assistant pull the right-hand wheel outwards while the right-hand driveshaft is removed from the differential side gear. Hold the strut/carrier outwards with a block of wood.

9 Using a screwdriver lever the oil seals from the gearbox (photo).

10 Clean the oil seal seatings in the gearbox.

11 Press the new left-hand oil seal squarely into the gearbox until flush using a block of wood.

12 The new right-hand oil seal is supplied with a protector to be used when fitting the driveshaft. First remove the protector and press the oil seal squarely into the gearbox until flush using a block of wood. Refit the protector having applied a little grease to the seal lips (photos).

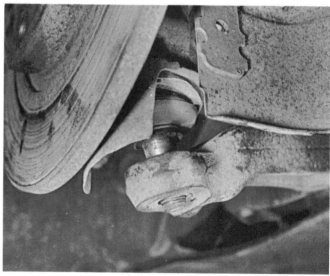

7.3 Disconnecting a front track control arm

13 Insert the right-hand driveshaft while guiding the intermediate bearing in the bracket (photo).

14 Pull out the protector and discard it. The protector is split so that it will pass over the driveshaft.

15 Slide the rubber dust seal next to the oil seal, where applicable (photo).

16 Refit and tighten the intermediate bearing bolts or cap and nuts as applicable.

17 Apply a little grease to the left-hand oil seal lips then insert the left-hand driveshaft (photo).

18 Reconnect the front track control arms to the stub axle carriers.

19 Lower the vehicle to the ground and refill the gearbox with oil as described in Section 2.

7.9 Levering a driveshaft oil seal from the gearbox

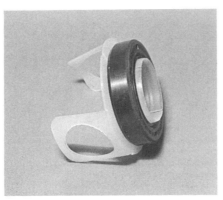

7.12A The right-hand driveshaft oil seal is supplied with a protector

7.12B Right-hand driveshaft oil seal installed ready for driveshaft refitting

7.13 Refitting the right-hand driveshaft

7.15 Right-hand driveshaft rubber dust seal

7.17 Refitting the left-hand driveshaft

Chapter 5 Braking system

Contents

Specifications

Type .... Front disc brakes, rear drum brakes, servo assistance by vacuum pump (exhauster) belt-driven from camshaft

Vacuum pump
Oil capacity .... 40 cc
Lubricant type/specification .... Multigrade oil, viscosity SAE 15W/40 to API SF/CC (Duckhams Hypergrade)

Brake hydraulic fluid
Type/specification .... Hydraulic fluid to SAE J1703 or DOT 3 (Duckhams Universal Brake and Clutch Fluid)

Torque wrench setting

	Nm	lbf ft
Vacuum pump diaphragm nut/screw	9	7

1 General description

The braking system is identical to petrol-engine versions except for the addition of a vacuum pump. Since there is no throttle valve in the diesel engine, there is insufficient vacuum in the inlet manifold to operate the brake servo unit; the vacuum pump provides the necessary vacuum. It is mounted on the inlet manifold, and belt-driven from a pulley on the end of the camshaft. The discharge hose is connected to the inlet manifold.

2 Routine maintenance

Carry out the following procedures at the intervals given in *Routine Maintenance* at the beginning of the manual. These are additional to the routine checks specified in the appropriate manual for petrol-engined models.

Check vacuum pump and hoses for leaks
1   Examine the vacuum hose between the brake servo unit and vacuum pump for cracks, deterioration or damage. Renew if necessary.

2   Check the main body for signs of oil leakage.

Check vacuum pump oil level
3   Turn the engine so that the mark on the vacuum pump pulley shoulder is in line with the mark on the pump (ie uppermost).

4   Unscrew the plug and check that the oil is level with the bottom of the hole (photo). If not, top up with the specified oil.

5   Refit and tighten the plug.

Check vacuum pump drivebelt
6   Check the drivebelt for cracking and deterioration. Also check its tension and if necessary adjust it as described in Section 3.

2.4 Filler/level plug (arrowed) on the vacuum pump

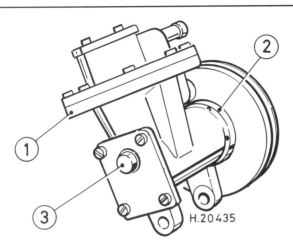

Fig. 5.1 Early vacuum pump (Sec 2)

1 *Type number location*
2 *Alignment marks for checking oil level*
3 *Oil filler/level plug*

3 Vacuum pump – removal and refitting

1 Remove the air cleaner and ducting with reference to Chapter 3.

2 Disconnect the vacuum and discharge hoses (photo).

3 Loosen the pivot and adjustment bolts, swivel the pump towards the engine and slip the drivebelt from the pulleys.

4 Remove the pivot and adjustment bolts, and withdraw the vacuum pump from the inlet manifold.

5 Refitting is a reversal of removal, but before tightening the pivot and adjustment bolts swivel the pump away from the engine until the deflection of the drivebelt midway between the pulleys is approximately 5.0 mm (0.2 in) under firm finger or thumb pressure (photo). Check and if necessary top up the pump oil level as described in Section 2.

4 Vacuum pump – testing and overhaul

1 A vacuum gauge is required to test the vacuum pump. Connect the gauge to the inlet port on the pump using a T-piece and two lengths of hose as shown in Fig. 5.2. The push valve is necessary to accurately time the test period.

2 Start the engine and let it idle, then close the push valve and check that a minimum of 500 mm Hg is recorded after 1 minute. Stop the engine.

3 If the correct result is not obtained, either the drivebelt is slipping or the vacuum pump is faulty.

4 To renew the valves, extract the two screws and lift off the cover and gasket, followed by the springs, valves and seals. Fit the new valves, together with new seals and a new cover gasket. Tighten the two screws.

5 To renew the diaphragm, first mark the cover in relation to the main body. Remove the screws and lift off the cover. Unscrew the nut or screw and remove the diaphragm and support plates from the piston. Prise the O-ring from the recess in the piston where fitted.

6 Turn the pulley so that the piston is at the top of its stroke, then attempt to move the top of the piston from side to side. If excessive wear is evident renew the complete vacuum pump.

3.2 Vacuum (1) and discharge (2) hoses on the vacuum pump

3.5 Checking vacuum pump drivebelt tension

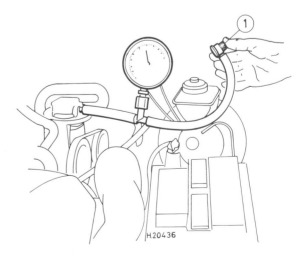

Fig. 5.2 Testing the vacuum pump with a vacuum gauge (Sec 4)

1 *Push valve*

7   Clean the components and commence reassembly by fitting a new piston O-ring (where applicable).

8   Fit the new diaphragm and support plates on the piston, making sure that the curved edges of the plates are next to the diaphragm. Where applicable, the smaller of the two plates should be fitted on top of the diaphragm.

9   Apply locking fluid to the threads of the nut or screw then fit and tighten to the specified torque.

10 Refit the cover and tighten the screws progressively.

11 Check and if necessary top up the oil level with reference to Section 2.

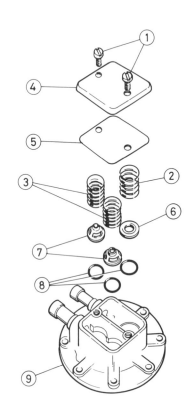

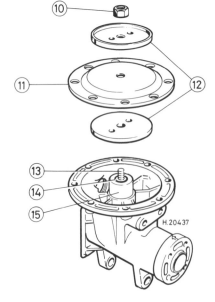

Fig. 5.3 Exploded view of the vacuum pump (Sec 4)

1   Cover screws
2   Inlet valve spring
3   Outlet valve springs
4   Cover
5   Gasket
6   Inlet valve
7   Outlet valves
8   Seals
9   Diaphragm cover
10 Nut
11 Diaphragm
12 Support plates
13 Screw
14 O-ring
15 Piston

H.20437

Chapter 6 Steering, wheels and tyres

Contents

Specifications

Power-assisted steering

Fluid capacity	0.65 litre (1.1 pint)
Fluid type/specification	Dexron type automatic transmission fluid (Duckhams D-Matic)
Drivebelt tension:	
Belt deflection between pulleys	5.0 mm (0.2 in)
Using a torque wrench:	
New belt	57 Nm (42 lbf ft)
Used belt	30 Nm (22 lbf ft)

Front wheel alignment

Toe-in:	
205	2.5 ± 1 mm (0.098 ± 0.04 in)
305	4.0 ± 1 mm (0.158 ± 0.04 in)
309	2.0 ± 1 mm (0.079 ± 0.04 in)
Horizon	0 ± 1 mm (0 ± 0.04 in) per wheel
Camber:	
205	0° 30′ ± 30′
305	0° 25′ ± 30′
309	0° ± 30′
Horizon	0° ± 30′
Castor:	
205	1° 40′ ± 30′
305	1° 45′ ± 30′
309	0° 30′ ± 30′
Horizon	2° ± 30′
Steering axis inclination:	
205	8° 50′ ± 30′
305	9° 20′ ± 30′
309	9° 30′ ± 30′
Horizon	12° ± 45′

Wheels and tyres

Wheel sizes:	
205	450 B13 FH 435 or 500 B13 FH 428
305	500 B14 FH 425
309	500 B13 FH 420
Horizon	4$\frac{1}{2}$J x 13 or 5J x 13
Tyre sizes:	
205 (except GRD)	145 SR 13
205 GRD	165/70 SR 13
305	155 R 14 S
309	165/70 SR 13
Horizon	155 SR 13

Tyre pressures in bar (lbf/in²):	Front	Rear
205 (except Van)	2.0 (29)	2.0 (29)
205 Van	2.0 (29)	2.6 (38)
305	1.9 (28)	2.1 (30)
309	2.0 (29)	2.2 (32)
Horizon	1.9 (28)	1.9 (28)

Torque wrench settings

	Nm	lbf ft
Power steering:		
Pump union	23	17
Steering gear mounting	35	26
Tie-rod to rack	55	41
Track rod end	35	26

1 General description

The procedures are identical to those on petrol engine models except for the addition of power steering on 305, 309 and Horizon models. On the diesel engine the power steering pump is belt-driven by a pulley on the end of the camshaft, since the location of the injection pump precludes its location at the timing end of the engine (as on petrol versions).

2 Routine maintenance

Carry out the following procedures at the intervals given in *Routine Maintenance* at the beginning of the manual. These are additional to the routine checks specified in the appropriate manual for petrol-engined models.

Check power steering fluid level
1 Set the front wheels in the straight-ahead position.

2 With the engine stopped, unscrew the pump reservoir filler cap and wipe clean the dipstick. Refit and remove the cap and check the fluid level on the dipstick. If the fluid is cold (ie after cooling for several hours) the level should be on the lower mark. If the vehicle has been in use, and the fluid is hot, the level should be on the upper mark.

3 If necessary top up the reservoir then refit the cap.

Check power steering pump drivebelt
4 Examine the full length of the drivebelt for cracks and excessive wear or deterioration. Use a mirror to view the concealed sections.

5 Check that the deflection of the drivebelt midway between the pulleys is approximately 5.0 mm (0.2 in) under firm finger or thumb pressure.

6 If adjustment is necessary, loosen the mounting/adjustment bolts, reposition the pump, and retighten the bolts. On early models three slotted holes are provided in the bracket, but on later models the pump pivots on a single bolt.

7 A torque wrench may be used on the later type to adjust the belt tension using the 12.7 mm (^{1}/$_2$ in) square hole provided (Fig. 6.5). With both bolts loose, apply the torque given in the Specifications then tighten the adjustment bolt, followed by the pivot bolt.

3 Power steering system – draining and refilling

1 Disconnect the battery leads.

2 Where necessary remove the air cleaner and ducting.

3 On 305 and Horizon models unscrew the union nut and disconnect the high pressure pipe from the steering gear valve, then drain the fluid into a suitable container.

4 On 309 models, loosen the clips and disconnect both hoses from the fluid cooler, then drain the fluid into a suitable container.

5 To ensure complete draining, turn the steering slowly from lock to lock at least three times.

6 Reconnect the pipe or hoses and tighten the nut or clips.

7 Remove the reservoir cap and refill to approximately 25 mm (1.0 in) below the rim.

8 With the engine stopped, turn the steering slowly from lock to lock several times. Top up with fluid to the lower cold mark on the filler cap dipstick.

Fig. 6.1 Power steering pump filler cap (1) on 305 models (Sec 2)

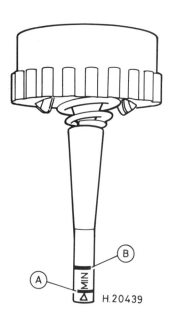

Fig. 6.2 Filler cap level marks (Sec 2)

a *Minimum cold level*   b *Maximum hot level*

9 Run the engine at idling speed and continue to turn the steering slowly from lock to lock several times. Top up the fluid as the level drops.

10 Switch off the engine and top up with fluid to the lower cold level mark. Refit the filler cap.

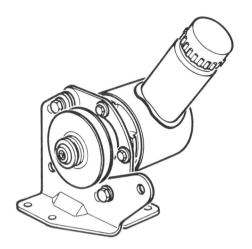

Fig. 6.3 Early type power steering pump (Sec 2)

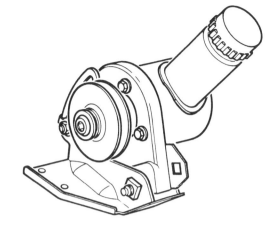

Fig. 6.4 Later type power steering pump (Sec 2)

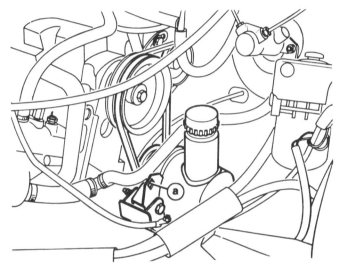

Fig. 6.5 Square hole (a) for adjusting the belt tension on the later type pump (Sec 2)

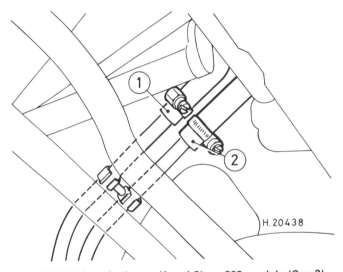

Fig. 6.6 Fluid cooler hoses (1 and 2) on 309 models (Sec 3)

4 Power steering pump – removal and refitting

1   Remove the air cleaner and ducting as described in Chapter 3.

2   Disconnect the leads, unbolt the mounting clamp and remove the battery.

3   Loosen the power steering pump mounting and adjustment bolts, as applicable, move the pump upwards, and slip the drivebelt from the pulleys.

4   Drain the power steering system as described in Section 3.

5   Using two spanners, unscrew the high pressure union nut on the pump while holding the union stationary. Disconnect the high pressure pipe.

6   Loosen the clip and disconnect the low pressure return hose.

7   Unscrew the mounting bolts and remove the pump from the bracket on the gearbox.

8   Refitting is a reversal of removal, but tension the drivebelt as described in Section 2. On 309 models, position the high pressure hose up to 20° rearwards (Fig. 6.7) before tightening the union nut. Fill the system with fresh fluid as described in Section 3.

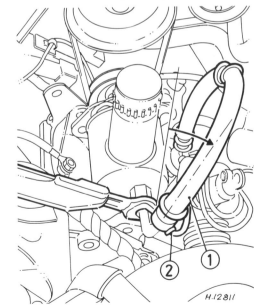

Fig. 6.7 High pressure (1) and low pressure (2) hoses on the 309 power steering pump (Sec 4)

Note angle of high pressure hose

5 Power steering gear (305 models) – removal and refitting

1 Apply the handbrake then jack up the front of the car and support on axle stands. Remove both front wheels.

2 Disconnect the battery negative lead.

3 Remove the air cleaner and ducting as described in Chapter 3.

4 Loosen the power steering pump mounting and adjustment bolts, as applicable, move the pump upwards, and slip the drivebelt from the pulleys.

5 Unscrew the mounting bolts and remove the pump from the bracket on the gearbox. Tie or support the pump in an upright position towards the front of the engine compartment.

6 Drain the power steering system as described in Section 3 by disconnecting the high pressure pipe.

7 Disconnect the low pressure return hose from the steering gear valve.

8 Detach the gearchange assembly from the steering gear by removing the cap and bolt and prising out the clip. Tie the assembly to one side.

9 Mark the steering column in relation to the flexible coupling then unscrew and remove the pinchbolt. Push the column upwards as far as possible.

10 Unscrew the nuts and disconnect the track rod ends from the steering arms.

11 Unscrew and remove the mounting bolts from the subframe.

12 Unclip the fuel supply and return pipes from the underbody.

13 Rotate the steering gear until the control valve points rearward then turn the flexible coupling to full left-hand lock. Move the steering gear to the right and release the left-hand track rod from the subframe. Lower the steering gear from the car.

14 Refitting is a reversal of removal, but tighten the nuts and bolts to the specified torques. Refill the power steering system as described in Section 3. Adjust the drivebelt tension with reference to Section 2. Check and, if necessary, adjust the front wheel alignment as described in the petrol engine manual.

6 Power steering gear (309 models) – removal and refitting

1 Apply the handbrake then jack up the front of the car and support on axle stands. Remove both front wheels.

2 Drain the power steering system as described in Section 3.

3 Unscrew the union nuts and disconnect the high and low pressure pipes from the steering gear valve.

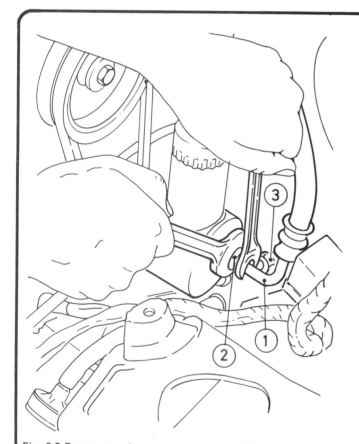

Fig. 6.8 Power steering pump unions on 309 models (Sec 6)

1 High pressure pipe   3 Low pressure pipe union
2 High pressure pipe union

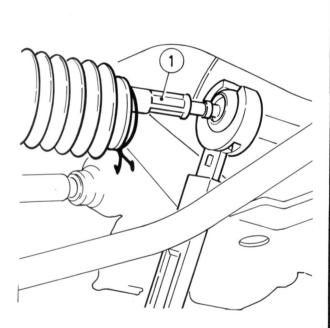

Fig. 6.9 Removing the left-hand tie-rod (1) from the power steering gear on 309 models (Sec 6)

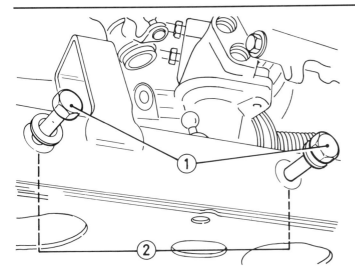

Fig. 6.10 Power steering gear mounting bolts (1) and spacer tubes (2) on 309 models (Sec 6)

4   Mark the steering column universal joint in relation to the pinion then unscrew and remove the pinchbolt.

5   Unscrew the nuts and disconnect the track rod ends from the steering arms.

6   Release the strap and pull the left-hand rubber bellows from the steering gear housing.

7   Unscrew the left-hand track rod from the rack.

8   Disconnect the gearchange control rods from the relay levers, prise out the clip, and tie the assembly to one side.

9   Unscrew and remove the mounting bolts from the subframe noting the location of the spacer tubes.

10 Release the steering gear from the column universal joint and rest it on the subframe.

11 Turn the rack fully to the left.

12 Move the steering gear to the right then lift the left end over the gearbox and withdraw.

13 Refitting is a reversal of removal, but tighten the nuts and bolts to the specified torques. Refill the power steering system as described in Section 3. Check and, if necessary, adjust the front wheel alignment as described in the petrol engine manual. Make sure that the low pressure hose is positioned clear of the gearchange rods.

Chapter 7 Electrical system

Contents

Specifications

System type .... 12 volt, negative earth, battery, alternator, and pre-engaged starter motor

Battery
Type .... 60 Ah

Alternator
Type .... 3-phase, 750 watt
Regulated voltage .... 13.8 to 14.8 V

Starter motor
Type .... Pre-engaged
Minimum brush length .... 12.7 mm (0.5 in)

Torque wrench settings

	Nm	lbf ft
Alternator pivot bolt	39	29
Alternator adjustment bolt	20	15
Starter motor	34	25

1 General description

The electrical system is of 12 volt negative earth type. The main components are a 12 volt battery, an alternator with integral voltage regulator, and a pre-engaged starter motor (with reduction gears on some models). The starter motor incorporates a one-way clutch on its pinion shaft in order to prevent the engine driving the motor when it starts.

It is important to disconnect the battery leads before charging the battery, removing the alternator, or working on wiring circuits which are permanently live. Additionally the alternator wiring must be disconnected before using electric arc welding equipment.

2 Routine maintenance

The procedures are as described for petrol models, but refer to Section 3 of this Chapter when adjusting the alternator drivebelt tension.

3 Alternator – removal and refitting

1 Disconnect the battery negative lead.

2 Disconnect the two wires from the rear of the alternator (photo).

3 Loosen the pivot and adjustment bolts then swivel the alternator towards the engine and slip the drivebelt from the pulleys. On later models a tension adjustment bolt is provided, and this must be slackened so that the alternator will swivel inwards (photos).

4 Remove the adjustment bolt(s) and withdraw the alternator from the engine. Note that it is not necessary to remove the pivot bolt, as the alternator housing is slotted.

5 Refitting is a reversal of removal, but tension the drivebelt so that it deflects by approximately 6.0 mm (0.236 in) midway between the pulleys under firm finger or thumb pressure (photo).

3.2 Alternator wires (arrowed)

3.3A Alternator pivot bolt

3.3B Alternator adjustment locknut (1) and adjustment bolt (2)

3.5 Checking tension of alternator drivebelt

4.3A Starter motor solenoid wiring (Bosch)

4 Starter motor – removal and refitting

1   Disconnect the battery negative lead.

2   Remove the air cleaner and ducting (Chapter 3).

3   Unscrew the nut and disconnect the large cable from the solenoid. Also disconnect the small trigger wire (photos).

4   Using a hexagon key, unscrew the three mounting bolts.

5   Withdraw the starter motor from the gearbox (photo).

6   Refitting is a reversal of removal, but tighten the bolts evenly to the specified torque.

5 Starter motor (Mitsubishi/Melco) – dismantling and reassembly

1   Clean the starter motor exterior surfaces.

2   Mark the yoke, drive end bracket and commutator end cover in relation to each other.

3   Unscrew and remove the through-bolts (photo). Unscrew the small screws and lift off the commutator end cover.

4   Remove the spacer from the end bearing (photo).

5   Using a hooked instrument, lift the springs in turn and extract the field brushes from the brush holder (photos).

4.3B Starter motor solenoid wiring (Mitsubishi/Melco)

4.5 Removing the starter motor (Mitsubishi/Melco)

5.3 Removing the through-bolts

5.4 End bearing spacer removal

5.5A Brush holder prior to removal

5.5B Field brush (1) and armature brush (2)

5.6 Brush holder removed from starter motor

5.8 Removing the yoke

5.9 Armature and bearing removal

6 Similarly lift the springs and extract the armature brushes. Remove the brush holder (photo).

7 Unscrew the nut and disconnect the main cable from the solenoid terminal.

8 Withdraw the yoke over the armature (photo).

9 Lift the armature and bearing from the intermediate bracket (photo).

10 Turn the drive end bracket over. Using a suitable metal tube, tap the stop ring clear of the spring clip. Extract the spring clip followed by the stop ring, pinion and spring (photos).

11 Remove the two screws and lift off the pinion shaft end cover (photo).

12 Prise out the C-clip and remove the thrust washer (photos).

13 Unscrew the cross-head screws securing the solenoid to the drive end bracket (photo).

14 Unhook the solenoid from the fork and remove the gasket (photo).

15 Unscrew the bolt and lift the intermediate bracket from the drive end bracket (photos).

5.10A Extract the spring clip ...

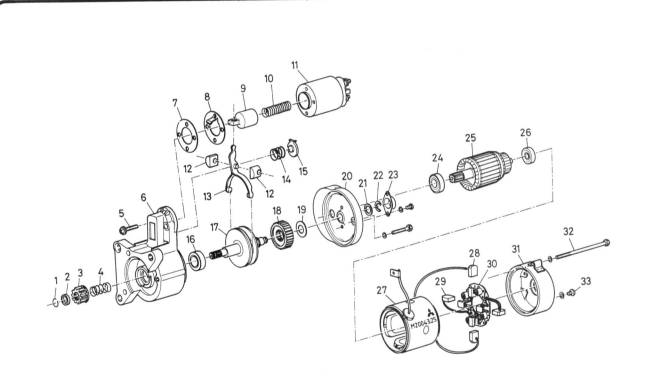

Fig. 7.1 Exploded diagram of the Mitsubishi/Melco starter motor (Sec 5)

1 Spring clip	10 Spring	18 Reduction gear	26 Ball-bearing
2 Stop ring	11 Solenoid	19 Thrust washer	27 Yoke
3 Pinion	12 Bush halves	20 Intermediate bracket	28 Field brush
4 Spring	13 Fork	21 Thrust washer	29 Armature brush
5 Solenoid securing screw	14 Spring	22 C-clip	30 Brush holder
6 Drive end bracket	15 Rubber plug	23 End cover	31 Commutator end cover
7 Gasket	16 Ball-bearing	24 Ball-bearing	32 Through-bolt
8 Shim	17 One-way clutch	25 Armature	33 Cover screw
9 Plunger			

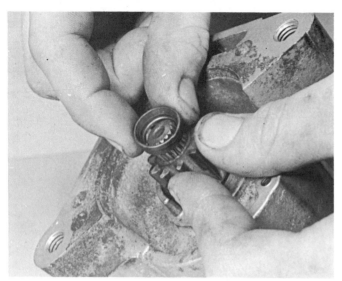

5.10B ... followed by the stop ring ...

5.10C ... pinion ...

5.10D ... and spring

5.11 Removing the pinion shaft end cover

5.12A Prise out the C-clip ...

5.12B ... and remove the thrust washer

5.13 Solenoid mounting screws

5.14 Solenoid gasket removal

5.15A Unscrew the bolt ...

5.15B ... and remove the intermediate bracket

5.16 Removing the rubber plug and spring

5.17A Remove the thrust washer ...

16 Prise out the rubber plug and spring from the fork pivot (photo).

17 Remove the thrust washer from the pinion shaft, followed by the reduction gear (photos).

18 Lift out the pinion shaft and fork then release the fork from the engagement groove (photos).

19 Remove the pivot bush halves from the fork (photo).

20 Clean all the components and examine them for wear and damage. Spin the ball-bearings on the armature shaft and in the drive end bracket and renew them if they feel rough or have excessive play. A puller will be required to remove the shaft bearings, and a suitable metal tube to drive out the bearing from the drive end bracket (photo).

21 Commence reassembly by fitting the new bearings. Use a metal tube on the inner track when fitting the bearings to the armature shaft, and a metal tube on the outer track when fitting the bearing to the drive end bracket.

22 Lightly grease the pivot bush halves and fit them to the fork.

23 Grease the fork ends and engage the fork with the groove in the pinion shaft. Locate the assembly in the drive end bracket.

24 Fit the reduction gear and thrust washer.

25 Locate the spring and rubber plug over the fork in the drive end bracket.

26 Grease the shaft then refit the intermediate bracket and secure with the bolt.

27 Locate the gasket, hook the solenoid onto the fork, and secure with the cross-head screws (photos).

28 Push the pinion shaft into the drive end bracket and fit the thrust washer and C-clip (photo).

29 Refit the end cover then insert and tighten the screws.

30 Locate the spring, pinion, and stop ring on the pinion shaft. Insert the spring clip in the groove and draw the stop ring back over it.

5.17B ... and reduction gear

5.18A Pinion shaft and fork in the drive end bracket

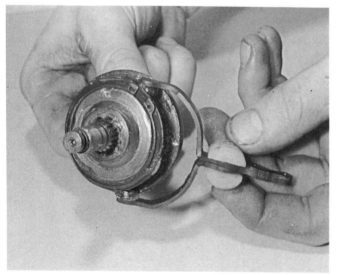

5.18B Separating the fork from the engagement groove

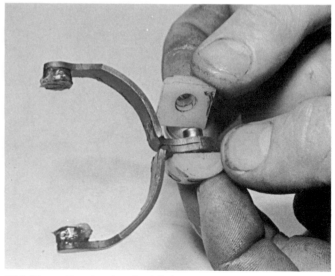

5.19 Dismantling the pivot bush halves

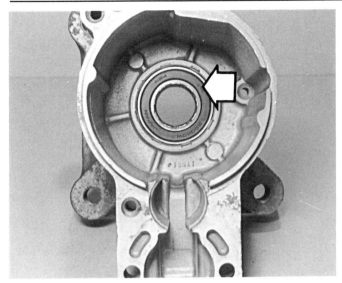

5.20 Drive end bracket bearing

5.27A Fork arm in drive end bracket

5.27B Refitting the solenoid and gasket

5.28 Inserting the C-clip into the pinion shaft groove

31 Grease the gear teeth and refit the armature and bearing into the intermediate bracket.

32 Refit the yoke with the previously made marks aligned.

33 Reconnect the main cable to the solenoid terminal and tighten the nut.

34 Refit the brush holder. Lift the springs and insert the brushes then release the springs.

35 Locate the spacer on the end bearing.

36 Refit the commutator end cover with the previously made marks aligned. Insert and tighten the through-bolts and small screws.

Wiring diagrams overleaf

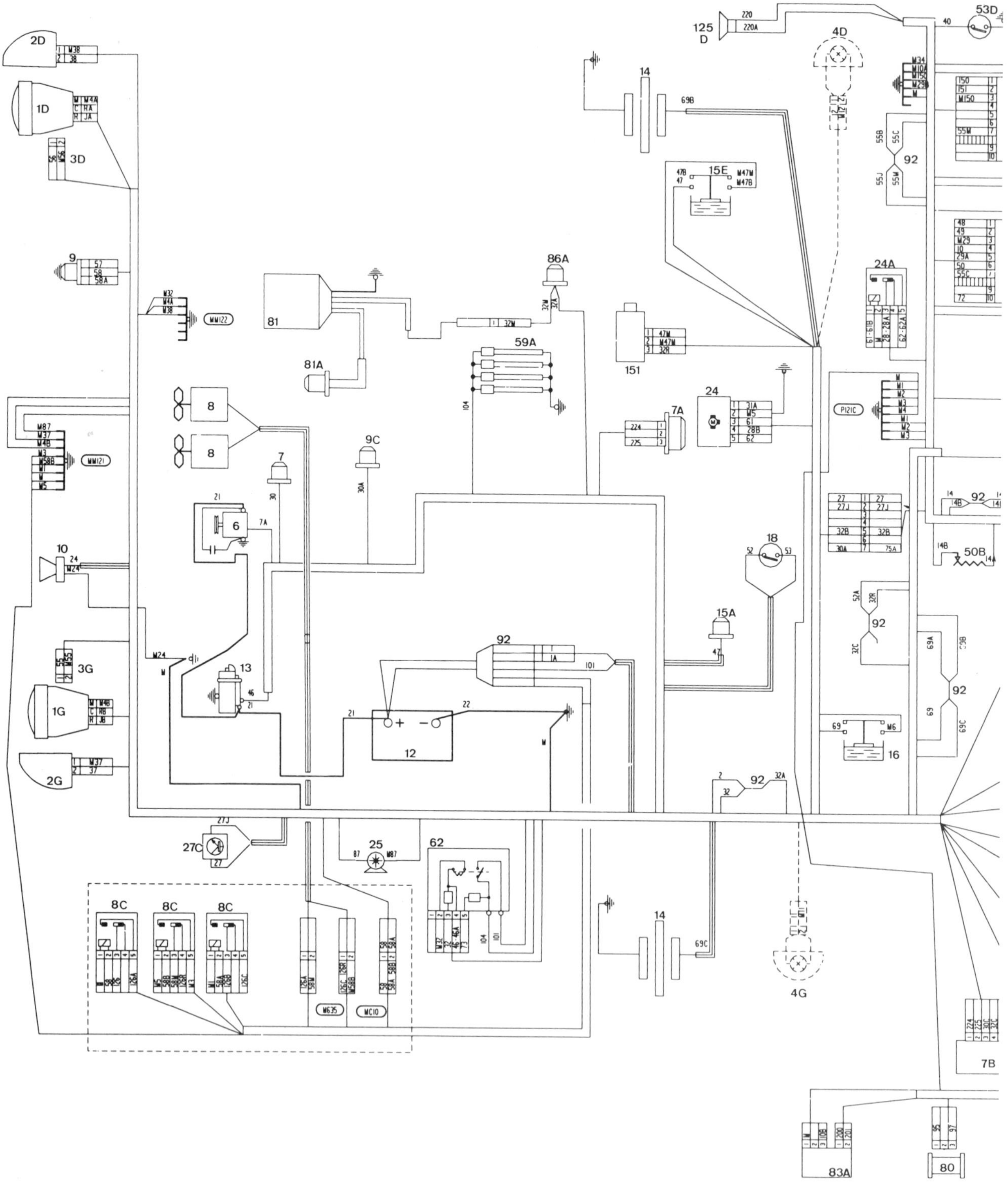

Fig. 7.2 Wiring diagram for Peugeot 205 models up to 1985

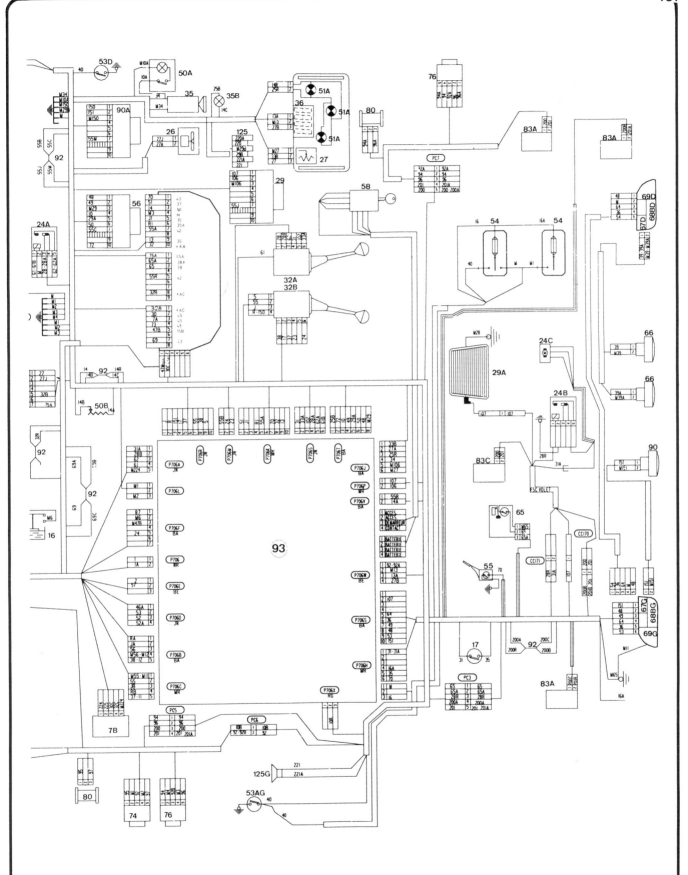

Fig. 7.2 Wiring diagram for Peugeot 205 models up to 1985 (continued)

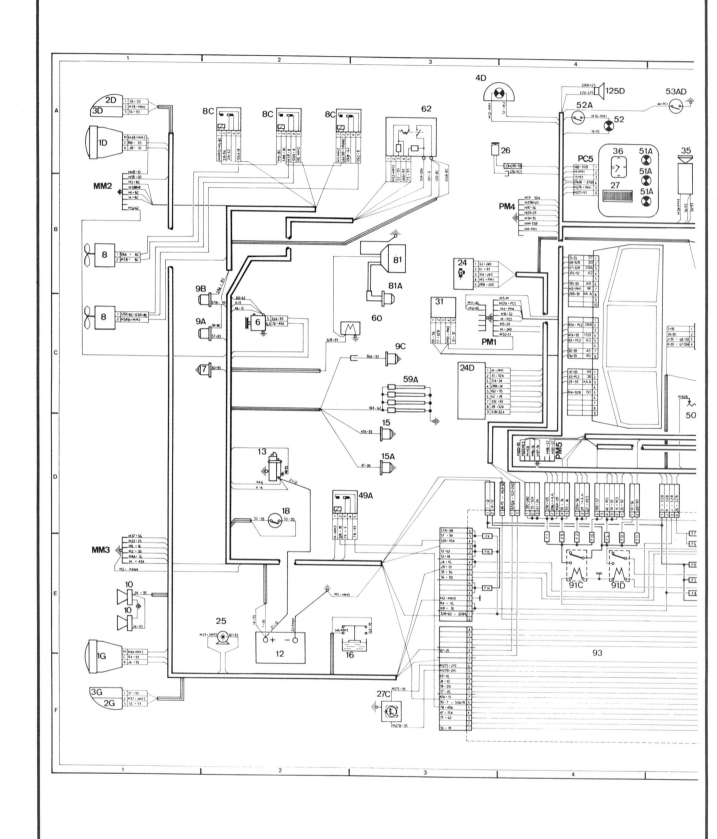

Fig. 7.3 Wiring diagram for Peugeot 305 models up to 1985

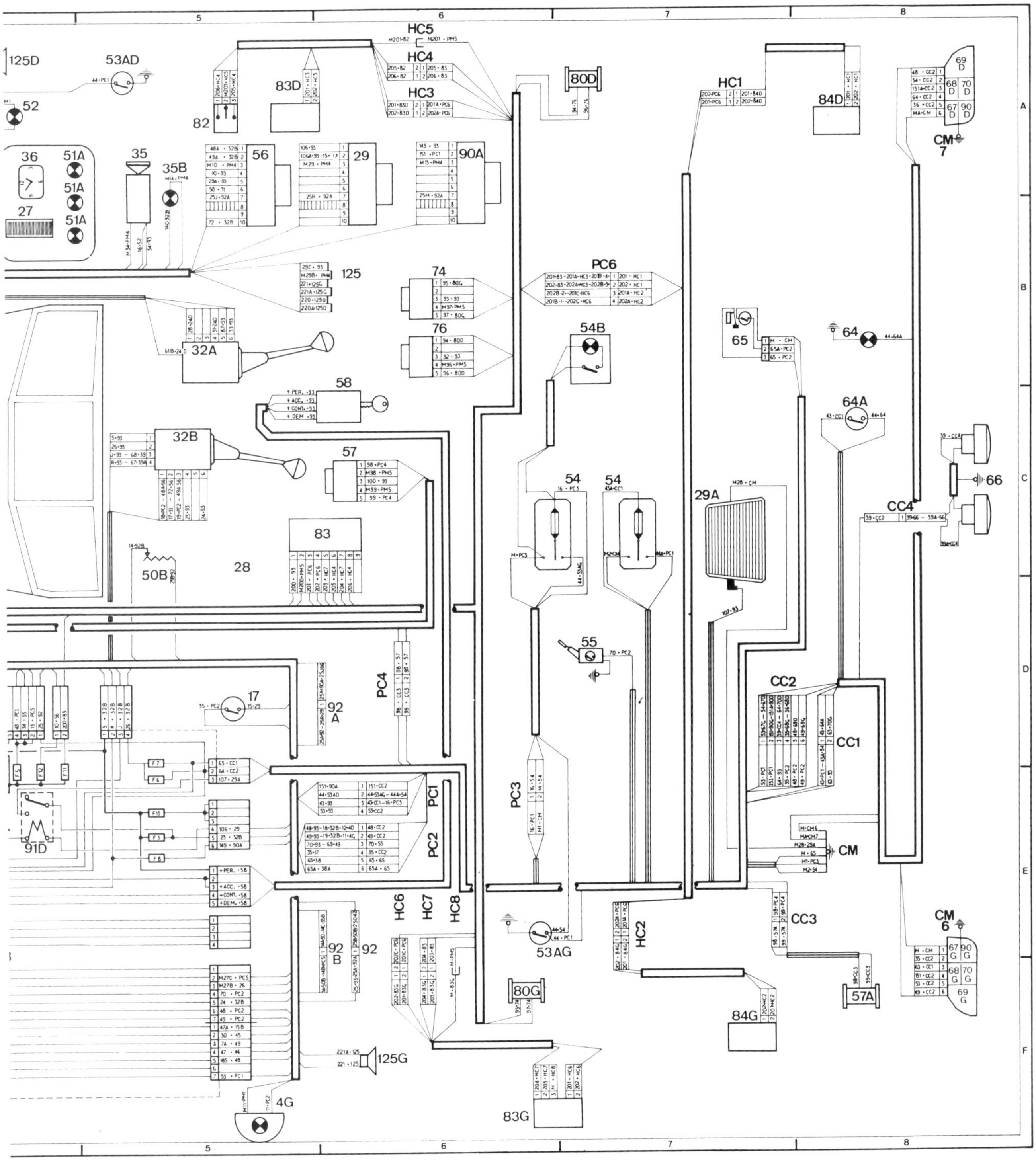

Fig. 7.3 Wiring diagram for Peugeot 305 models up to 1985 (continued)

Key to Figs. 7.2 and 7.3

1D	Headlamp, RH
1G	Headlamp, LH
2D	Direction indicator, front RH
2G	Direction indicator, front LH
3D	Sidelamp, RH
3G	Sidelamp, LH
4D	Indicator repeater, RH
4G	Indicator repeater, LH
5	Starter relay
5A	Neutral safety relay
6	Alternator
7	Sender unit, oil pressure
7A	Sensor, engine oil level
7B	Control unit, engine oil level
7C	Checking diode, engine oil level
8	Motor, engine cooling fan
8A	Disengaging fan relay
8B	Air conditioning electric fan
8C	Electric fan relay
8D	Diodes
8	Motor, engine cooling fan
8F	Resistor, cooling fan motor
9	Temperature switch, fan motor
9A	Temp. switch, fan clutch, cooling system
9B	Temp. switch, fan clutch, lube system
9C	Sender unit, oil temperature gauge
10	Horn
11	Headlight relay
12	Battery
12A	Battery cutout
13	Starter motor
14	Brake pads
15	Sender unit, coolant temperature
15A	Switch, coolant temperature
15B	Coolant temp, warning light switch or coolant temp. warning light
15C	Resistor, coolant temp. gauge
15D	Checking diode, coolant temp. warning light
15E	Switch, coolant level
16	Brake fluid reservoir
17	Stop switch
18	Reversing light switch
19	Starter safety cut-out
21	Regulator
24	Windscreen wiper
24A	Windscreen wiper relay
24B	Windscreen wiper timer
24C	Rear window wiper
24D	Windscreen wiper unit
25	Windscreen washer pump
25A	Rear window washer pump
26	Heating/ventilation fan, front
26A	Rear heating/ventilation fan
26B	Heating/ventilation fan switch
26C	Air conditioning blower
26D	Relay, air conditioning blower

27	Heating/ventilation switch or rheostat
27A	Rheostat resistor or heating/ventilation fan resistor
27B	Rear heating/ventilation switch
27C	Air conditioning control unit
29	Heated rear window switch
29A	Heated rear window
30	Windscreen wiper/windscreen washer switch
30A	Rear window wiper/washer switch
31	Direction indicator flasher unit
32	Lighting – windscreen wiper/windscreen washer switch
32A	Windscreen wiper/windscreen washer switch
32B	Lighting/direction indicator/horn control switch
33	Headlights flasher relay
34	Sidelamps
35	Cigar lighter, front
35A	Cigar lighter, rear
35B	Illumination, cigar lighter
36	Clock
37	Direction indicator repeater light
38	Fuel gauge
38A	Warning light, low fuel level
39	Main beam warning light
39A	Dip beam warning light
40	Hazard warning light
41	Rev counter
42	Sidelamp warning light
43	Brake safety warning light
43A	Brake safety warning light checking diode
44	Coolant temperature gauge
44A	Warning lamp, minimum coolant level
45	Warning light, low oil pressure
45A	Warning light, high oil temperature
45B	Warning light, oil pressure and temp.
46	Choke warning light
47	Oil and water warning light
48	Preheater warning light
49	Charge/discharge warning light
50	Instrument panel lighting
50A	Gear change gate light
50B	Rheostat, gear change gate light
50C	Switch lighting
51	Heater lighting
51A	Console lighting
51B	Console lighting rheostat
52	Glove compartment light
52A	Glove compartment light switch
53	Front door switch
53A	Rear door switch
53AD	Courtesy switch, RH front door
53AG	Courtesy switch, LH front foor
54	Interior lamp
54A	Light under facia panel
54B	Map reading light
54C	Illumination, courtesy mirror
55	Handbrake switch

56	Hazard warning light switch
57	Sunroof switch
57A	Sunroof motor
57E	Locking relay, sunroof
58	Steering lock
58B	Ignition switch light
59	Preheat – starter switch
59A	Preheater plugs
60	Pump cut-out motor or solenoid valve
61	Preheater warning light switch
62	Preheater relay
63	Direction indicator and horn control
64	Boot or rear compartment lighting
64A	Boot lid or tailgate switch
65	Fuel gauge tank with or without low fuel warning
65A	External tank unit resistor
65B	Rheostat, fuel gauge
66	Number plate light
67	Reverse lamps
67D	Reverse lamp, RH
67G	Reverse lamp, LH
68	Stop-lamp
68B	Stop/tail lamp (twin filament)
68BD	Stop/tail lamp, RH
68BG	Stop/tail lamp, LH
69	Rear direction indicator
69D	Direction indicator, rear, RH
69G	Direction indicator, rear, LH
70	Tail lamp
71	Tailgate switch
72	Door mounted light
73	Left hand rear window winder switch
73A	Locking relay, LH rear window winder
74	Window winder switch, LH front
74A	Locking relay, LH front window winder
75	Interlock, rear window winder
76	Window winder switch, RH front
76A	Locking relay, RH front window winder
76D	Switch, RH electric window, front, RH
76G	Switch, LH electric window, front, RH
77	Window winder switch, RH rear
77A	Locking relay, RH rear window winder
78	Left-hand window winder rear switch
79	Right-hand window winder rear switch
80	Window winder motor
80A	Window winder relay
80D	Motor, electric window, front, RH
80G	Motor, electric window, front, LH
81	Diagnostic socket
81A	TDC sensor, diagnostic socket
82	Door lock switch
83	Control box, central door locking
83A	Actuator, door lock
83B	Actuator, fuel filler flap
83C	Actuator, tailgate lock
83D	Actuator, door lock, front, RH

83G	Actuator, door lock, front, LH
83AD	Actuator, door lock, rear, RH
83AG	Actuator, door lock, rear, LH
86	Fuel pump
86A	Primary fuel pump
87	Solenoid valve
87A	Solenoid valve control switch
90	Rear foglights
90A	Rear foglight switch
90B	Rear foglight warning light
91	Relay
91B	Tachymetric relay
91C	Accessory relay
91D	Heated rear window relay
92 to 92F	Multi-plug/connectors
93	Connector board
93A	Fuse box No 1
93B	Fuse box No 2
94	Conductive tailgate stay
95	Brake servo vacuum switch
96	Brake pedal travel switch
97	Headlight washer/wiper switch
98	Headlight washer pump
99	Headlight wiper motor
99A	Headlight wiper relay
100	Pressure drop indicator
101	Tachograph
102	Flasher light
102A	Flasher light switch
103	Centre interior light
103A	Centre interior light switch
104	Feed warning light
104A	Feed warning light switch
105	Air fan
105A	Air fan switch
106	Warning bell
106A	Warning bell switch
107	Electrical plug
107A	Socket, towing attachment
108	Compressor clutch
108A	Compressor clutch switch
108B	Relay, compressor clutch
109	Thermostat
109A	Protection diode, thermostat
110	Constant pressure unit
111	Idling speed compensation solenoid valve
111A	Air conditioning shut-off pressure switch
118	Control pressure regulator
119	Additional air control
120	Sensor plate switch
121	Cold starting injector
122	Thermal time switch
123	Speed regulator switch
123A	Speed regulator electronic unit
123B	Speed regulator servo
123C	Speed regulator safety switch

Key to Figs. 7.2 and 7.3 (continued)

123D	Speed regulator disengagement switch		172	Control unit, knock detector
123E	Speed regulator pick-up		172A	Knock detector
123F	Speed regulator fuse		173	Warning light, LED, knock detector
123G	Safety relay speed regulator		174	Relay, capsule venting
123H	Vacuum capsule		175	Electronic relay
123I	Safety relay		180	Relay, fuel injection system
123J	Main switch, speed regulator		181	Calculator, fuel injection system
125	Radio connection		182	Airflow sensor
125D	Radio speaker, front RH		183	Injector
125G	Radio speaker, front LH		184	Throttle switch unit
125AD	Radio speaker, rear RH		185	Temperature sensor, engine
125AG	Radio speaker, rear LH		190	Sensor, fuel pressure
125E	Connector, radio speaker		191	Sensor, turbocharger excess pressure
129	Speed sensor		192	Gauge, turbocharger pressure
142	Tachymetric relay, fuel cut-off on over-run		195	100 mbar switch – turbo full load control, turbo injection intercooler
142A	Relay, fuel injection cut-off on over-run		196	Switch advance curve selector
142B	Control unit, for delay of fuel injection cut-off		197	Resistor, full load circuit, turbo injection intercooler
150	Warning light, economy		200	Control unit, voice synthesizer
150A	Vacuum pick-up		200A	Filter
151	Switch, water detector		201	Test button, voice synthesizer
151A	Warning light, water detector switch		210	Trip computer
152	Connector, front foglamps		211	Display control
152A	Switch, front foglamps		212	Fuel flow sensor
152B	Relay, front foglamps		213	Digital display
153	Sensor, oil pressure		+AA	Supply to accessories
153A	Oil pressure gauge		F	Fuse
165D	Long range driving lamp, RH		M	Earth
165G	Long range driving lamp, LH		+P	Supply from battery
170	Relay ignition system			
171	Calculator, ignition advance			

Not all items fitted to all models

Key to Figs. 7.4 to 7.9

1	Cigar lighter, front
3	Cigar lighter, rear
5	Distributor, ignition
9	Idling actuator (idling solenoid)
10	Alternator
11	Transistor, heater blower control (power transistor)
13	Strut (earth connection)
14	Ammeter (battery charge)
20	Radio aerial, electric
25	Horn
25A	Horn, low note
25B	Horn, high note
27	Connector, towing attachment
28	Dimmer, dipped beams
30	Radio
35	Actuator, fuel output (VP15)
40	Radio balance control, front
41	Radio balance control, front/rear
45	Battery
46	Control unit, positive supply
47	Diodes unit
48	Unit, electric pump group (EPG)
49	Unit, fuse board group (FBG)
50	Ignition coil
53	Control box, exhaust emission, for pilot carburettor
54	Emission control unit (ignition advance modulator)
55	Emission control unit (idle retard)
56	Control unit, automatic transmission (idle speed)
57	Alarm unit, theft protection
58	Control unit, injection
60	Control unit, air conditioning
61	Electronic unit, brake antilock
65	Control unit, screen wiper
66	Control box, power steering
75	Control unit, ignition, or pick-up amplifier module
76	Detector unit, bulb failure
80	Cruise control unit
85	Indicator unit, oil level
86	Indicator unit, coolant level
90	Control unit, central door locking
95	Infra red signal receiver (PLIP)
96	Control unit, knock detector
97	Thermostat unit (passenger compartment)
98	Electronic control unit for differential locking
110	Control unit, preheater
111	Control unit, fuel cut-off on overrun
112	Control unit, fuel flow (trip computer)
113	Electronic control unit, advance
114	Control box, coolant temperature, air conditioning
115	Preheater plug
120	Terminal connector
121	Buzzer (P4, warning, coolant temperature, oil pressure, charge warning light)
122	Buzzer, direction indicator (P4)
125	Audible warning, seat belt
126	Audible warning (key in the ignition/steering lock with the driver's door open)
127	Audible warning, excessive speed
128	Audible warning, (lights on, door open or 'STOP' warning lamp on)
129	Condenser, radio interference
130	TDC sensor
131	Altitude sensor
132	Knock detector
133	Sensor, engine speed
134	Sensor, absolute pressure
135	Sensor, potentiometer (econoscope vacuum)
136	Sensor, demisting the rear glass
137	Pressure sensor, inlet manifold
138	Pressure sensor
140	Speed sensor, speedometer cable
141	Speed sensor, trip computer
142	Sensor, oil pressure
143	Sensor, No 1 cylinder
144	Sensor, diesel injector needle lifted
145	Direction indicator flasher unit
146	Antilock sensor, LH front wheel
147	Antilock sensor, RH front wheel
148	Antilock sensor, LH rear wheel
149	Antilock sensor, RH rear wheel
150	Air temperature sensor, (air conditioning)
15	Load sensor (Diesel)
155	Pilot carburettor
160	Battery isolator
165	Instrument panel
167	Connector, emission control setting
169	Switch, starter/preheater
170	Switch, luggage compartment lamp
171	Switch, enrichment (LPG)
172	Switch, air filter clogging warning lamp
173	Switch, number plate
175	Switch, door lock
176	Switch, vacuum (LPG)
177	Switch, LH front lock (door open detector)
178	Switch, RH front lock (door open detector)
179	Switch, LH rear lock (door open detector)
180	Switch, RH rear lock (door open detector)
181	Switch, luggage compartment lock (lid open detector)
182	Switch, bonnet lock (bonnet open detector)
185	Switch, stop-lamps
186	Switch, brake pedal travel
190	Switch, handbrake
195	Switch, low pressure (Freon)
196	Switch, mean pressure (Freon)
200	Thermal switch (Freon)
205	Switch, glovebox lamp
210	Switch, seat belt
211	Switch, display (trip computer)
215	Switch, starter inhibitor
216	Switch, reverse lamp

Key to Figs. 7.4 to 7.9 (continued)

217	Switch, reverse lamp/starter inhibitor
220	Switch, heating/ventilation fan
221	Switch, heating/ventilation fan (rear)
225	Switch, choke warning light
229	Switch, ignition/steering lock
230	Door switch, LH front
231	Door switch, RH front
232	Door switch, LH rear
233	Door switch, RH rear
234	Control switch, audible warning (ignition key 'in')
235	Switch, brake fluid pressure drop
236	Switch, brake fluid level
237	Switch, coolant level
238	Switch, water sensing, fuel system
239	Switch, washer bottle level
240	Limit switch, sunroof
241	Switch on accelerator pedal (idle speed)
242	Switch, idle speed
243	Switch, power take-off (P4)
247	Switch, rear differential lock
248	Switch, front differential lock
249	Switch, windscreen wiper lockout (P4)
250	Disengaging switch, cruise control (brake)
250A	Disengaging switch, cruise control (clutch)
251	Throttle switch (idling + full load)
252	Level switch, brake anti-lock
253	Switch, driver's passive seat belt
254	Switch, passenger's passive seat belt
260	Control, lighting/direction indicators/horn
261	Control, lighting/screen wiper/screen wash
262	Control, lighting/screen wiper/direction indicator/horn
263	Control, screen wiper/wash
264	Control, lighting/horn
265	Control, direction indicator/horn
266	Switch, cruise control
267	Switch, cruise control/direction indicator
268	Switch, flasher unit
269	Switch, lighting/blackout (P4)
270	Switch, windscreen wiper (P4)
275	Control, driver's seat position
276	Control, rear view mirror LH
277	Control, rear view mirror RH
280	Supplementary air device (cold start)
281	Corrector, fuel reheating
285	Capacitor, coil positive
286	Capacitor, direction indicator flasher unit
290	Tachometer
295	Compressor
296	Compressor, air horn
300	Starter motor
301	Vapour relief valve (LPG)
302	Diode, relay protection
303	Diode, rear foglamps
304	Protection diode, electronic control unit
305	Checking diode, coolant temperature warning light
306	Checking diode, brake warning light
307	Diode, air conditioning control
308	Diode, lighting dimmer
309	Diode, electric fan
310	Diode, compressor
311	Diode, roof lamp
312	Diode, speech synthesizer
313	Flow sensor
314	Diode, boot locking
328	Solenoid valve, turbo-charge regulator
329	Solenoid valve, cruise control deceleration
330	Solenoid valve, air conditioning
331	Solenoid valve, EGR (pilot carburettor)
332	Solenoid valve, opening the carburettor throttle valve
333	Solenoid valve, injection cut-off on over-run
334	Solenoid, emission control advance modulator
335	Solenoid, exhaust emission
336	Solenoid, carburettor breather
337	Main solenoid, brake anti-lock
338	Control solenoid, brake anti-lock
340	Solenoid, pump stop
343	Solenoid valve, air intake
344	Solenoid, turbine fan
345	Solenoid valve, fast idle stabiliser
346	Solenoid, canister
347	Solenoid, cruise control
348	Advance solenoid, diesel
349	Solenoid valve, temperature control
350	Switches, illumination
351	Illumination, instrument panel
355	Illumination, heating/ventilation control
360	Illumination, console
361	Courtesy lamp
364	Illumination, cigar lighter
365	Illumination, luggage compartment (or tailgate)
375	Illumination, glovebox
380	Illumination, engine compartment
385	Illumination, number plate LH
386	Illumination, number plate RH
390	Illumination, ignition switch/steering lock
395	Floor illumination, driver's side
396	Floor illumination, passenger's side
397	Sill illumination, driver's side
398	Sill illumination, passenger side
400	Illumination, gear selector lever
410	Clutch, compressor
420	Idling cut-off, carburettor
425	Map reading lamp
440	Sidelamp LH
441	Sidelamp RH
445	Tail lamp cluster LH
446	Tail lamp cluster RH
452	Marker lamp, LH rear
453	Marker lamp, RH rear
455	Door marker lamp LH

Key to Figs. 7.4 to 7.9 (continued)

456	Door marker lamp RH		522	Switch, window winder, LH rear
457	Front foglamp RH		523	Switch, window winder, RH rear
458	Front foglamp LH		524	Switch, window winder, LH rear (in rear compartment)
459	Fuse holder (front foglamps)		525	Switch, window winder, RH rear (in rear compartment)
460	Rear foglamp LH		526	Child safety switch, rear window winders
461	Rear foglamp RH		527	Switch, main/dip beams
462	Reverse lamp		530	Switch, sunroof
463	Stop-lamp		532	Switch, heated rear window
464	Reverse lamp + foglamp (rear)		535	Switch, driver's seat heating
465	Suppression filter, tachometer		536	Switch, passenger's seat heating
466	Fuse holder (+ accessories, brake anti-lock)		540	Switch, preheater
467	Fuse holder (for warning light, brake anti-lock)		545	Switch, central roof lamp
468	Fuse holder (power circuit, brake anti-lock)		548	Test switch, brake wear warning light
469	Fuse holder, LAMBDA sensor heater		549	Diagnostic switch, diesel
470	Fuses (fusebox)		550	Switch, rear screen wiper
471	Fuse holder (radio)		552	Switch, headlamp wiper
472	Fuse holder (locks)		555	Switch, fuel supply warning light
473	Fuse holder (dipped beams)		556	Switch, police horn
474	Fuse holder (speech synthesizer)		557	Switch, rotating lamp
475	Fuse holder (carburettor heater)		558	Switch, air fan
476	Fuse holder (cruise control)		560	Switch, warning bell
477	Fuse holder (supply pump)		565	Switch, pressure drop
477A	Fuse holder (injection and ignition control unit supply)		566	Switch, air conditioning control
478	Flashing lamps, priority		567	Switch, cruise control
479	Fuse holder (pump, brake anti-lock)		570	Switch, hazard warning
480	Direction indicator lamp, LH front		571	Test switch
481	Direction indicator lamp, RH front		572	Switch, lamps (police)
482	Direction indicator lamp, LH rear		574	Injectors
483	Direction indicator lamp, RH rear		575	Cold start injector
484	Sidelamp/direction indicator, LH front		576	Information display, injection control box
485	Sidelamp/direction indicator, RH front		580	Fuel tank unit
486	Suppression filter, speech synthesizer		590	Map reading lamp
487	Fuse holder (control unit, fuel output VP15)		591	Indicator, coolant temperature
488	Fuse holder (control unit, advance regulator VP15)		592	Gauge, turbocharger pressure
489	Fuse holder, cooling fan group (CFG)		593	Fuel gauge
490	Impulse generator (speed)		594	Gauge, engine oil temperature
491	Rotating lamp		595	Gauge, engine oil pressure
500	Loudspeaker, LH front		598	Electronic control unit, ignition
501	Loudspeaker, RH front		600	Motor, screen wiper
502	Loudspeaker, LH rear		601	Motor, window wiper, rear
503	Loudspeaker, RH rear		605	Wiper motor, headlamp LH
505	Hour meter (P4)		606	Wiper motor, headlamp RH
510	Switch, front foglamps		607	Motor, heater control flap
511	Switch, rear foglamps		610	Motor, sunroof
512	Switch, auxiliary driving lamp		615	Motor, LH front window winder
513	Switch, siren		616	Motor, RH front window winder
514	Switch, rotating lamp		617	Motor, LH rear window winder
515	Switch, rheostat, instrument panel illumination		618	Motor, RH rear window winder
516	Switch, parking lights		620	Motor, heating/ventilation fan
517	Switch, general (military P4)		625	Actuator, LH front door lock
518	Test switch, oil, coolant or charging fault (P4)		626	Actuator, RH front door lock
519	Switch, horn (P4)		627	Actuator, LH rear door lock
520	Switch, window winder (driver's)		628	Actuator, RH rear door lock
521	Switch, window winder (passenger's)		629	Actuator, luggage compartment lock
521A	Switch, passenger's window winder		630	Motor, fuel filler flap lock

Key to Figs. 7.4 to 7.9 (continued)

631	Motor, driver's passive seat belt	747	Relay, CLT
632	Motor, passenger's passive seat belt	748	Relay, ECU, exhaust emission
635	Motor, engine cooling fan	749	Relay, cold cut-off
636	Motor, air conditioning fan	750	Relay, front foglamps
640	Clock	751	Relay, rear foglamps
645	Pressure switch, brake servo	752	Relay, compressor cut-out (105°)
646	Pressure switch, power steering	753	Relay, pump, brake anti-lock
647	Pressure switch, air conditioning cut-out	754	Relay, power circuit, brake anti-lock
650	Oil pressure switch	755	Relay, headlamp wiper
651	Vacuum-pressure switch	756	Relay, headlamp wiper timer
652	Pressure switch, turbocharger cut-out	757	Relay, advance curve selection
653	Full throttle enrichment switch	758	Relay, brake warning lamp (anti-lock brake system)
654	Advance curve selection switch	760	Relay, heated rear window
660	Trip computer	761	Relay, rear electric window
660A	Keyboard, trip computer	762	Relay, front electric window
660B	Display, trip computer	763	Relay, sunroof
668	PTC (positive temperature coefficient resistance)	764	Relay, sunroof tilt + central locking
669	Potentiometer, throttle	765	Relay, front screen wiper
669A	Potentiometer, accelerator pedal (Diesel)	766	Relay, rear window wiper
670	Headlamp LH	767	Relay, warning light occultation (P4)
671	Headlamp RH	770	Relay, accessories
672	Headlamp blackout (P4)	771	Relay, visual warning
673	Driving lamp LH	772	Relay, two-speed (mixture control)
674	Driving lamp RH	773	Relay, carburettor heater
675	Brake pads, LH front	775	Relay, starter motor isolator
676	Brake pads, RH front	776	Relay, cruise control disengagement
677	Brake pads, LH rear	777	Relay, pilot carburettor supply
678	Brake pads, RH rear	778	Relay, scavenge pump
679	Vacuum pump, cruise control	779	PTC resistance control relay
680	Washer pump, front	780	Relay, lighting dimmer
681	Washer pump, rear	781	Relay, excessive speed
682	Washer pump, headlamp	782	Relay, ignition supply
683	Fuel supply pump	783	Relay, injection supply
684	Scavenge pump	784	Relay, trip computer/cruise control/speech synthesizer information
685	Coolant heater matrix		
686	Hydaulic pump, brake anti-lock	785	Relay, brake warning (Australia)
688	Interior lamp, front	786	Resistor, coil
689	Interior lamp, rear	787	Resistor, heating/ventilation fan
690	Interior lamp, centre	788	Resistor, two-speed cooling fan
691	Interior lamp, LH front	789	Resistor, lighting dimmer
692	Interior lamp, RH front	790	Heater, diesel fuel
693	Interior lamp, LH rear	791	Heater, carburettor
694	Interior lamp, RH rear	793	Resistor, preheater (P4)
697	PLIP	794	Resistor, injection matching
700	Pressure switch	795	Rheostat, instrument illumination
705	Connector board	800	Regulator, voltage
706	Services connector board	801	Regulator, control pressure
710	Battery supply socket	810	Side repeater flasher LH
720	Diagnostic socket	811	Side repeater flasher RH
721	Test socket (injection)	812	Rheostat, temperature display
723	Front foglamp LH	814	Rear view mirror LH
724	Front foglamp RH	815	Rear view mirror RH
727	Lambda sensor heating relay	817	Heater seat, front LH
728	Relay, passive seat belt (non motorised)	818	Heater seat, front RH
729	Relay, emission control	820	Bell
730	Relay, starter motor	821	Diagnostic test socket
731	Relay, preheater	829	Servo, power steering
732	Relay, fan clutch	830	Servo, cruise control
733	Relay, electric fan motor	832	Sensor, evaporator
734	Relay, hour meter (P4)	833	Sensor, blown air
735	Relay, main beams	834	Sensor, interior air temperature
736	Relay, auxiliary driving lamps	835	Sensor, oil level
737	Relay, dipped beams	836	Sensor, fuel flow (trip computer)
738	Relay, heating/ventilation fan, fast speed	837	Sensor, coolant level
740	Relay, coil	838	Sensor, mixture regulator
741	Relay, coil resistance	840	Sensor, high temperature
742	Relay, cold start control	841	Siren
743	Relay, compressor	845	Speech synthesizer
744	Tachymetric relay or pump control relay	846	Sensor, body temperature (exhaust)
745	Relay, air horn compressor	847	Sensor, passenger compartment temperature regulation
746	Tachymetric relay (cut-off on over-run)	848	Lambda sensor

Key to Figs. 7.4 to 7.9 (continued)

849 Sensor, external air temperature
850 Thermal switch, cooling fan (coolant)
852 Thermal switch, transmission oil
853 Thermal switch, 18°C (coolant temperature)
855 Thermal switch, coolant
861 Thermal switch, 40°C (coolant temperature)
862 Thermal switch, 60°C (coolant temperature)
865 Thermostat, electronic (air conditioning)
870 Thermal time switch (cold start opening)
871 Temperature switch 15 degrees (air temperature)
880 Tachograph
885 Timer switch, seat belt
886 Timer switch, interior lamp
887 Timer switch, headlamp wash
888 Sender unit, oil temperature gauge
889 Temperature sender unit, injection
890 Sender unit, coolant temperature gauge
891 Temperature sender unit, electronic (heating/ventilation)
892 Sender unit, engine oil temperature
893 Timer switch, rear screen wiper
893A Timer switch, windscreen wiper
894 Temperature sender unit, controlling cooling fan motors by ECU (liquid cooling)
895 Sender unit, exhaust emission
896 Thermal resistor, inlet air temperature
897 Tester, anti-lock
898 Sender unit, oil pressure
899 Test unit, variable power steering
929 Proportioning valve, cruise control
930 Fan, electromagnetic clutch
935 Fan, heating/ventilation
936 Fan, heating/ventilation, rear
945 Heater rear window
950 Fan
955 Ram, driver's seat
960 Fan, air conditioning
965 Cold start flap
970 Voltmeter
+ AA Supply from accessories terminal
+ AC Supply from ignition switch

Not all items fitted to all models

BL Screened cable
+ D Supply from starter motor
L1 Warning lamp, seat belt
L2 Warning lamps, direction indicator
L3 Warning lamp, low fuel level
L4 Warning lamp, main beams
L5 Warning lamp, hazard warning
L6 Warning lamp, side/tail lamps 'on'
L7 Warning lamp, no battery charge
L8 Warning lamp, preheater
L9 Warning lamp, choke control
L10 Warning lamp, oil pressure
L11 Warning lamp, oil and coolant
L12 Warning lamp, coolant temperature
L13 Warning lamp, brake safety
L14 Warning lamp, rear fog lamps
L15 Warning lamp, fuel supply
L16 Warning lamp, 'stop'
L17 Warning lamp, brake fluid/stop-lamps
L18 Warning lamp, sidelamp failure
L19 Warning lamp, tail lamp failure
L20 Warning lamp, screenwash level
L21 Warning lamp, coolant level
L22 Warning lamp, engine oil level
L23 Warning lamp, brake pad wear
L24 Manual test switch, instrument panel
L25 Warning lamp, oil temperature
L26 Warning lamp 'door open'
L27 Warning lamp, tail lamp or rear foglamp failure
L30 Warning lamp, rear differential lock
L31 Warning lamp, front differential lock
L32 Warning lamp, knock detector
L33 Warning lamp, diagnosis
L34 Warning lamp, water in fuel
L35 Warning lamp, dipped beams
L36 Warning lamp, trailer direction indicator
L37 Warning light, power take-off (P4)
L39 Warning lamp, catalytic converter
L39 Warning lamp, brake anitlock alert
M Earth connections
+ P Supply from battery

Colour code (where used)

AZ Sky Blue
BA White
BE Blue
GR Slate
JN Yellow
MR Brown
NR Black
OR Orange
RG Red
RS Pink
VE Green
VI Purple

Guidance for use

The vehicle is divided into 4 sections. Section codes are given before the component code

M Engine
P Facia
H Passenger compartment
C Luggage area

For connections between harnesses, the Section codes, followed by C, are used to indicate where the connection is eg MC indicates a connector between the engine and facia harnesses which is located in the engine compartment
For earthing points the Section code in followed by M
eg CM indicates an earthing point in the luggage area

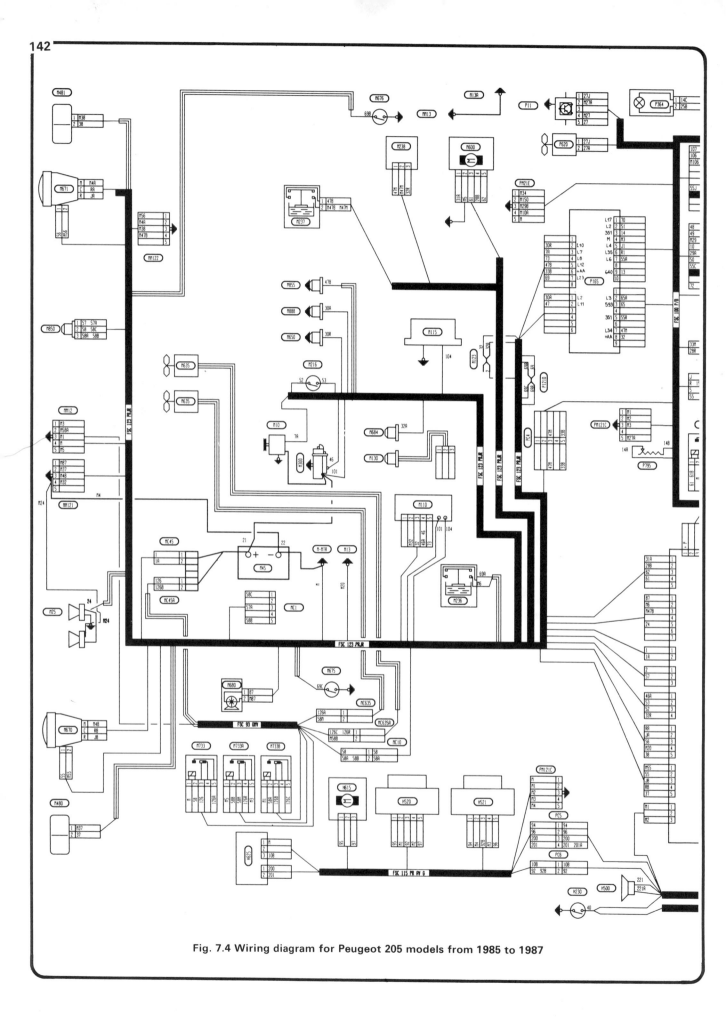

Fig. 7.4 Wiring diagram for Peugeot 205 models from 1985 to 1987

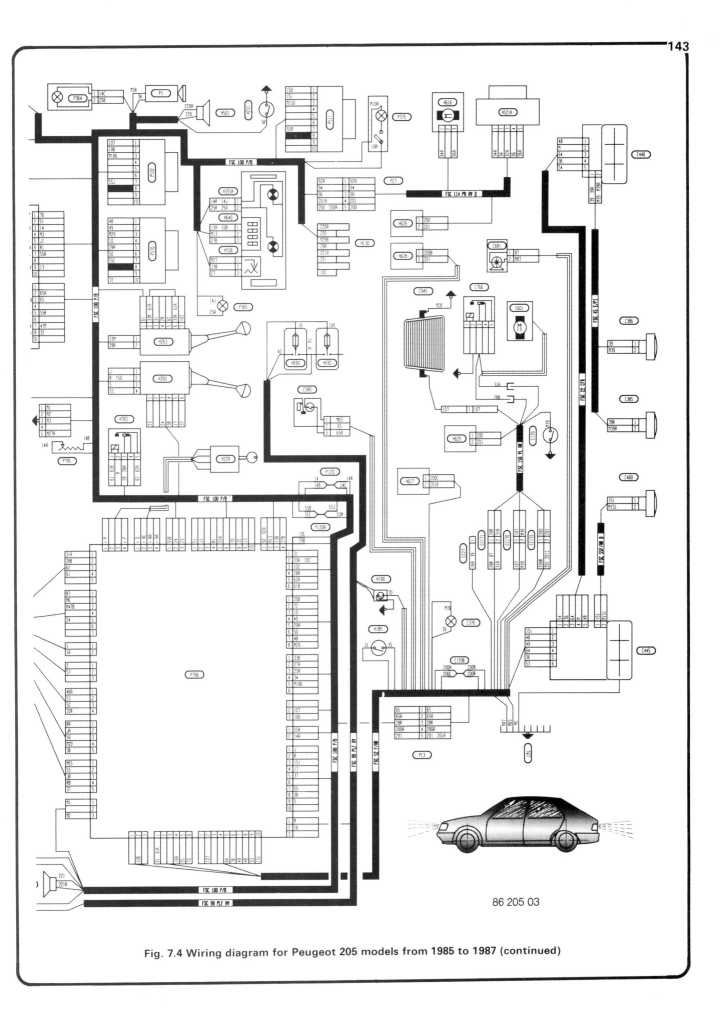

Fig. 7.4 Wiring diagram for Peugeot 205 models from 1985 to 1987 (continued)

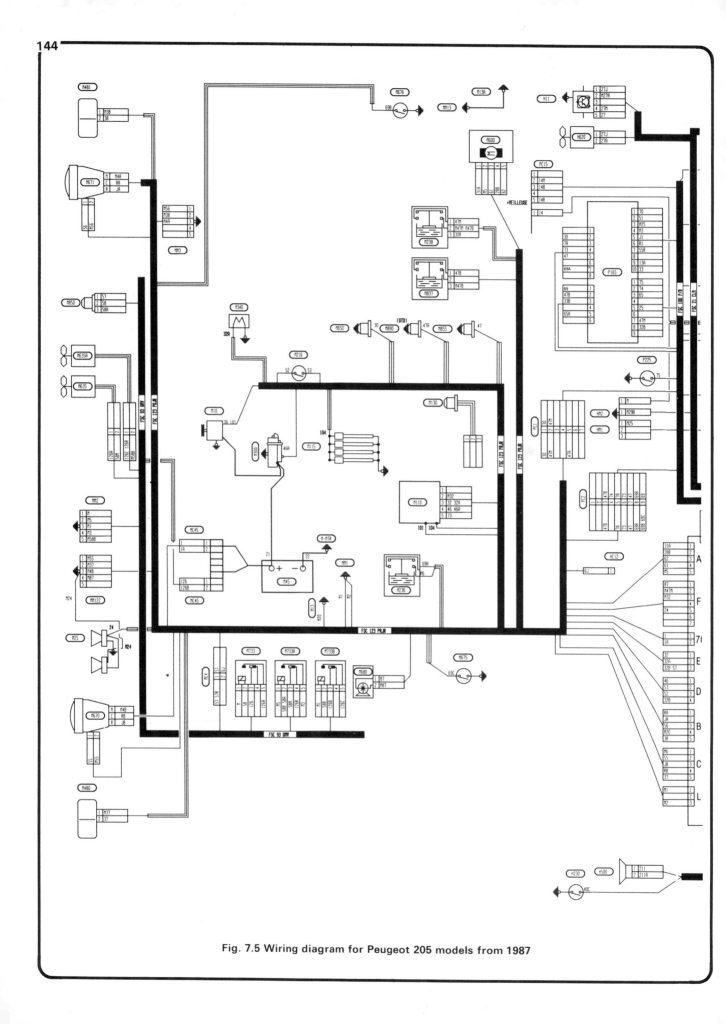

Fig. 7.5 Wiring diagram for Peugeot 205 models from 1987

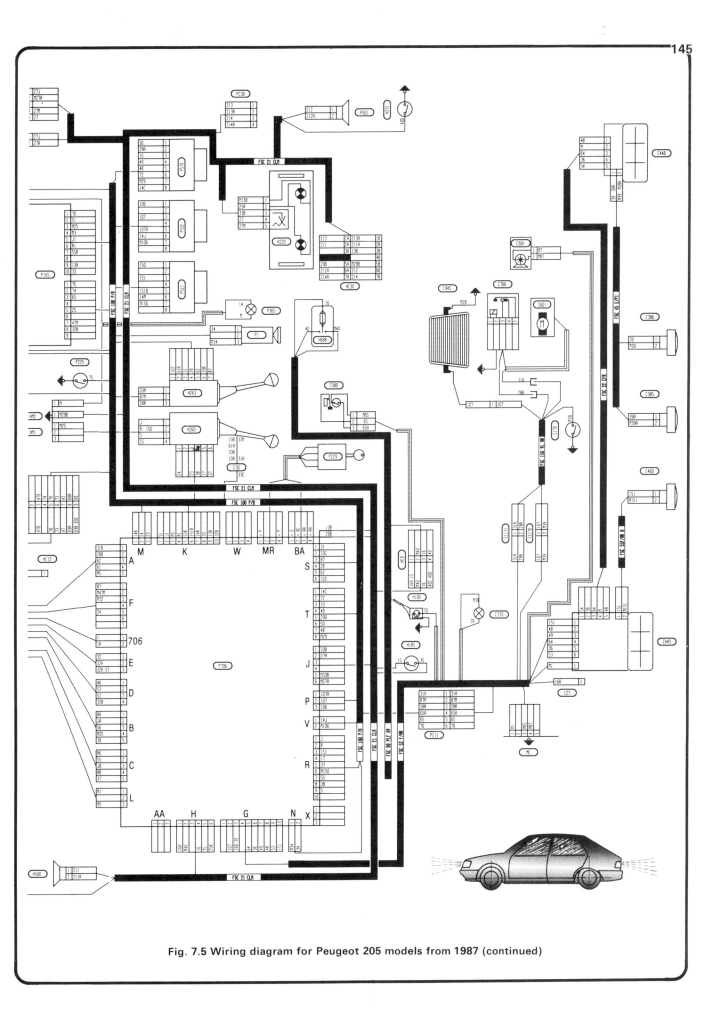

Fig. 7.5 Wiring diagram for Peugeot 205 models from 1987 (continued)

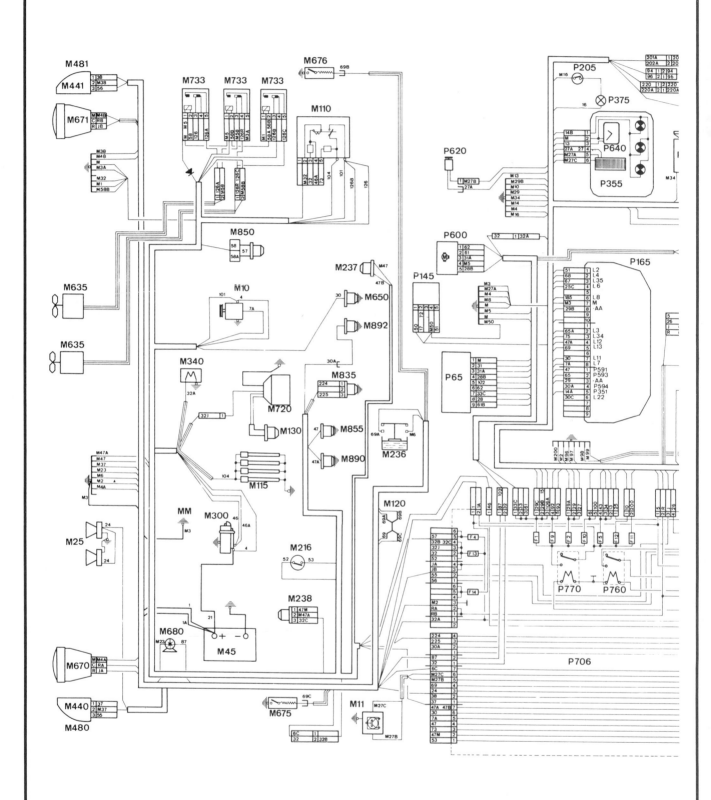

Fig. 7.6 Wiring diagram for Peugeot 305 models from 1985

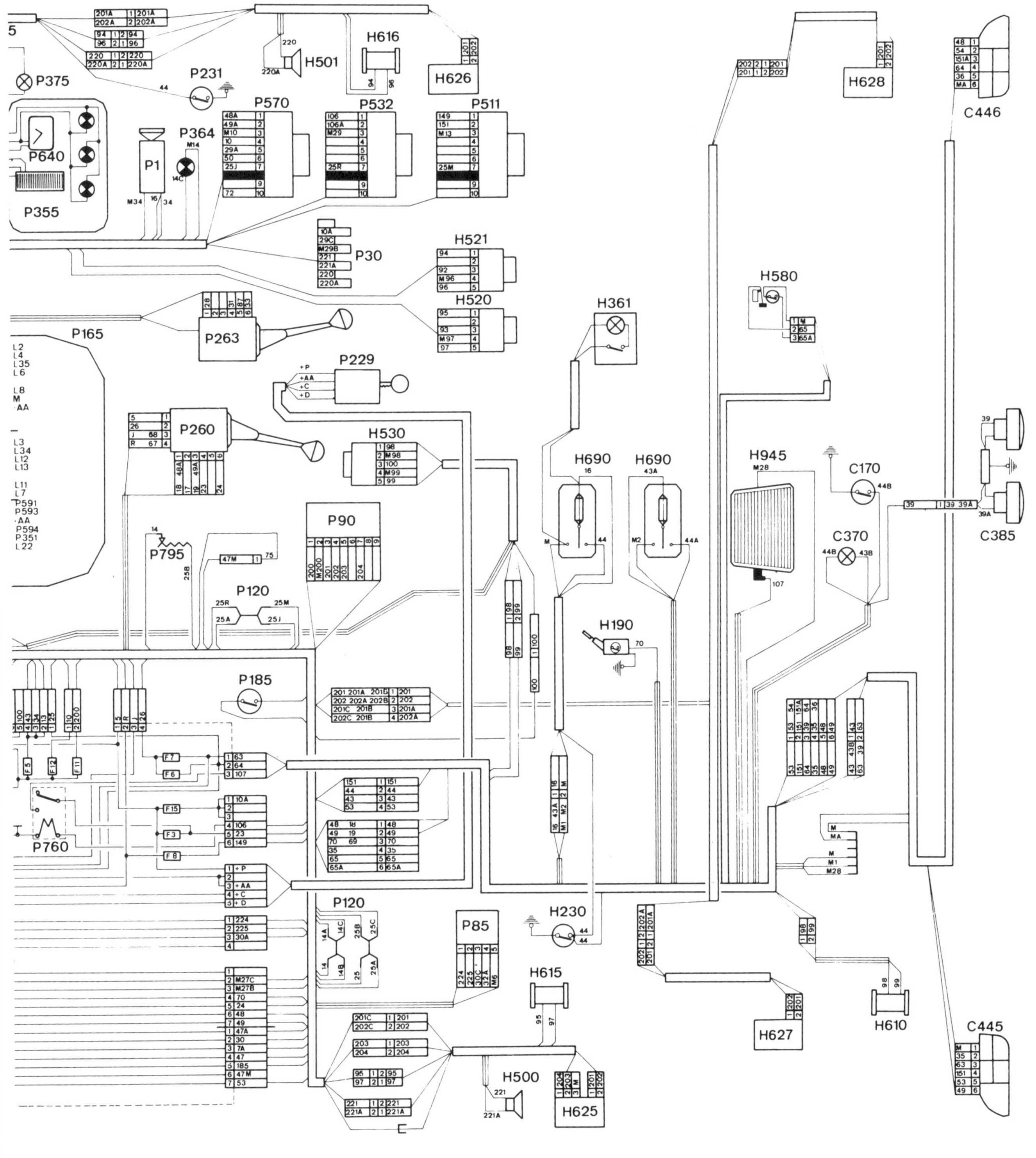

Fig. 7.6 Wiring diagram for Peugeot 305 models from 1985 (continued)

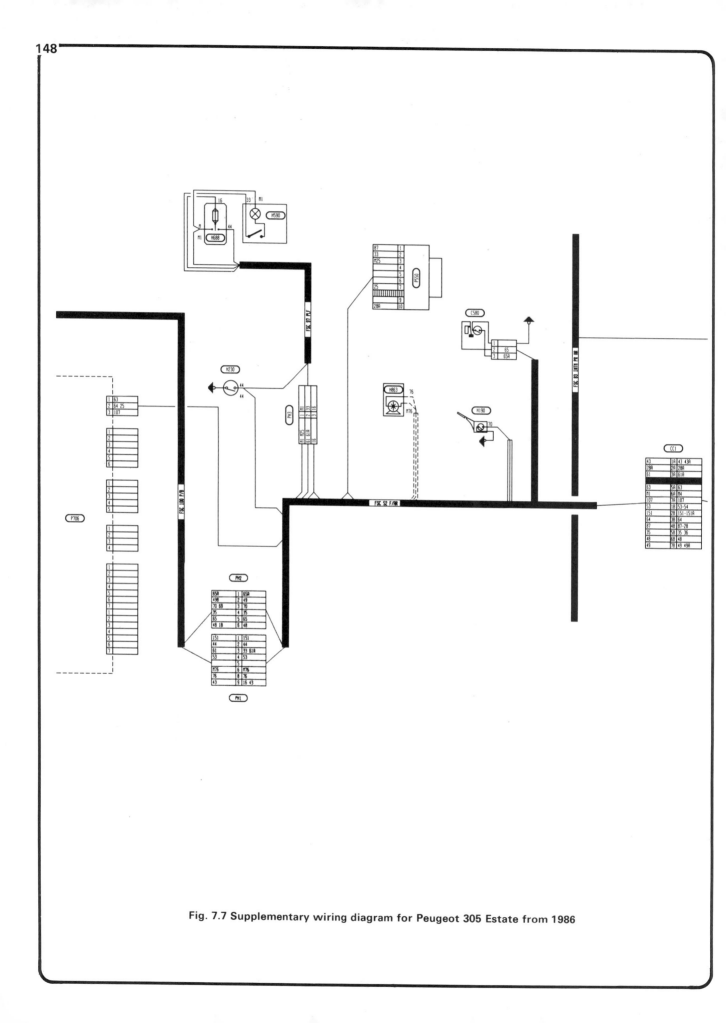

Fig. 7.7 Supplementary wiring diagram for Peugeot 305 Estate from 1986

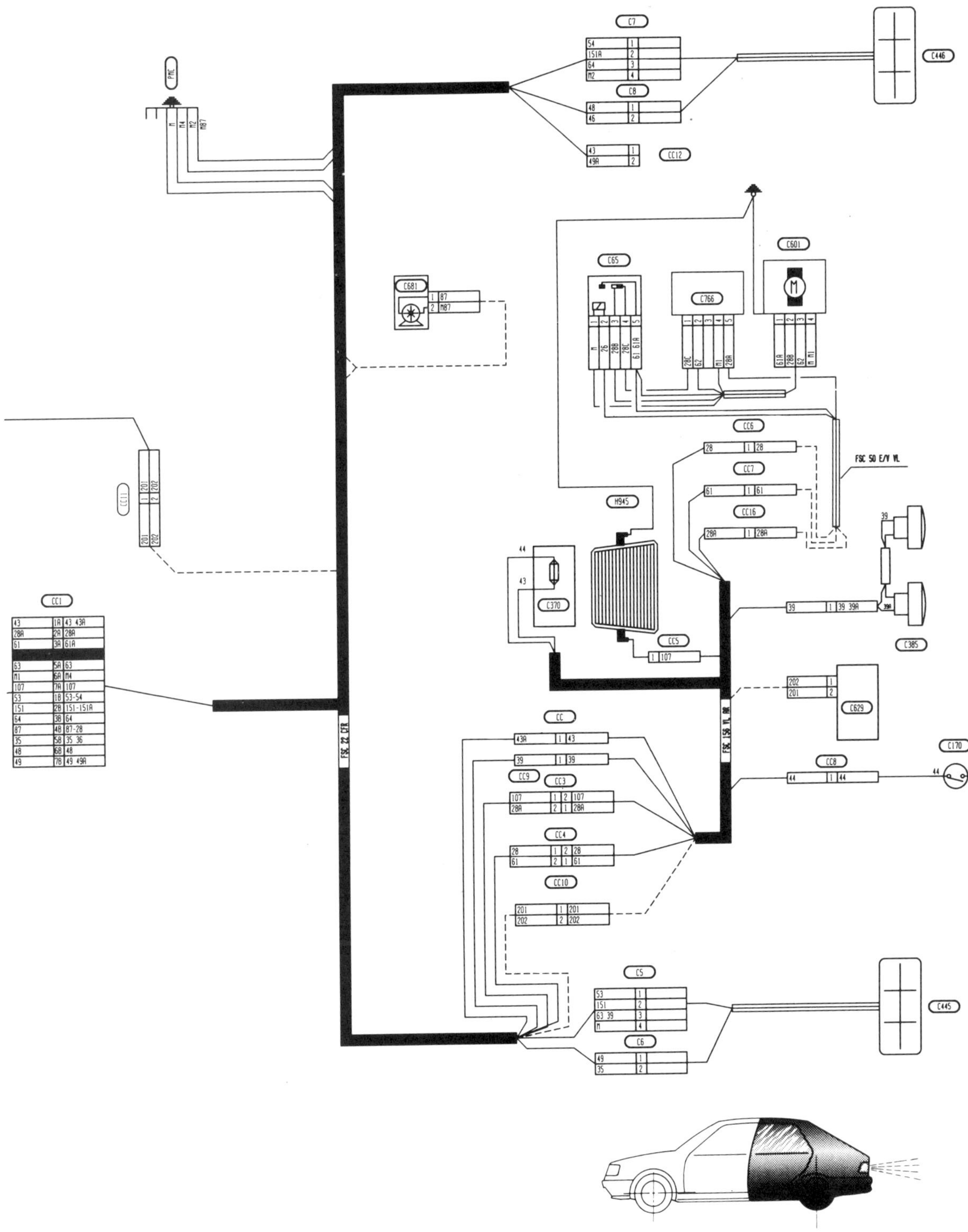

C7

S4	1
151A	2
64	3
M2	4

C446

C8

| 48 | 1 |
| 45 | 2 |

| 43 | 1 |
| 49A | 2 |

CC12

PHC

C681

| | 1 | 87 |
| | 2 | M87 |

C65   C601

C766   M

CC11

	1	201
	2	202
201		
202		

CC1

43	1A	43 43A
28A	2A	28A
61	3A	61A
63	5A	63
M1	6A	M4
107	7A	107
53	1B	53-54
151	2B	151-151A
64	3B	64
87	4B	87-28
35	5B	35 36
48	6B	48
49	7B	49 49A

CC6

| 28 | 1 | 28 |

CC7

| 61 | 1 | 61 |

CC16

| 28A | 1 | 28A |

FSC 50 E/V M

H945

| 44 | |
| 43 | |

C370

39

| 39 | 1 | 39 39A | 39A |

C385

CC5

| | 1 | 107 |

| 202 | 1 |
| 201 | 2 |

C629

C170

FSC 22 E/R   FSC 150 M M

CC

| 43A | 1 | 43 |
| 39 | 1 | 39 |

CC9   CC3

| 107 | 1 | 2 | 107 |
| 28A | 2 | 1 | 28A |

CC8

| 44 | 1 | 44 |

CC4

| 28 | 1 | 28 |
| 61 | 2 | 61 |

CC10

| 201 | 1 | 201 |
| 202 | 2 | 202 |

C5

53	1
151	2
63 39	3
M	4

C445

C6

| 49 | 1 |
| 35 | 2 |

87 305 06

Fig. 7.7 Supplementary wiring diagram for Peugeot 305 Estate from 1986 (continued)

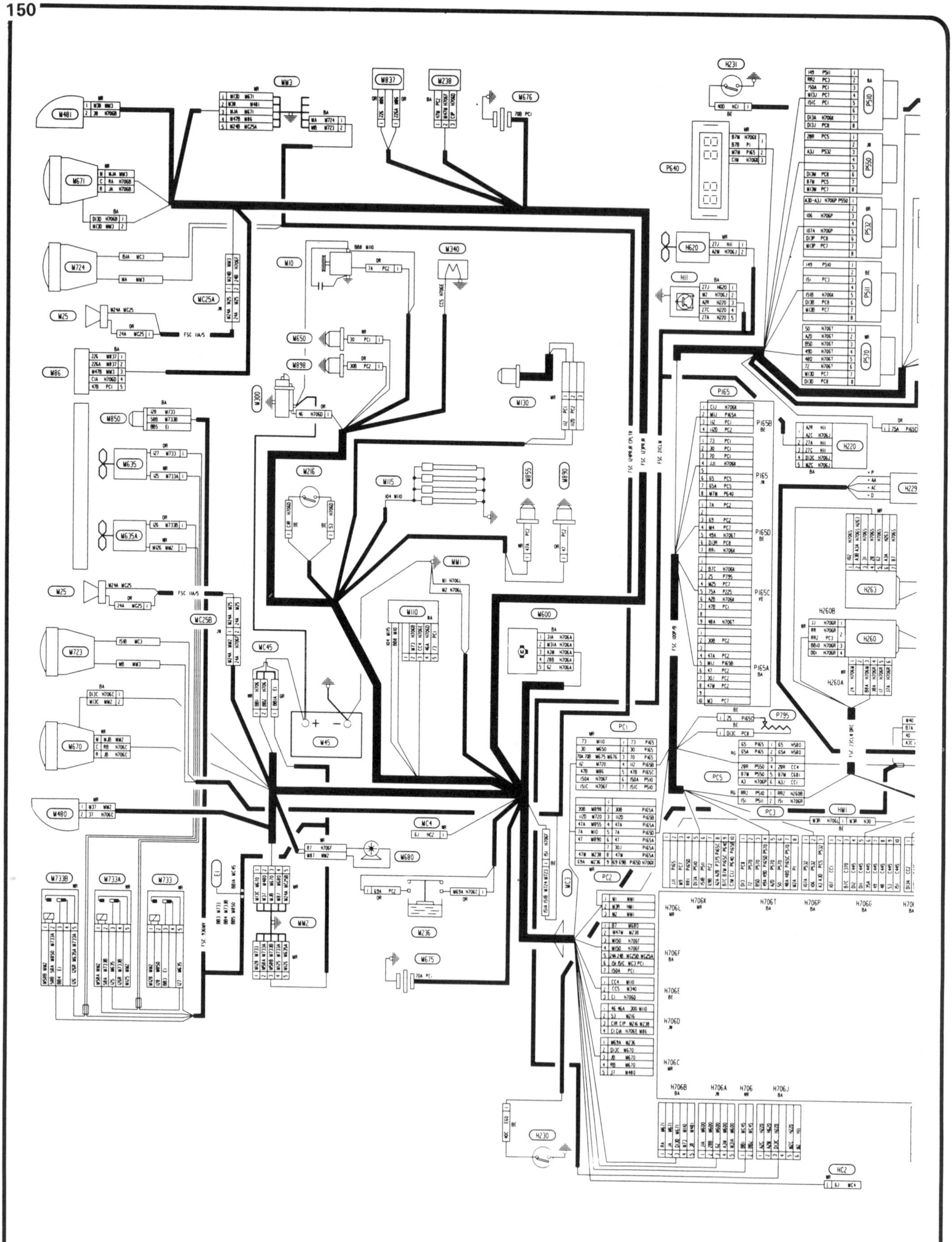

Fig. 7.8 Wiring diagram for Peugeot 309 models up to 1987

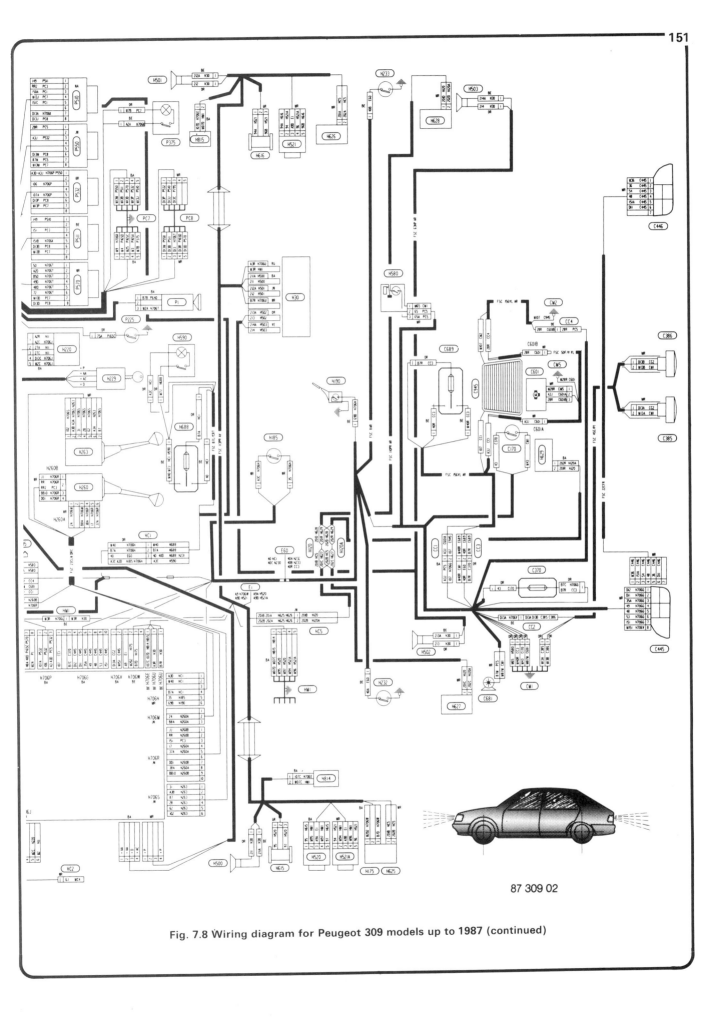

87 309 02

Fig. 7.8 Wiring diagram for Peugeot 309 models up to 1987 (continued)

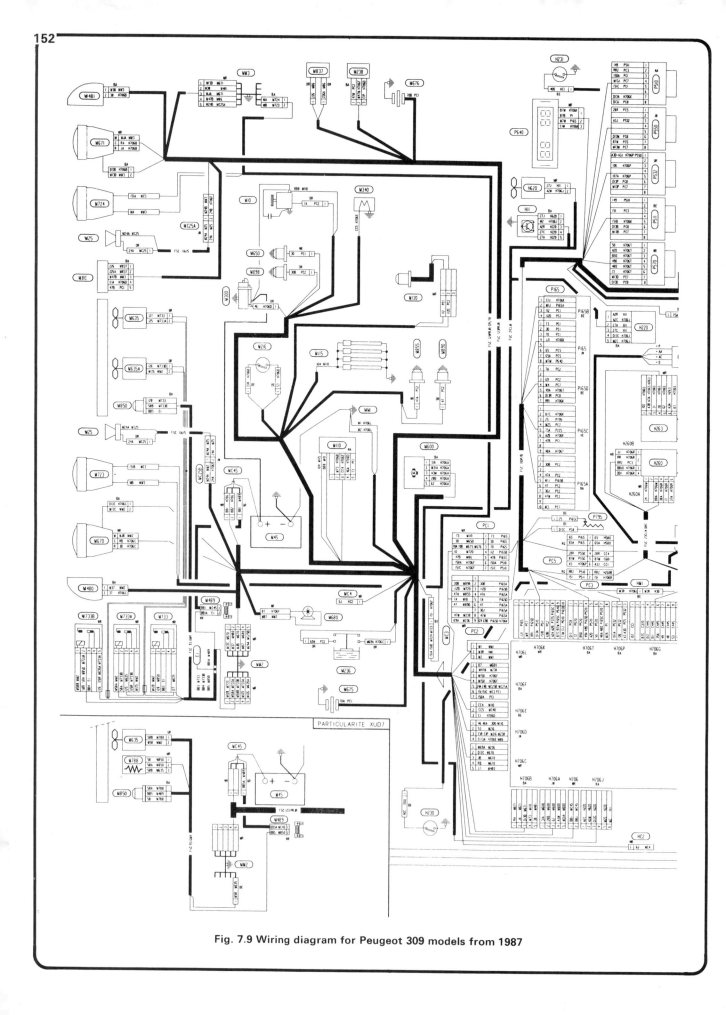

Fig. 7.9 Wiring diagram for Peugeot 309 models from 1987

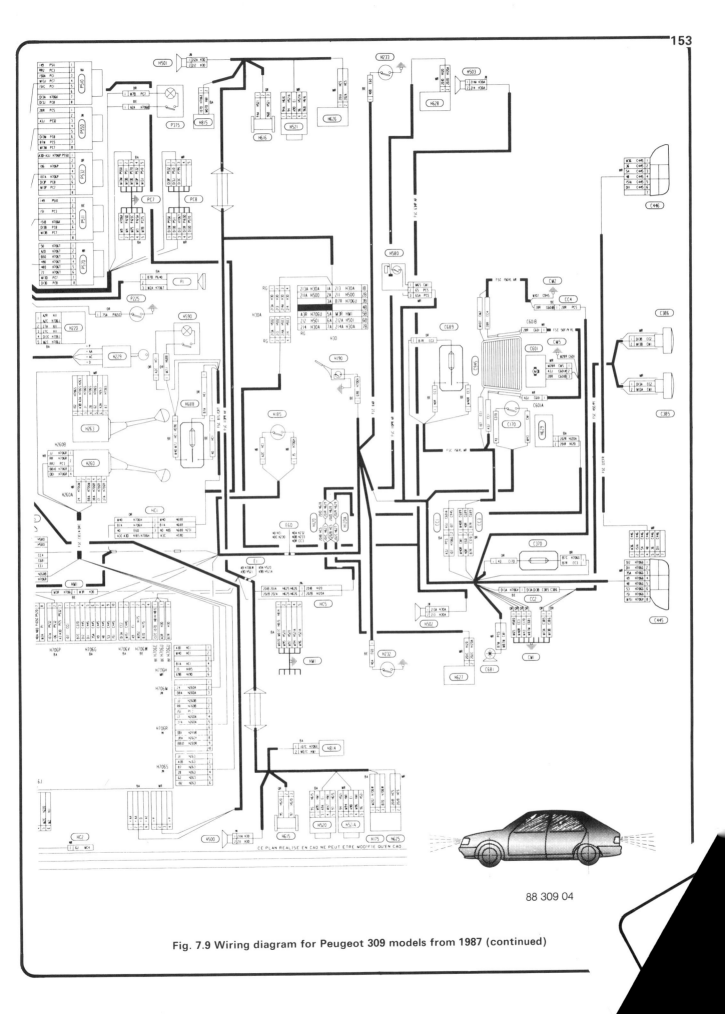

88 309 04

Fig. 7.9 Wiring diagram for Peugeot 309 models from 1987 (continued)

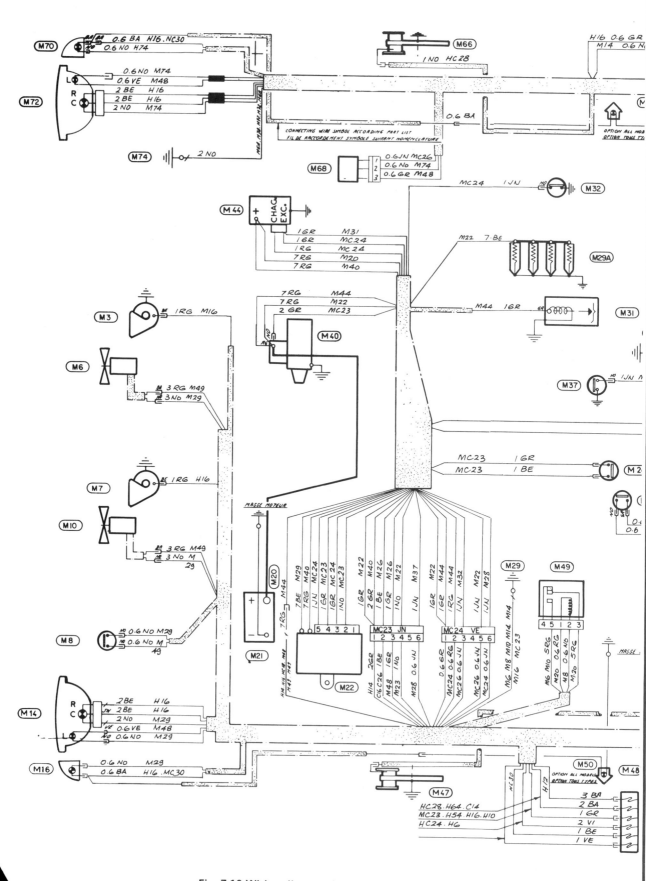

Fig. 7.10 Wiring diagram for Talbot Horizon

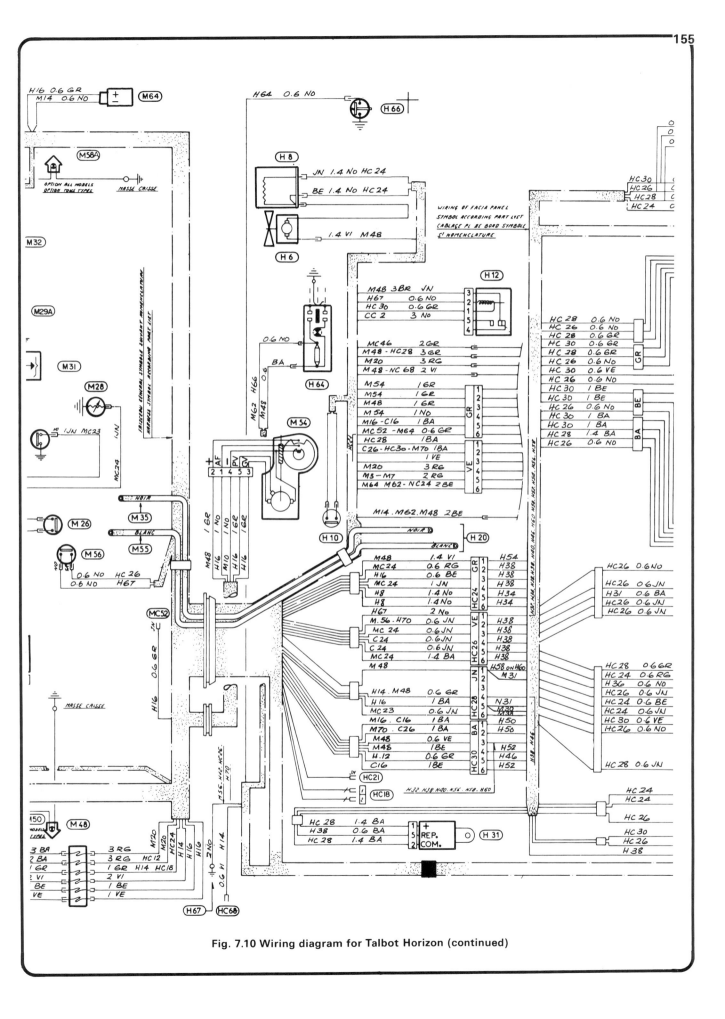

Fig. 7.10 Wiring diagram for Talbot Horizon (continued)

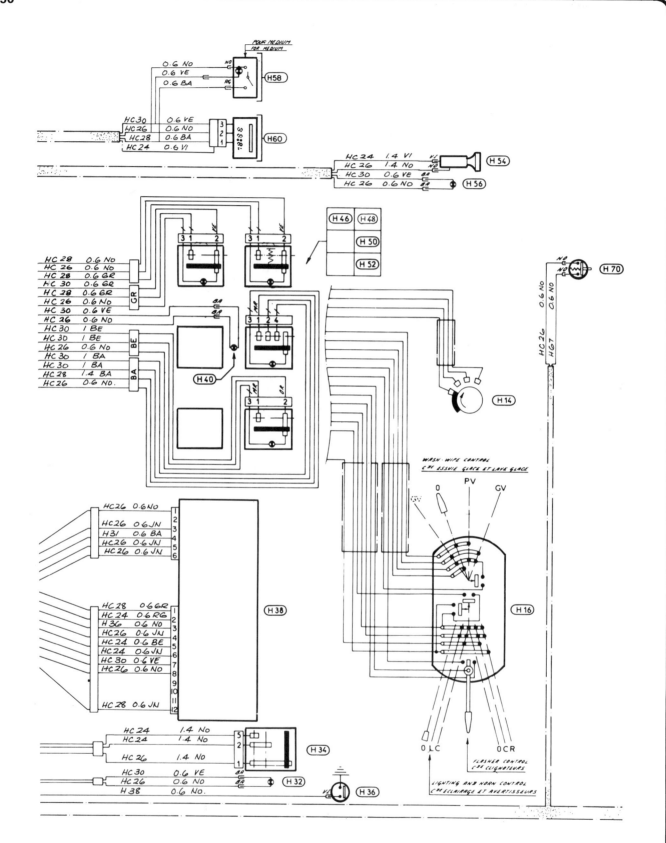

Fig. 7.10 Wiring diagram for Talbot Horizon (continued)

157

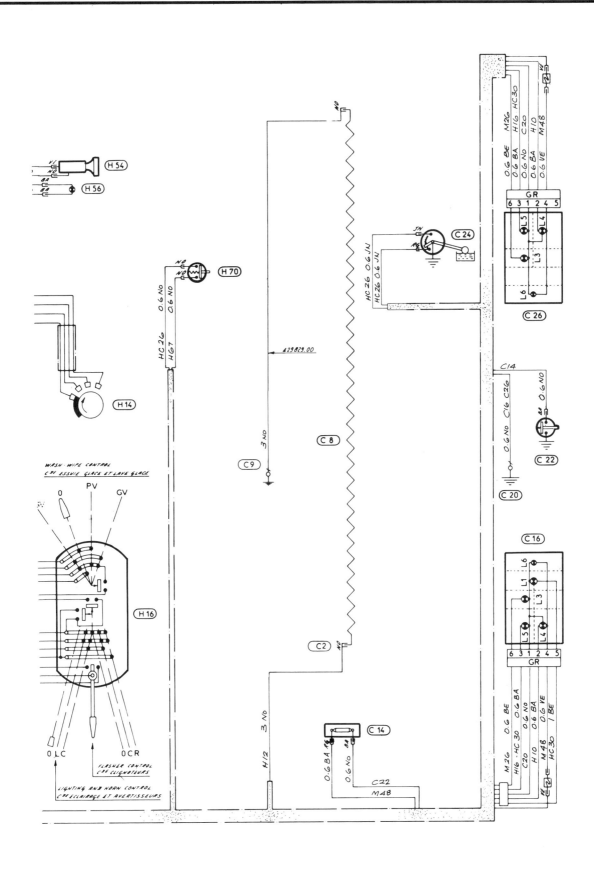

Fig. 7.10 Wiring diagram for Talbot Horizon (continued)

Key to Fig. 7.10

C8	Heated rear window		M3	Horn RH
C9	Earth on body		M6	Cooling fan motor
C14	Illumination, luggage compt		M7	Horn LH
C16	Rear lamp cluster LH		M10	Cooling fan motor
C20	Earth on body		M10	Earth on body
C22	Switch, luggage compt lamp		M14	Headlamp LH
C24	Fuel tank gauge unit		M16	Direction indicator LH
C26	Rear lamp cluster RH		M19	Indicator repeater LH
H6	Heater blower motor		M21	Battery
H8	Resistor, heater motor		M22	Control unit, preheaters
H10	Switch, stop-lamps		M26	Switch, reverse lamps
H12	Relay, heated rear window		M28	Sender unit, coolant temperature
H14	Ignition/starter switch		M29A	Preheater plugs
H16	Combination switch		M30	Ignition coil
H20	Heater control		M31	Injection pump
H31	Flasher unit, direction indicators		M32	Sender unit, oil pressure
H32	Illumination, heater controls		M34	Connector, engine oil pressure
H34	Switch, heater blower motor		M35	Vacuum connection
H36	Switch, choke control		M36	Horn, high note
H38	Instrument panel		M37	Sender unit, coolant temp
H40	Illumination, push-push		M30	Starter motor
H46	Switch, heated rear window		M42	Horn, low note
H50	Switch, hazard warning		M44	Alternator
H52	Switch, rear foglamps		M45	Diagnostic socket
H54	Cigar lighter		M47	Wear indicator, LH brake
H56	Illumination, ashtray		M48	Fusebox
H58	Clock, analogue		M49	Relay, cooling fan
H60	Clock, digital		M50	Control unit, ignition
H62	Courtesy switch LH		M50	Indicator repeater LH
H64	Interior lamp		M53	Capacitor
H66	Courtesy switch RH		M54	Motor, windscreen wiper
H67	Earth on body		M55	Heater valve
H70	Switch, handbrake		M56	Indicator, brake fluid level
L1	Foglamps, rear		M57	Wear indicator, RH brake
L2	Reverse lamps		M58	Pump, windscreen washer
L4	Stop/tail lamps		M58A	Indicator repeater
L5	Direction indicators		M68	Detector, water in diesel fuel
L6	Illumination, number plate			

Colour code

BA	White
BE	Blue
GR	Slate
JN	Yellow
MR	Brown
NO	Black
RG	Red
VE	Green
VI	Purple

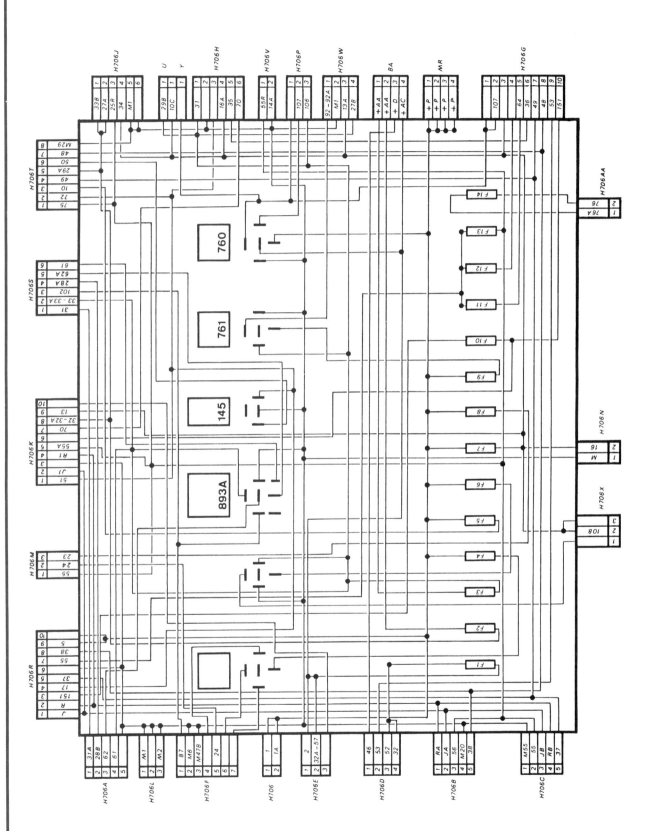

Fig. 7.11 Fuse/relay board connections – Peugeot 205, chassis numbers 5820 001 to 7330 000

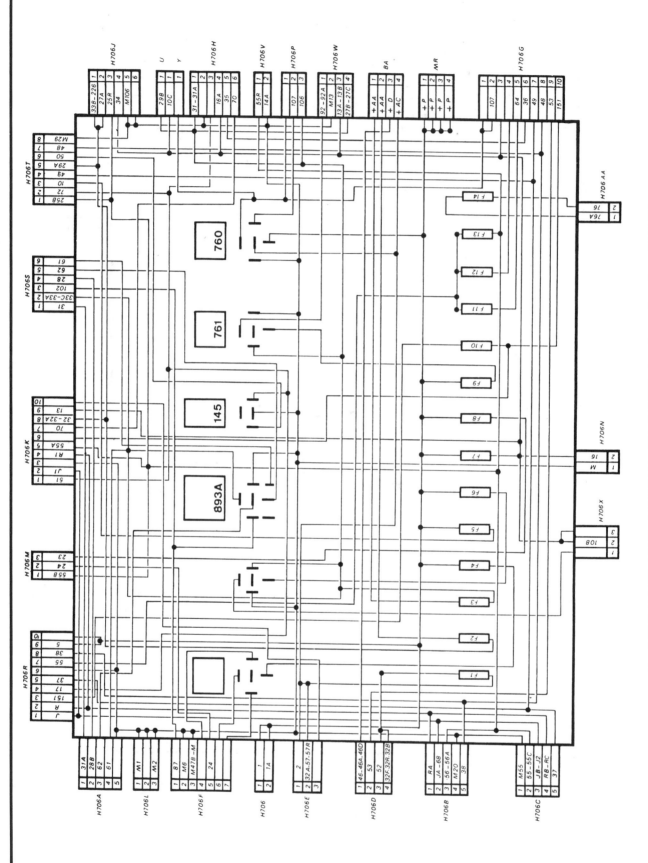

Fig. 7.12 Fuse/relay board connections — Peugeot 205, chassis numbers from 7330 001

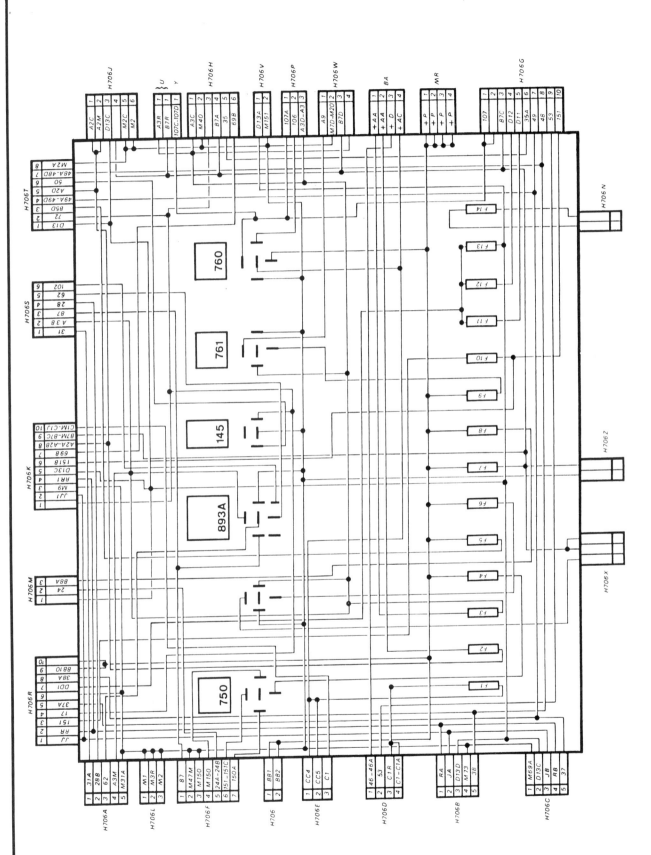

Fig. 7.13 Fuse/relay board connections – Peugeot 309

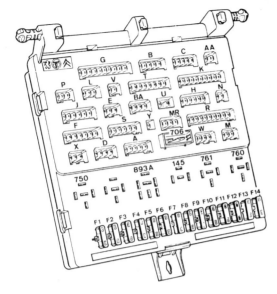

Fig. 7.14 Wiring socket locations on fuse/relay board – Peugeot 205

The socket code corresponds to the connector suffix in Figs. 7.11 and 7.12

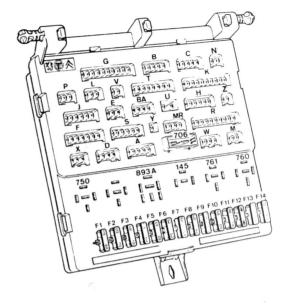

Fig. 7.15 Wiring socket locations on fuse/relay board – Peugeot 309

The socket code corresponds to the connector code suffix in Fig. 7.13

Index